WEST GERMAN FOREIGN AID, 1956–1966

ITS ECONOMIC AND POLITICAL ASPECTS

WEST GERMAN
FOREIGN AID
1956-1966

ITS ECONOMIC AND POLITICAL ASPECTS

KAREL HOLBIK
HENRY ALLEN MYERS

BOSTON UNIVERSITY PRESS
1968

©Copyright 1968 by the Trustees
of Boston University

Library of Congress Catalog Card Number 68-58498
Printed in the United States of America

We must not waver on the importance of aid. It is not a luxury of modern foreign policy. It is, in fact, the obvious accommodation between countries where saving is easy and automatic and those where it is difficult and painful. It is the principal basis for harmonious coexistence between the rich countries and the poor.

—JOHN KENNETH GALBRAITH

Economically, development policy is of vital importance for us because this country's economic growth will in the future be even more dependent on the development of our foreign trade than is the case today.

—WALTER SCHEEL

PREFACE

This book is intended to provide an analysis of the first decade of the West German foreign-aid program in terms of its economic results and its effectiveness as an instrument of foreign policy. The German Federal Republic has ranked fourth and occasionally third as donor-nation to the underdeveloped world for ten years; it has considered its development-aid efforts sufficiently important to create a new ministry to manage them. In spite of these facts, no study of any depth on the German aid program has appeared in West Germany except for several publications compiled by government officials and organs. As these latter have served chiefly to justify the program to the German people and publicize it rather uncritically to foreign readers, the authors felt that a detailed study from a non-governmental point of view was needed. It has been our purpose to make a critical evaluation of the economic, political, and sometimes psychological aspects of the West German foreign-aid program, treating it as a chapter in the history of modern Germany. It has not been our intention to take issue at length with authors who have touched on isolated aspects of this topic with or without the benefit of a thorough investigation.

The West German Ministerium für wirtschaftliche Zusammenarbeit was extremely cooperative in furnishing veritable mountains of material on which to base this work, as was the Kreditanstalt für Wiederaufbau in Frankfurt am Main, to which we are indebted for the map of projects backed by loans. We would also like to thank the Deutsche Bundesbank for permission to reprint three of their charts. Because of the general accessibility of the daily, German-language *Bulletin des Presse-und Informationsamtes der Bundesregierung,* which (not to be confused with the very summary, weekly, English-language *The Bulletin,* issued by the same source) contains official texts of almost all important speeches, agreements, and regulations dealing with foreign aid, we have cited texts from it wherever possible, rather than from the original press communiqués.

The writers owe special thanks for further documentary material to Dr. Albert F. Ernecke, Director of the Economics Branch of the Federal Republic's embassy in Washington, to Economics Advisor Bernd von Arnim of the Federal Republic's embassy in Vienna, and to Inter Nationes staff member Sigrid Lanzrath in Bonn. For critical material from the East German standpoint, discussed particularly in the last chapter, we are indebted to *Verlag Zeit im Bild,* Dresden.

Boston
November 1967

Karel Holbik
Henry Allen Myers

CONTENTS

TABLES

CHARTS

MAPS

THE FREE WORLD EFFORT

Aid for Development: The Cold War and the Sense of International Cohesion

The thought that progressive Western nations have some duty to aid less-advanced countries to utilize their dormant potentialities has been a familiar one throughout most of the twentieth century. More than forty-five years ago, Sir Frederick Lugard, an advocate of rule through native institutions and leaders (indirect rule) in British African colonies, could point to "the high ideal of leading the backward races, by their own efforts, in their own way, to raise themselves to a higher plain of social organization" as a perfectly plausible goal.[1] But earlier in the century, European advocates of aid for development tended to assume that the logical first step in any program should be political tutelage by the mother country, to assure the reliability of those aided. Such spokesmen desired speed in helping Asian and African peoples to advance, but they could not inspire any feeling of urgency.

With the end of World War II and the onset of the Cold War, several factors severely undermined the basic Western assumption that outstanding political trustworthiness must precede gradual economic advancement, aided by patron European nations. Over the past two decades, most of the "backward" parts of the old national empires have made the transition from colony to complete independence or membership in a loose federation with the former mother country. The new freedom of the emerging states has brought a new politesse into Western attempts to deal

1. *The Dual Mandate in British Tropical Africa* (Edinburgh: William Blackwood and Sons, 1922), p. 215. This classic work of its type, while acknowledging "that European brains, capital and energy have not been and never will be, expended in developing the resources of Africa from motives of pure philanthropy," still describes aid to less-advanced regions rather much in white-man's-burden terminology: "By railways and roads, by reclamation of swamps and irrigation of deserts, and by a system of fair trade and competition, we have added to the prosperity and wealth of these lands, and checked famine and disease ... We are endeavouring to teach the native races to conduct their own affairs with justice and humanity, and to educate them alike in letters and in industry" (p. 617).

1

with them; their peoples are no longer "backward," but only "underdeveloped" or "developing."

In the Cold-War competition between the Western and Eastern blocs, the new politesse is an absolute necessity. No longer can a less-advanced people be expected to accept the rule of whatever outside power gains momentary ascendance in their region. Instances, such as that of Tibet, in which imperialist expansion has proceeded by the nineteenth-century method of a military takeover, have recently been rare in the underdeveloped countries; even where military struggles have been open, as in Laos or Viet-Nam, they have often remained at least partly subordinate to political and psychological warfare. The assumption now prevailing to varying degrees in both Western and Eastern camps in the sixties amounts to this: the peoples coming into their own outside the main power blocs must be courted. Further, the Communist and non-Communist worlds seem equally convinced that the emerging nations must be appealed to with all possible speed. Western proponents of extensive foreign aid appear to be certain that unless the populations of the underdeveloped regions learn to trust democratic capitalism *now*, they will soon fall into the Communist camp and be irretrievably lost.

From the Communist side, even the Russians—however less theoretically drastic than the Chinese they may be on other issues—insisted in their party program of 1961 that the moment for transition to Communism by Asian and African countries is now. Western aid attempts must be discredited or made irrelevant by "national-liberation" warfare.[2] To most Western minds, there are two conflicts here: one between the desire for peaceful coexistence and the encouragement of warfare in the underdeveloped areas; and the other between the ideas of historical inevitability and the necessity of making predetermined events happen immediately. In Communist ideology, however, peaceful coexistence and national "wars of liberation" in the underdeveloped areas are perfectly harmonious ideas, since they effect the transition to socialism by different means, conditioned by different time and place coordinates. "Peaceful coexistence" means peace only among existing states or power blocs, but not necessarily within those countries whose social systems, in Communist eyes,

2. "The imperialists are using new methods and new forms to maintain colonial exploitation of the peoples . . . Under the guise of 'aid', they are trying to retain their old positions in those [newly independent] countries and capture new ones, to extend their social basis, lure the national bourgeoisie to their side, implant military despotic regimes and put obedient puppets in power . . . In many countries, the liberation movement of the peoples that have awakened proceeds under the flag of nationalism. Marxists-Leninists draw a distinction between the nationalism of the oppressed nations and that of the oppressor nation. The nationalism of an oppressed nation contains a *general democratic element* directed against oppression, and Communists support it because they consider it historically justified at a given stage." "Programme of the Communist Party of the Soviet Union," adopted Oct. 31, 1961 [English edition] (Moscow: Foreign Languages Publishing House, 1961), pp. 44–45.

cry out for change.[3] Then, too, historical inevitability does not mean that the agents for change (the already-committed Communist nations) can shirk their responsibility for contributing to the predestined overthrow of capitalism at the historically opportune moment—which all signs proclaim to be in the 1960's. Ultimately, this means that time is of the essence in foreign-aid dealings with underdeveloped areas, for Communist nations as well as for those of the West.

In the non-Communist world, the idea of foreign aid has from the beginning been more closely linked with Cold War strategy in the United States than elsewhere. The responsibility of the United States to oppose Communism was presented as following logically from the responsibility already accepted in defeating fascism. In 1947, when the world-wide role to be played by the United States in containing Communism was still not self-evident to anyone, President Truman backed the first major program of foreign aid to Greece and Turkey in terms of protecting the American investment made during World War II: "The United States contributed $341,000,000,000 toward winning World War II. This is an investment in world freedom and world peace. The assistance that I am recommending for Greece and Turkey amounts to little more than one-tenth of 1 percent of this investment. It is only common sense that we should safeguard this investment and make sure that it was not in vain."[4] The basic thought behind that original request for $400 million was that effective opposition to Communism depends on making an independent government work in a flourishing economy, which can be decisively furthered by Western funds and expert supervision: "It is of the utmost importance that we supervise the use of any funds made available to Greece, in such manner that each dollar spent will count toward making Greece self-supporting, and will help to build an economy in which a healthy democracy can flourish."[5]

3. "Peace and peaceful coexistence are not quite the same thing. Peaceful coexistence does not merely imply absence of war; it is not a temporary unstable armistice between two wars but the coexistence of two opposed social systems, based on mutual renunciation of war as a means of settling disputes between states." "Report of the Central Committee of the CPSU to the 22nd Congress of the Communist Party of the Soviet Union," delivered by N.S. Khrushchev, Oct. 17, 1961. In *Documents of the 22nd Congress of the CPSU*, Vol. I (New York: Crosscurrents Press, 1961), p. 46.

4. "Address of the President of the United States—Greece, Turkey and the Middle East" (House Document 171), *Congressional Record—House*, March 12, 1947, p. 1,981.

5. Ibid., p. 1,980. Whether the Greeks, in retrospect, attach much importance to American aid in having kept Greece self-supporting during its civil war and thus politically and militarily viable is, of course, another question. A recent and otherwise thorough English-language history of modern Greece sums up the whole postwar crisis and development episode as follows: "Hardly had she (Greece) begun to rise from her ruins than the terrible 'civil war' was unleashed upon her. Pacified by Marshal Alexander Papagos and thanks to the vitality of the people, spurred by their consciousness of the mission which history has assigned to them and their inexhaustible capacity for work, Greece has marched to complete rehabilitation. Today Greece ranks among those nations with rare political stability, military preparedness, and economic prosperity. It is a nation vehemently attached to democratic ideals and permanently aligned with the Western World in its opposition to international Communism." S. M. Sophocles, *A History of Greece* (Thessalonike: Institute for Balkan Studies, 1961), p. 370.

All this has a familiar sound. To be sure, the idea of encouraging democracy through development aid has been expanded, if that is the word, to include aid to faithful (although undemocratic) anti-Communists, such as those in Spain and Formosa, and aid with the thought of encouraging a national brand of Communism which might present less of a worldwide threat than the formerly monolithic Soviet empire. But the rhetoric that couches the notion of gaining friends for the Western system through frugal but effective expenditures, calculated to combat the distress on which Communism is felt to thrive, is scarcely distinguishable in President Johnson's 1965 foreign-aid message from that of the Truman speech: "The Communists are hard at work to dominate the less developed nations of Africa, Asia and Latin America. Their allies are the ancient enemies of mankind: tyranny, poverty, ignorance and disease. If freedom is to prevail, we must do more than meet the immediate threat to free world security, whether in Southeast Asia or elsewhere. We must look beyond—to the long-range needs of the developing nations."[6]

Although United States foreign aid for economic development purposes has been viewed over the past two decades as an instrument in Western competition for the loyalties of poorer nations, there has been a marked shift in geographical emphasis during this time. Aid for those countries bordering the Communist bloc in Europe, something thought of in the late forties as a temporary measure, has been replaced in importance by aid for countries in Asia, Latin America, and Africa, to counter much more vague threats without any time limitation.[7] Another shift has been equally important: where the United States bore nearly all of the burden in 1947, between 1956 and 1963 its share became a rough but consistent five-eighths.[8]

The Cold War tie-in of Western aid for development emerges clearly in frequent dramatic comparisons by foreign-aid advocates of the scope and success of free-world efforts with those of the Communist bloc. Thus, in order to underline Western achievements, Gerhard Schröder, then West German foreign minister, noted in 1963 that aid emanating from industrial countries of the West and Japan was forty-five times that of the total Soviet-Chinese bloc in 1960, and that the latter had fulfilled only one-quarter of its promises.[9] So also, in order to drive home the different

6. Address to Congress. Text in the *New York Times*, Jan. 15, 1965, p. C12:1.

7. In the period since 1960, Asia has received about 40 per cent of Western developmental assistance, Africa 30 per cent, Latin America 20 per cent, (Southern) Europe 10 per cent. On a per capita basis, however, Africa has recently ranked first.

8. "Beachtliche Hilfe zur Selbsthilfe: Finanzielle Leistungen an Entwicklungsländer in den Jahren 1956 bis 1963," *Bulletin des Presse-und Informationsamtes der Bundesregierung* (hereinafter referred to as *Bulletin*), No. 40 (March 6, 1965), pp. 317–318. A 1961 U.S. State Department table affixes the U.S. share at a slightly higher nine-fourteenths during the earlier years of the period in question. United States Senate Committee on Foreign Relations, *Organization for Economic Cooperation and Development: Report* (Washington, 1961), Appendix 2, p. 121.

9. Statement in *Scala International: Sonderheft Entwicklungshilfe* (Dec., 1963), p. 8.

point of increasing competition for Western achievements, President Johnson's 1965 foreign-aid message noted that Russia and Communist China had more than tripled their promises of aid in the past year.[10] Such an added emphasis by the Communists evidently implies needed countermoves in development-aid efforts by the wealthier free nations. The prize in this competition appears throughout as a measure of political and economic favor among the countries of Asia, Africa, and Latin America.

In the spring of 1964, seventy-seven developing nations presented their problems to the United Nations Conference on Trade and Development, meeting in Geneva. They went on record as finding their rates of growth in recent years generally unsatisfactory and sustained development impossible on the basis of their resources alone; they said the urgently needed acceleration in growth would require efforts both by themselves and the developed countries.[11] Their problem of economic growth is complicated by several factors. Many of the less-developed countries still lack a sense of national unity and are far from possessing the political stability and authority essential to economic growth and to solving concomitant problems. In many cases the skills necessary to carry out new activities are only beginning to emerge. This, coupled with the fact that the needs of developing countries differ greatly from country to country, presents a challenge to the donor nations.

Of course, development-aid problems are not unique to the developing countries. It is important to remember that the industrial nations of the West have their own difficulties in connection with giving economic assistance; it is one thing to assent to the general idea of wealthy nations helping poorer ones and an entirely different one to suggest that one's own country assume responsibility for particular projects. Historical ties between developed and underdeveloped nations have proved an asset in

10. Address to Congress, p. C12:1. Writing on behalf of the Trade-Expansion Act of 1962, President Kennedy used the same reasoning to justify the measure's urgency: "The Communist aid and trade offensive has also become more apparent in recent years. Soviet bloc trade with 41 non-Communist countries in the less-developed areas of the globe has more than tripled in recent years; and bloc trade missions are busy in nearly every continent attempting to penetrate, encircle, and divide the free world." Reciprocal Trade Agreements Program—Message from the President of the United States (House Document 314), *Congressional Record—House*, Jan. 25, 1962, p. 953.

Communist foreign-aid obligations amounted to $1,246 million and $685 million in 1964 and 1965, respectively. The U.S.S.R. contributed $618 million (1964) and $369 million (1965). "Die Kapitalbewegungen nach den Entwicklungsländern," *Neue Zürcher Zeitung*, June 18, 1966.

11. Willard L. Thorp, *Development Assistance Efforts and Policies of the Members of the Development Assistance Committee* (Paris: Organization for Economic Cooperation and Development), Sept., 1964, p. 9. See also the following works, which treat the problem of growth acceleration in the developing countries: Max F. Millikan, W. W. Rostow, and P. N. Rosenstein-Rodan, *A Proposal: Key to an Effective Foreign Policy* (New York: Harper, 1957); F. Benham, *Economic Aid to Underdeveloped Countries* (New York: Oxford University Press, 1961); Walter Birmingham and A. G. Ford, editors, *Planning and Growth in Rich and Poor Countries* (New York: Praeger, 1965); and Lauchlin Currie, *Accelerating Development: The Necessity and the Means* (New York: McGraw-Hill, 1966).

gaining legislative support for aid programs in Western countries. England, France, and Belgium have shown a special affinity for aiding their former colonies, while the United States has inherited a feeling for responsibility in the Southeast Pacific from the days of its mandate to resist the Spanish enemy and Japanese invader. President Kennedy justified responsibility for aid to Latin America under the Alliance for Progress in terms of historical continuity from the time when, together, "we" achieved independence and established the Monroe Doctrine.[12] But for industrial nations whose ties to underdeveloped regions are neither very strong nor very recent, other reasons must be found to go beyond token support of development aid. Motivation in Cold War terms varies greatly among Western powers and does not fix individual responsibility. In most cases, development assistance is financed, directly or indirectly, through budgeted funds and has to compete with local political projects, which promise more visible results in less time. There would probably be stronger support for various assistance programs if examples of aid resulting in substantial progress occurred more frequently.[13]

It is likely that Communist bloc donor countries also have problems with development aid. Difficulties are inevitable when political considerations of development aid overshadow the economic capability of the donor nations to sustain the burden. But in a controlled economy, purely economic forces can give way to political expediency with relative ease. In this economic environment, situations such as Communist China's giving grain to other nations in the face of domestic shortages are not uncommon, as totalitarian governments need not account to the people for their actions.

The Free-World Effort

Almost all free-world development aid for the past six years has been coordinated by the Organization for Economic Cooperation and Develop-

12. "In the late 18th and early 19th century we struggled to throw off the bonds of colonial rule, to achieve political independence, and to establish the principle that never again would the Old World be allowed to impose its will on the nations of the New." Add to this the good-neighbor policy, and any United States failure to correct its (presumably recent) indifference to Latin America becomes historically unjustifiable: "For too long my country, the wealthiest nation on a poor continent, failed to carry out its full responsibilities to its sister Republics. We have now accepted that responsibility." President John F. Kennedy, "Fulfilling the Pledges of the Alliance for Progress" (White House Press Release, March 13, 1962), U.S. *Department of State Bulletin*, April 2, 1962, pp. 539.

13. President Johnson touched upon this fact in his fiscal 1966 foreign-aid message when he said that the United States was "ready and willing to cooperate with the industrious, but unwilling to subsidize those who do not assume responsibility for their own fate." the *New York Times*, Feb. 2, 1966. See also John D. Montgomery, *The Politics of Foreign Aid* (New York: Praeger, 1962); Ronald Robinson, *Industrialization in Developing Countries* (Cambridge, England: Overseas Study Committee, 1965); and A. H. Lovell, "How Should Overseas Aid Be Given?" *Lloyds Bank Review*, April 1966, pp. 19–32.

ment (OECD). This association of states is a successor to the Organization for European Economic Cooperation (OEEC), founded in 1948 to deal with the problems of European postwar recovery, to make recommendations for Marshall Plan allocations, and to aid in liberalizing trade among western European states. By 1960 the participating governments had come to agree that the purpose for which the OEEC had been founded was largely achieved. A conference of their representatives took place in Paris during January of that year, partly to deal with problems of relationships between the members of the European Common Market and the Outer Seven and partly to consider what more meaningful tasks the OEEC could undertake. A four-member committee with representatives from France, Great Britain, Greece, and the United States submitted its report on April 20, recommending that the OEEC be renamed the Organization for Economic Cooperation and Development and reorganized to meet the task of aiding underdeveloped countries to achieve economic growth. On July 23, 1960, Thorkil Kristensen of Denmark was named secretary-general of the nascent OECD; and on September 30, 1961, the change in title and stated purpose became official at the first meeting of the new organization, which retained virtual continuity in membership.[14] One noteworthy change was full membership in the new organization by the United States and Canada, which had participated in some functions of the earlier organization. Canada's Minister of Finance, Donald Fleming, became the first chairman of the OECD. Ratification of the treaties enabling participation by the member nations followed quickly, with the Senate approving United States membership on March 16, 1961, by a vote of 72 to 18. Although the first significant activities of the OECD in 1962 were primarily directed toward providing technical assistance to Greece, Iceland, Spain, Turkey, and Yugoslavia—the first four of which were continuing members from the OEEC—the primary emphasis since 1963 has been on dealing with the problems of Latin America, Asia, and Africa.

The problems inherent in the development-aid program have contributed to the variegated pattern of contributions by some countries within the OECD, although the totals from 1956 through 1964 indicate roughly a doubling of efforts on the part of the wealthier nations to improve the lot of the developing nations. (See Table I.) Of the world-wide total of aid donated to underdeveloped countries, by far the greatest quantity is coordinated by the Development Assistance Committee (DAC), an OECD agency, whose figures have accounted for virtually all the free-

14. Full members in both organizations were: Austria, Belgium, Denmark, France, German Federal Republic (also referred to in this book as "West Germany," or simply "Germany"), Greece, Ireland, Iceland, Italy, Luxembourg, Netherlands, Norway, Portugal, Sweden, Switzerland, and the United Kingdom. Japan, which had not belonged to the earlier organization, was admitted to membership in the OECD on July 26, 1963.

world aid recently contributed:[15] some $10,150 million out of $10,956 million in 1965. (See Table II.)

Table I.   The Flow of Official Financial Resources to Less-Developed Countries and Multilateral Agencies, 1956–1966 (in millions of U.S. dollars).[a]

Source	1956	1960	1961	1962	1963	1964	1965	1966
A. Official Aid								
Australia	34	58.9	70.9	73.8	96.9	(104.0)	121.6	128.8
Austria	—	−0.1	2.2	13.8	2.1	14.6	33.8	36.9
Belgium	20	101.0	92.1	79.8	89.9	81.7	112.4	92.1
Canada	30	75.2	61.5	54.4	98.0	127.7	124.3	208.5
Denmark	3	5.5	8.1	7.4	9.7	10.6	12.9	26.1
France	647	848.3	943.3	977.0	850.7	831.2	752.2	721.1
Germany	142	351.0	618.4	467.8	437.2	423.2	471.6	490.0
Italy	43	110.4	85.3	110.1	110.2	54.1	92.7	117.8
Japan	96	97.7	108.5	88.2	140.3	115.7	243.7	285.4
Nether- lands	48	46.7	69.3	90.8	37.8	48.4	59.6	95.4
Norway	8	10.1	9.0	6.9	20.6	17.1	11.8	13.4
Portugal	3	36.9	43.8	40.8	51.1	61.9	21.2	—
Sweden	3	6.7	8.4	18.5	22.9	32.8	38.1	55.5
United Kingdom	205	407.0	456.8	421.0	414.5	493.4	480.6	501.4
United States	2,006	2,776.0	3,447.0	3,536.0	3,699.0	3,445.0	3,626.8	3,634.0
Total DAC Aid	3,288	4,931.3	6,024.6	5,981.3	6,080.5	5,859.9	6,203.2	(6,466.2)
B. Private long-term net aid[b]	2,878.5	3,006.3	3,076.1	2,431.2	2,381.6	3,208.2	4,075.3	(3,426.1)
Total of official and private aid	6,166.5	7,937.3	9,100.7	8,417.5	8,462.1	9,068.1	10,278.6	(9,872.3)

Source: Compiled from tables appended to OECD, "Report of the Sixth High-Level Meeting of the Development Assistance Committee," Paris, July 20, 1967 (press release).
[a]Total sums in this and subsequent tables show minor deviations caused by rounding off component figures.
[b]Not including private export credits guaranteed by states.

In spite of the fact that aid coordinated by the Development Assistance Committee accounted for over 90 per cent of the total resources shown in Table II, the Development Assistance Committee considers the amount contributed by OECD countries too small to achieve its stated objective, namely, acceleration of the process of development in the less developed

15. The OECD countries not represented at all on the DAC: Ireland, Greece, Iceland, Spain, and Turkey, tend to be token donors or recipient nations. The odd fact that Portugal has become a fairly substantial donor country (Table I), while neighboring Spain has not, is probably to be explained by Portugal's vital interest in her own African territories. See Thorkil Kristensen, *Die wirtschaftlichen Beziehungen zwischen dem Westen und den Entwicklungsländern; in Kieler Studien*, new series, no. 22 (Kiel: Institut für Weltwirtschaft, Universität Kiel, 1962).

nations. The increase of OECD-member accomplishments over the $3,288-million figure of 1956 has been found not only inadequate in absolute terms; it has also been largely offset by population increases and increased costs of consumer goods in the underdeveloped countries. Because

Table II.   Total Net Flows to Less-Developed Countries 1960–1965 (in millions of U.S. dollars).

Source	1960	1961	1962	1963	1964	1965
A. DAC Members:						
Bilateral official	4,317	5,274	5,423	5,712	5,441	5,773
Bilateral private	2,784	2,986	2,231	2,402	3,044	3,589
Official to multilateral agencies	671	832	690	411	441	498
Private to multilateral agencies	174	75	219	−12	156	290
Total DAC outflow	7,947	9,168	8,564	8,513	9,081	10,150
B. Estimated flow from non-DAC members (including Soviet bloc)	360	533	567	647	662	(675)
C. Net additional multilateral outflow[a]	−604	−732	−537	+256	+195	+131
Total receipts of less-developed countries	7,703	8,969	8,594	9,416	9,938	(10,956)

Source: OECD, "What is Happening to Development Assistance?" Paris, October 18, 1966 (press release).

[a]Difference between disbursements by multilateral organizations in each year (net of capital subscriptions, bond purchases and repayments by less-developed countries) and total receipts in the same year, including those from non-DAC countries.

of free-world economic growth in the last decade, the developmental gap between the industrial nations of the West with Japan and those of the rest of Asia, Latin America, and Africa actually had widened rather than decreased by 1964.[16] A basic problem was that the DAC flow for 1962 and 1963 stayed in the vicinity of $8 billion, while the total aid available for the underdeveloped countries in either of these years remained slightly under the 1961 total. largely due to decreases in sums allotted to multilateral agencies by OECD countries. Figures for 1965 showed only a minor increase, bearing little relation to the increased annual require-

16. David A. Morse, Director-General of the International Labor Office, cited as source in press release of Bonn branch: "Industrie– und Entwicklungsländer, *"Bulletin,* No. 49 (March 19, 1965), pp. 392–393. see also Andreas Freund, "Flow of Funds to Poorer Lands is Termed Inadequate to Need," the *New York Times,* Jan. 15, 1965; "Europe is Warned by Thant on Aid," *ibid.,* May 4, 1966; and L. J. Zimmermann, *Poor Lands, Rich Lands; The Widening Gap* (New York: Random House, 1965). Those concerned about the lag in the flow of capital from the rich to the poor nations are impressed by the contrast between the gains realized in exports by the Western industrial and by the underdeveloped countries, since between 1963 and 1964 exports of the former group rose by 13.6 per cent but those of the latter group by 9.7 per cent. The fact, moreover, that the national products of both groups increased during the same period by 5 per cent (although the increase should have been higher in the developing countries) has caused despair among political and economic officials.

ments of the developing nations, chiefly as a result of still greater population pressures. A 1962 DAC admonition that some member countries are guilty of relative parsimony seems to have had little effect.[17] It has been contended that by 1970 between $15-20 billion must flow to the poor countries to sustain an average economic growth rate sufficient to take care of rapidly growing populations and to provide enough capital for significant investment.

Both the OECD and the United Nations have accepted the "one per cent of national income" formula as the target for expansion of developmental aid by individual donor nations. However arbitrary this standard is, it facilitates international evaluation of the efforts in question. Table III exemplifies this and corroborates the conclusion which can be drawn from preceding statistics, namely, that after 1961, Western aggregate developmental aid became stationary.

Table III. Disbursement of Assistance as Percentage of National Income.

	1962	1964	1965	1966
Average of DAC countries	1.04	0.96	1.00	0.40
U.S.A.	1.00	0.96	0.98	0.76
France	2.31	1.94	1.87	1.70
United Kingdom	0.97	1.09	1.26	1.16
Germany	1.00	0.94	0.85	0.81

Source: Derived from OECD, *1965 Review*, p. 55, with additions from *Neue Zürcher Zeitung*, "Entwicklungshilfe als Daueraufgabe," July 27, 1967. West German computations, based on net national product at factor cost, vary somewhat from those of the OECD; for 1964, the following proportions were arrived at: Total DAC, 0.86; U.S.A., 0.85; France, 1.74; U.K., 1.00; and Germany, 0.83. Kreditanstalt für Wiederaufbau, *XVII. Jahresbericht (1965)*, p. 22.

The $131 million disbursement from multilateral (international) agencies given in Table II does not reflect a lessening of the flow from these agencies to underdeveloped countries; on the contrary, such disbursements increased sharply from 1961 to 1964. The multilateral part of the problem of financing development aid is necessarily complicated by the longer route from donor to recipient. Funds for multilateral organizations are obtained from governments and through the sales of securities in private capital markets. Until 1963, the total input from these two sources provided the international aid institutions with more funds than they disbursed and, therefore, substantial funds accumulated. 1963 saw the beginning of an opposite tendency (see Table IV).

DAC spokesmen remained hopeful in 1965 that the unbalanced situation

---

17. "In relation to their resources and capabilities, some members of the Committee are contributing more than others. This indicates that, from the point of view of resources, there is scope for special emphasis on an increase in the aid effort of certain countries." "Resolution on the First Annual Aid Review and the Future Work of the Development Assistance Committee" (in press communiqué), *U.S. Department of State Bulletin*, Sept. 10, 1962, p. 396.

depicted in Table IV might right itself at least somewhat in the future. Disbursements were expected to continue to rise at a high rate, but projected budgets of free-world nations indicated that there would be some improvement in public contributions over the 1964 level. While their expectations were partly fulfilled in 1965, commitments by the Big Four of foreign aid—the United States, Great Britain, France, and Germany—each with pressing budgetary problems in 1966, ran lower that year than in 1965; their reductions were not offset by increases from the smaller DAC countries.[18]

Table IV.   Multilateral Flows (in millions of U.S. dollars).

	1961	1962	1963	1964
Public Contributions	811	602	396	367
Private Markets	75	214	—	153
Total Contributions	886	816	396	520
Disbursements	428	583	776	927

Source: Derived from Willard L. Thorp, Development Assistance Efforts and Policies of the Members of the Development Assistance Committee (Paris: OECD, September 1964), pp. 26–27; and OECD, 1965 Review, pp. 35–36.

The largest part of the flow of assistance to less-developed countries is based on bilateral arrangements between donor and recipient countries. These arrangements include the use of both public and private funds which are also the flows that most clearly reflect the policies and intentions of the donor countries. The Development Assistance Committee considers bilateral resources to include:[19]

1.   Financial grants.

2.   Grants in kind.

3.   Technical assistance contributions (funds for the technical education of persons on all levels in the recipient country).

4.   Sales of surplus agricultural commodities against local currencies.

5.   Public net lending for maturity periods exceeding five years.

Total public bilateral net disbursements of OECD countries reached a level of $5,680 million in 1963 and $5,555 million in 1964. This decrease was a minor one (2 per cent), and the DAC would probably not like to view it as a trend. The largest 1964-1965 increases in disbursing public bilateral aid occurred in the United Kingdom ($76 million), the German Federal Republic ($55 million), and Canada ($21 million). In contrast, U.S. disbursements fell off by $336 million.

In addition to disbursements, new commitments are also indicators of trends, particularly since the time lag inherent in projects frequently

18. Neue Zürcher Zeitung, "Entwicklungshilfe als Daueraufgabe," July 27, 1967, and Bernard Nossiter, "While the Rich Get Richer . . ." International Herald Tribune, July 22–23, 1967.

19. Thorp, p. 21. The items listed constitute the basis for all DAC bilateral aid computations.

spans several years. New bilateral commitments by DAC members declined between 1962 and 1963, but gained in 1964 by $1.3 billion. However, the West German increase between 1962 and 1963 was lost by 1964.

Within the framework of bilateral aid, technical assistance expenditures have continued to rise significantly. As a portion of the total DAC flow of official long-term financial resources to less-developed countries, technical assistance rose from 13 per cent in 1962 to 15 per cent in 1963 and to 16 percent in 1964.[20] While this reflects a strong desire among donor nations to improve human skills (human capital) in the developing countries, a major obstacle to effective technical assistance by free-world nations remains the difficulty of providing adequate numbers of qualified experts to be used as instructors.

Most donor nations would prefer to see a greater portion of development aid accomplished through the use of private funds. President Johnson's 1965 foreign-aid message noted: "We are placing increasing emphasis on the role of private institutions and private enterprise in the development process."[21] The strong West German feeling on this subject will become increasingly apparent in subsequent chapters. Private investment is conspicuously absent from the DAC's official listing of bilateral resources given above, undoubtedly because private investment requires no contractual relationship between donor and recipient states. Constitutional or other guarantees to the effect that taxes on foreign enterprise will be limited and prohibitions against outright confiscations in many ways serve the purpose of agreements between industrial and less-developed nations, since they remove the greatest barrier to private investment in these countries.[22] In its "Resolution on the First Annual Aid Review and the Future Work of the Development Assistance Committee," the DAC had already pointed out in 1962: "There should be a further exploration of ways and means to promote and safeguard the flow of private capital

20. *Ibid.*, p. 23. The same tendency is even more evident within UNESCO under Director René Maheu, whose total budget for 1965–1966 was raised by 20 per cent over the previous corresponding period, to effect a doubling of activity in technical education projects. "Bildungshilfe muß der Entwicklungshilfe vorangehen: zum Besuch des General-Direktors der UNESCO in der Bundesrepublik," *Bulletin*, No. 138 (Sept. 9, 1964), p. 1,288. See also William N. Parker, W. Paul Strassmann, E. A. Wilkening, and Robert S. Merril, *The Diffusion of Technical Knowledge as an Instrument of Economic Development* (Washington: National Institute of Social and Behavioral Science, 1962); and Yonah Alexander, *International Technical Assistance Experts* (New York: Praeger, 1966).

21. "Address to Congress..." p. C12:1. In 1964, David Bell, Director of the U.S. Agency for International Development (AID), presented Walter Scheel, then West German minister for economic cooperation, with a catalog outlining more than 1,500 possibilities for private investment. Press release of the Bundesministerium für wirtschaftliche Zusammenarbeit, "Verstärkte Koordinierung bei der Entwicklungshilfe," *Bulletin*, No. 38 (March 4, 1965), p. 307.

22. Kurt Schmücker, now West German Federal Treasurer, in the Erhard Cabinet Minister for Economic Affairs, "Entscheidende Rolle der Weltbank: Entwicklungshilfe eine politische und wirtschaftliche Notwendigkeit dieser Zeit," *Bulletin*, No. 139 (Sept. 11, 1964), p. 1,294.

to less-developed countries."[23] But exactly what can be done here without indirectly affronting the sensitive feelings of national sovereignty of the developing nations remains as vague now as then. The flow of private long-term capital in all forms from DAC countries to the less-developed countries decreased slightly in 1963. In 1964 it rose again, but its rise to a record high in 1965 was almost cancelled out by a reversion in 1966 to only a small fraction over the 1964 level in absolute terms. Of the 1964 official—private total of $9,068 million shown in Table I, public funds accounted for 64-2/3 per cent, while the remaining 35-1/3 per cent was obtained from private sources; the 1966 portion of 34-2/3 per cent reflects the comparative stability of the proportion of aid from private sources in recent years. Such stability is, of course, not enough for DAC leaders, whose hopes for substantial increases from the private sector have been disappointed, probably as a result of the poor investment environment existing in many areas.

The difficulties in assessing the effectiveness of worldwide development aid measures are increased by the long-term nature of the economic growth process, which must be measured in decades rather than years. While it is easy to point to current problem areas, specific gains are not always readily apparent. Again the DAC is hopeful that progress is being realized in the following ways:

1. New institutions are being formed, ranging from agricultural demonstration centers to development banks.

2. Developing nations are facing economic problems with greater realism.

3. Planning is being facilitated by improved statistics within developing countries.

4. Some countries are developing cadres of government officials capable of operating with greater competence in the public interest.

5. Donor countries are showing a wider geographic distribution of aid with increased variety and flexibility in operations.[24]

West Germany and the Free World Team

All in all, there remains a certain residue of conflict in descriptions of what is happening in the worldwide development-aid program, even when these are made by the best-informed spokesmen for contributing countries. There are expressions of disappointment with insufficient achievements that contrast sorely with what seem to be potentialities: donor countries are too stingy and recipient countries are too reckless; aid appropriations are only a fraction of what the industrial countries

23. Text in U.S. Department of State Bulletin, Sept. 10, 1962, p. 396.
24. Thorp, p. 13.

can afford, and new nations' failure to dissipate fears of confiscation frightens private capital away.[25] There are also words of hope and assurance that progress can be expected if new intelligence is shown by donor and recipient alike: donor countries can pinpoint feasible economic targets and recipient countries are awakening to a sense of urgency and responsibility. Most information available on development aid is filtered through one official source or another; and probably nothing comes more naturally to an agency spokesman than singling out lack of courage or responsibility somewhere outside his own agency as a severe impediment to fulfilling the agency's program—a program which will contribute to the national interest, world peace, and the like. But, according to the same agency spokesman, the impediments cannot be insurmountable; the agency may just *possibly* be able to overcome them, *if* it can awaken enough interest, secure sufficient funds, and count on the support of complementing officials and agencies at home and abroad.

In dealing with the free-world development-aid effort, there is not only the natural official tendency to equivocate in this fashion with regard to present success and future hopes. There is also a very real uncertainty—because of huge numbers of human variables, because the program is new, and because the international organizational framework coordinates national efforts only in the broadest sense of the term (without exercising any actual control over the all-important matter of how much the individual nation states are going to participate).[26] Many interpretations can be placed on the decline in flow to multilateral organizations and from private sources in contrast to the slight rise in the total net flow of official and private resources from Development Assistance Committee countries which occurred in 1963 as a result of concentration on bilateral aid. A study of different motives and relative degrees of committedness on the part of members of the free-world team on an individual basis seems necessary in order to analyze the total effort.

In spite of the comparative recentness (1956) of the Federal Republic's role in post-war intercontinental economic politics, its importance as a member of this team is unquestioned. Figures presented so far show West Germany to be among the major contributors to the free-world effort, of which her aid policies are to constitute an integral—though distinctly identifiable—part. In this spirit the West Germans have contributed signi-

25. Cf. Hans J. Morgenthau, "Preface to a Political Theory of Foreign Aid" in Robert A. Goldwin, ed., *Why Foreign Aid?* (Chicago: Rand McNally & Co., 1963), pp. 70–89.

26. One somewhat rough and ready but friendly account of the problems that beset non-Communist international planners sums them up: "The only piece of paper that binds the Atlantic partnership says a nation may ignore any decision it chooses to be against." Charles A. Cerami, *Alliance Born of Danger: America, the Common Market, and the Atlantic Partnership* (New York: Harcourt, Brace and World, Inc., 1963), p. 121. As for the DAC's development-aid efforts: "This is all voluntary, as everything connected with OECD is" (p. 125).

ficantly to the pooling of international bilateral assistance through consortia sponsored by the World Bank and the OECD.

Succeeding chapters will examine the objectives, adequacy, and effectiveness of West Germany's development-aid efforts, along with the interplay between her development-aid policies or programs and her foreign policy—an intriguing aspect of the problem. First to be considered is the question of West Germany's supporting economy, a fundamental consideration in assessing the continuing importance of any country's development-aid program.

THE ECONOMIC BASIS OF GERMANY'S FOREIGN AID

The very nature and purpose of development aid postulates that it be furnished by nations whose economic power enables them to shoulder the long-term commitments involved. The West German economy possesses that power since it constitutes one of the world's most productive economic systems and represents one of the world's most important markets.[1] These two attributes of the nation's economy have not been seriously affected by the four business cycles which have developed since 1950, with peaks in 1951, 1955, 1959–1960 and 1964, and slumps in between (including the present one). Neither have internal developments interfered with Germany's determination to fulfill her foreign-aid programs, although budgetary considerations have imposed some strain on their financing.

In view of the above-mentioned economic fluctuations (partially reflected in Table VI)[2] the West German economy can no longer be referred to as "one of the stablest and healthiest," as former Chancellor Erhard described it, or as one with "a lasting and strongly running favorable turn of the market," as characterized by Kurt Schmücker, Erhard's successor in the Ministry of Economics.[3] Nevertheless, the economy remains a very modern and viable one, of which the steadily increasing per capita income is an eloquent proof.

The sinews of German economic achievements can be explained in several ways because they depend on numerous variables. If Marshall Plan aid and West European regional cooperation are disregarded, students

1. In 1966, West Germany's GNP compared with those of three other industrial leaders as follows: Germany, $119 billion; U.S., $740 billion; U.K., $95 billion; Japan, $97 billion. (International Monetary Fund, *International Financial Statistics,* September, 1967.) The 1965 per capital imports and exports revealed the following comparative capacities—Germany: imports, $296; exports $303; U.S., $109 and $139; U.K., $295 and $251; Japan, $83 and $86. Statistical Office of the European Communities, *Basic Statistics of the Community, 1966* (7th edition), p. 101.

2. The recession which started in 1965 is especially evident in 1965–1966 data for "GNP at 1954 prices," "gross investment in fixed assets," "imports" (all of which declined) and "exports" (which rose).

3. Arthur J. Olsen, "Erhard Sums Up Germany: Position One of Stablest and Healthiest in World," the *New York Times,* Jan. 15, 1965; Kurt Schmücker, "Die Stabilität hat den Vorrang," radio address, Jan. 4, 1965, *Bulletin,* No. 3 (Jan. 7, 1965), p. 22.

of the Republic's development will probably agree that its progress has been brought about by the economic policies which the Federal Republic has pursued since World War II, from which a *dirigiste* ingredient has not been absent. This progress has been also predicated on the country's organizational spirit and methods; export-oriented capital-goods industries; industrial relations permitting gains in productivity to be translated into profitable enterprise; vigorous investment which has claimed more than one-fourth of the GNP; adequate supply of skilled labor; the "general staff mentality" of German managers; the close links existing between the country's industries and financial institutions; and last but certainly not least, fiscal policies encouraging business activity.

All commentators on West German economic accomplishments are agreed that they have resulted from a basic economic institution: competition. With a few exceptions—notably transportation, where the government assigns the carriers' tasks; agriculture, where special protection has been demanded by German farmers; and housing, where controls were essential to meet postwar requirements—the Federal Republic has promoted competition in all fields.

But competition is only the most obvious characteristic of the postwar German economy, which has another important side. Partly because of the traditional strength of the state for most of the last century and partly because of the strength of the Social Democrats in the Bundestag, the social duties of the state play a much larger part in commentaries on the West German economy by its architects and advocates than in any discussion of the American economy. The Christian Democratic Union (Christlich-Demokratische Union, CDU), the party of Adenauer and Erhard, whom Americans generally think of as orthodox spokesmen for capitalism, prides itself upon its vastly increased expenditures for government pensions, support of the compulsory health insurance plan, sick pay, and the like, within the framework of a broad social program or welfare policy *(Sozialpolitik)*.[4] The government of the Federal Republic includes a special Ministry for Family and Youth Affairs in addition to the Ministry for Labor and Social Affairs. Thinking of all components of national economics and politics as potential elements in the government's social-political plan is second nature to West German officials regardless of party affiliation. Characteristically, the Federal Republic's gross national product is termed "gross *social* product" *(Bruttosozialprodukt)*. When asked to characterize the nature of German foreign aid, former Economic Cooperation Minister Walter Scheel chose the words "social policy on a world-wide scale."[5] If competition has largely determined the size of the revenues over which the Bonn govern-

4. Theodor Blank, Minister for Labor and Social Affairs, "Eine Bilanz, die sich sehen lassen kann: Die Sozialleistungen sind noch stärker gewachsen als das Sozialprodukt," *Bulletin*, No. 2, (Jan. 6, 1965), pp. 9–10.

5. Statement in *Scala International: Sonderheft Entwicklungshilfe* (Dec. 1963), p. 9.

ment has disposed in the postwar period, the notion of social purpose has determined in large part how these revenues have been spent. This explains to some extent why government development aid has had to compete—not always successfully—with other uses of budgetary funds, especially those allocated to social security programs, construction and national defense expenditures.

It is unlikely that the economic policies of the Kiesinger government, in which Professor Karl Schiller, a Social Democrat, is economics minister, will depart from previous policies to any drastic degree. Unquestionably, Schiller's stabilization policy of "controlled expansion" owes much to governmental determination to terminate the current (post-1965) recession and to resort, therefore, to deficit spending and, generally, Keynesian anti-cyclical measures. However, the Economics Minister has reassured the public not only that in the new system (with medium-term financial planning) "spontaneity of the market and competition will retain their central functions," but also that his policies will be carried out in full awareness of this time-honored fact: "the dynamic market economy and the socially conscious state condition *(bedingen)* each other reciprocally."[6] Still, it would be reasonable to expect that the international economic and financial policies of the Kiesinger administration will undergo some change which may very well affect West German foreign aid. The latter may be also affected by the realization of the present Grand Coalition government that the German "economic miracle" is definitely over and that only a 5 per cent annual growth rate is to be aimed at.

The National Product

The generally expanding nature of the West German economic system can be seen in a comparison of the gross national products of the Federal Republic and other Western nations based on the data given in Table V. The economic progress demonstrated in this table is particularly noteworthy if one takes into account that the 1953–1958 increase reflects only part of the beginning of postwar economic growth in Germany. The Federal Republic's need to recover markets lost during and immediately after World War II complemented the modernization of its industrial structure forced by wartime destruction, providing an impetus for vigorous international competition in comparison with the lesser efforts of France, the United Kingdom, and the United States. The influx of several million refugees by the early fifties ultimately aided both infrastructural and industrial expansion, as state

6. For an excellent statement of Schiller's economic objectives see his article "Stabilität und Wachstum als wirtschaftspolitische Aufgabe," *Neue Zürcher Zeitung,* Feb. 9, 1967.

governments granted land and tax advantages to owners of new factories in order to deal with the sudden increase in the laboring population; new establishments were given government assistance to obtain easy access to highways and railroads, and they were subsidized by special freight rates.[7] The Korean War stimulated world trade at the same time. All these factors contributed toward making the annual growth rate figure even larger—9 per cent—for the period 1951–1953 than for the subsequent years given in Table V.

Table V.   Average Annual Growth Rates of GNP at Constant Prices.

Country	Aggregate GNP	
	1953-58	1955-65
Germany	6.9%	5.6%
France	4.6	5.0
Italy	5.2	5.6
United Kingdom	2.2	3.1
U.S.A.	1.7	3.4

Source: Statistical Office of the European Communities, *Basic Statistics of the Community,* Sixth Edition (Brussels, 1965), p. 35, and Seventh Edition (1966), p. 74.

Although Table VI verifies the described development and reveals adequately the enviable West German economic strides taken during the years since the inception of the country's formal foreign-aid program (1960), it is necessary to supplement this statistical view of the nation's economic vigor by a few additional comments about its progress and capacity to be even more impressive.

First, the expansionary process was free of tensions because 1) it drew on rising private savings; and 2) it was supported by a relatively resourceful capital market, sufficient to meet not only internal but also foreign demand

7. Friedrich Edding, *Die wirtschaftliche Eingliederung der Vertriebenen und Flücht- linge in Schleswig-Holstein* (Berlin: Dunker & Humblot, 1955), p. 34. There is, of course, a natural reluctance to refer to the uprooting of millions of Germans and the first un- certain years of their economic existence in the Federal Republic as an economic good. Most official West German commentators describe the West German economy of the early fifties with special reference to its chronic unemployment—which the influx of refugees could have been expected to aggravate—in order to contrast the bright present with the dark past. For many such spokesmen, the huge numbers of refugee workers for whom new jobs had to be found during the rest of the decade pointed up the uncanny ability of the social-market economy to overcome all obstacles. Others, particularly Eastern commentators, emphasized the refugees' competition for jobs as a prime factor in keeping prices for industrial goods stable within West Germany: "The division of Germany called forth a steady flow of refugees from East to West Germany, thus creating some sort of a 'reserve labour force' which enabled wages in West Germany to be maintained at a comparatively low level." Janez Stanovnik, *World Economic Blocs: The Nonaligned Countries and Economic Integration* (Beograd: Edition Jugoslavija, 1962), p. 46.

Table VI.   Sources and Uses of West German Gross National Product.

A.   Sources (at current prices)

	1966 propor- tions (in %)[b]	percentage change from preceding year					
		1961	1962	1963	1964	1965[a]	1966[a]
Agriculture, forestry, fisheries	4.2	+ 1.2	+ 0.2	+ 7.3	+ 6.4	− 2.2	+ 0.2
Producing industries	51.9	+10.5	+ 8.7	+ 4.8	+10.0	+ 8.6	+ 4.5
Trade and transport	19.1	+ 8.4	+ 9.9	+ 6.1	+ 9.1	+ 8.5	+ 6.0
Services	24.8	+13.2	+ 9.6	+10.9	+10.3	+11.5	+11.4
Total	100.0	+10.1	+ 8.7	+ 6.5	+ 9.6	+ 8.7	+ 6.2
Total at 1954 prices		+ 5.4	+ 4.1	+ 3.2	+ 6.6	+ 4.8	+ 2.6

B.   Uses

	1966 propor- tions (in %)	1961	1962	1963	1964	1965[a]	1966[a]
Private consumption	57.1	+ 9.8	+ 9.2	+ 5.4	+ 8.0	+ 9.5	+ 7.0
Government consumption	15.7	+14.0	+15.3	+11.4	+ 4.3	+12.7	+ 7.9
Gross investment in fixed assets	25.7	+14.3	+11.8	+ 5.2	+14.5	+ 9.1	+ 2.8
Inventory changes	0.2	−	−	−	−	−	−
Export surplus	1.4	−	−	−	−	−	−
Exports	21.5	+ 4.6	+ 4.8	+ 8.8	+11.4	+ 9.1	+12.7
Imports	−20.1	+ 5.9	+10.6	+ 7.2	+11.8	+17.5	+ 4.7
GNP at market prices	100.0	+ 9.9	+ 8.7	+ 6.5	+ 9.6	+ 8.7	+ 6.3

Source: Report of the Deutsche Bundesbank for the Year 1964, p. 79; ibid., 1966, p. 74.
[a]Provisional figures.
[b]In billions of DM, the 1966 GNP total was 478.7 (331.5 at 1954 prices), broken down as follows: agriculture, forestry, and fisheries, 20.1; producing industries, 248.4; trade and transport, 92.7; and services, 117.5.

for investable funds.[8] (Table VII indicates the scope of long-term capital exports and imports.)

This twofold use of German savings made the nation's authorities more than ever conscious of the importance of (monetary and fiscal) policies capable of safeguarding the internal as well as the international value of the mark (DM). The latter gave rise to some concern when, in 1965, Germany's balance of payments worsened considerably and her international reserves began to decline. The competitiveness of the country's exportables was at stake.

8. While between 1960 and 1965 savings deposits rose from DM 53 billion to DM 111 billion (equal to 12 per cent of disposable income), in 1966 the increment was as much as DM 16 billion. Thus domestic formation of material and monetary assets proceeded without interruption. Between 1960 and 1964 the value of floated debt securities expanded from DM 5.4 billion to DM 16.9 billion. But as soon as the 1965 recessionary tendency appeared, these issues declined to only DM 9.4 billion in 1966. The corresponding amounts of corporate shares were DM 1.9 billion (1960), DM 2.6 billion (1965), and DM 2.0 billion (1966). Report of the Deutsche Bundesbank for the Year 1966, pp. 155, 162.

Another decisive factor underlying the acceleration of West German production prior to 1965 must be seen in the remarkable rise in labor productivity (6 per cent in 1964) which—for the good of the entire country, to be sure—failed to induce workers and employees to raise their wage and salary claims. The existing employment vacancies spared the German industries and labor market some major tensions.

Table VII.   Net Long-Term Capital Movements (in billions of DM).

Investments	1961	1964	1965	1966
A. German Investments Abroad (Export)				
1. Private	1.1	1.8	1.9	2.4
2. Official	1.9	1.2	1.2	3.0
Total	3.0	3.0	3.1	5.4
B. Foreign Investments in Germany (Import)	1.2	2.2[a]	3.9	2.8

Source: Report of the Deutsche Bundesbank for the Year 1966, p. 163.
[a]In 1963, capital imports amounted to an unprecedented DM 4.3 billion, but were cut by the 1964 coupon tax.

Finally, investment gains (gross investment in fixed assets) and government expenditures for civilian purposes such as social security pensions, civil administration, the federal railways, subsidies to agriculture, also played a significant role in Germany's economic expansion. But many started to sound the alarm when, in 1965, the indebtedness of public authorities increased by DM 9 billion to a total of DM 47.6 billion. (The 1963 and 1964 increases were also substantial, namely, DM 6 billion and DM 5 billion, respectively.)[9] Nevertheless, in the 1965 federal budget, the foreign-aid appropriation was not reduced. In fact, it was raised to a record level of $235 million—to be supplemented by government loans and guarantees.[10]

Foreign Trade

The development of West German foreign trade since World War II, and particularly since 1950, has indeed been impressive: imports jumped from DM 10.7 billion in 1950 to DM 55 billion in 1964, and to DM 68.9 billion in 1966; and exports rose from DM 8.4 billion to DM 80.4 billion over the same sixteen-year period. The gains during the years 1960–1966 were, respec-

9. *Ibid., 1965*, p. 74. Between 1963 and 1965, total government expenditures rose from DM 134 billion to DM 161 billion, i.e., by about 10 per cent per year. This process turned budgetary surpluses into deficits.

10. "A Record Budget Presented in Bonn," the *New York Times*, Oct. 15, 1965. In 1965, aggregate demand caught up with aggregate supply and some disturbing economic tensions appeared. Inflationary pressures were mitigated not only by a restrictive credit policy, but also by merchandise imports which made up 16 per cent of Germany's GNP. Whereas the index of production rose by 7 points between 1964 and 1965 (to 132, 1960 = 100), the import index climbed by 23 points (to 169, 1960 = 100).

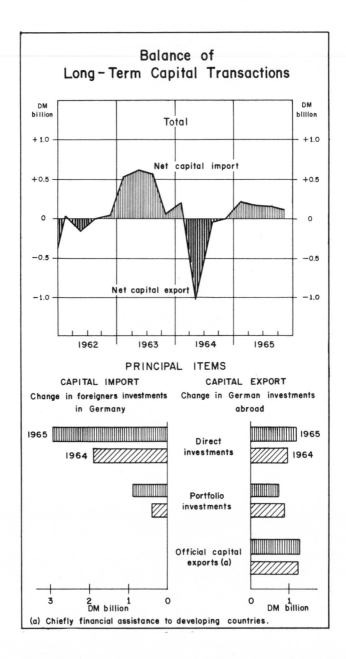

Balance of
Long-Term Capital Transactions

(Reproduced through the courtesy of the Deutsche Bundesbank.)

Chart I

FOREIGN TRADE

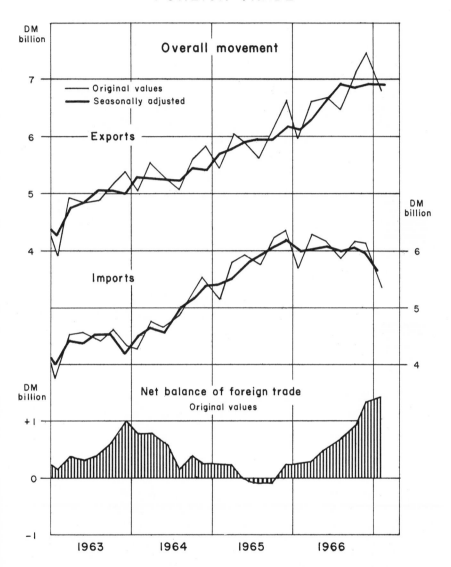

(Reproduced through the courtesy of the Deutsche Bundesbank.)

Chart II

tively, imports, DM 29.2 billion, exports, DM 32.5 billion.[11] These increases saw Germany assume third place in world trade after the United States and the United Kingdom—in imports since 1954 and in exports since 1953. By 1961, the Federal Republic still maintained third place in imports with 8.9 per cent of the world-wide total but had overtaken Great Britain to assume second place in exports with 10.7 per cent of the total. By the end of 1965, West Germany had arrived at second place in imports as well.

Various factors have contributed to the nation's success in achieving steady increases in foreign trade. First, the state of markets for German goods abroad has been excellent. The wide demand in the United States for economical and easy-to-park small cars, beginning in the early fifties and continuing to the present, has been only one example of constant demands from abroad for German products.[12] German economists are generally agreed that boomlike conditions in many of the Federal Republic's international markets have given a continued impetus to German industry and its exports. Secondly, the relatively stable price level in the country has made its goods additionally attractive to foreign customers. The viability of its domestic market economy, particularly its absence of industrial strife and its achievement of full employment, ultimately deserves credit for this. Then, too, Germany has always enjoyed a reputation for high quality products; unlike Japan, the Federal Republic did not have to overcome a prewar reputation for shoddiness in order to find postwar markets for its manufactured goods. During the current recession it is weakening internal demand, evident in both private consumption and business investment, that has benefited export sales.

West Germany's exports are much the same as those of analogous parts of the German Reich before World War II, with capital goods and other finished and semi-manufactured products making up the largest parts. Table VIII shows the breakdown for 1964–1966. With special attention to development aid, it is noteworthy that investment goods, which have made up the bulk (and in 1964, as much as two-thirds) of exported finished goods, have been consistently rising from year to year: in 1961 by 9.1 per cent; 1962, 5.8 per cent; 1963, 11.1 per cent; 1964, 10.7 per cent; and 1966, 12.8 per cent.

German imports fall somewhat less easily into categories of products, and their composition resembles the German prewar import structure less closely than exports do. Detailed statistics reveal that in the sixties the importation of finished and semi-finished goods has generally been growing more strongly than that of foodstuffs. (The small gains in 1966, as shown in Table IX, attest to a year of economic recession.) One would, of course, expect that the Federal Republic's separation from the eastern provinces

11. *Monthly Report of the Deutsche Bundesbank*, June 1966, p. 27.

12. Helmut Hesse, "Strukturwandlungen im Aussenhandel" in *Wandlungen der Wirtschaftsstruktur in der Bundesrepublik Deutschland* (Berlin: Duncker & Humblot, 1962), p. 279.

Table VIII.   Commodity Composition of Exports (in percentages).

Exports	1964 100% = DM 64.8 bill.	1965 100% = DM 71.5 bill.	Gain +10.4%	1966 100% = DM 80.4 bill.	Gain +12.5%
A. Foodstuffs	2.5	2.8	+22.7	2.4	− 0.6
B. Industrial Products	97.1	96.8	+10.0	97.1	+12.9
Raw Materials	3.9	3.6	+ 1.5	3.5	+10.9
Semi-Manufactures	8.8	8.7	+ 9.1	8.9	+14.4
Finished Products	84.4	84.5	+10.5	84.7	+12.8

Source: Der Bundesminister für Wirtschaft, *Die wirtschaftliche Lage in der Bundesrepublik Deutschland,*
4. Vierteljahr 1964, p. 44; and *ibid.*, 1. Vierteljahr 1967, p. 39.

of the German Reich (particularly Silesia and Pomerania which were agricultural regions) would force it to compensate by proportionately larger
increases in agricultural imports. This was indeed the situation in the immediate postwar years; however, since then, in considerable part because
of increasing agricultural efficiency at home, food imports have decreased.
Still, West Germany's agricultural imports remain considerable. As far as
trade with developing nations is concerned, most agricultural products of
Asia, Africa, and South America are not of such a type as to be greatly
affected by competitive domestic agriculture in West Germany at all. On
the contrary, the higher standard of living brought about during the 1950's
by the favorable state of business in the Federal Republic has produced increased consumer demands for such products of the less-developed nations
as tea, coffee, and cocoa; this became particularly evident after the reduction of the previously heavy taxes on these items, so that they are no longer
considered luxuries by most West Germans.

The comparatively high per capita volumes of West German exports
and imports point, clearly enough, to a lively governmental interest in
foreign trade; this, taken together with expanding domestic economy, should
favor a sound foreign-aid program. The developing nations of Europe (Spain,

Table IX.   Commodity Composition of Imports (in percentages).

Imports	1964 100% = DM 55 bill.	1965 100% = DM 66.5 bill.	Gain +19.7%	1966 100% = DM 68.9 bill.	Gain +3.2%
A. Foodstuffs	23.9	23.9	+20.1	24.0	+3.6
B. Industrial Products	75.1	75.1	+19.7	74.9	+2.8
Raw Materials	18.5	16.2	+ 4.7	16.3	+3.4
Semi-Manufactures	16.6	15.3	+10.5	14.9	+0.1
Finished Products	40.0	43.5	+30.4	43.7	+3.6

Source: Der Bundesminister für Wirtschaft, *Die wirtschaftliche Lage in der Bundesrepublik Deutschland,*
4. Vierteljahr 1964, p. 44; *ibid.*, 1. Vierteljahr 1967, p. 39.

Greece, Turkey and Yugoslavia), Asia, Africa, and Latin America have been significant purchasers of German manufactured exports and sellers of certain foodstuffs and raw materials which the Germans import. Table X shows that they account for some 20 per cent of Germany's total foreign trade.[13] It is noteworthy that while West German commercial relations with the emerging nations have grown steadily in the sixties, the rates of the increases in question have been substantially lower than those pertaining to trade with industrialized countries. Then, too, exchange of goods and services with the developing areas is partially explained by, as well as predicated on, outflow of West German long-term capital, private as well as official.

Table X. Balance of Trade by Groups of Countries (in billions of DM).

	Percentage of Total Trade (1966)	1960	1961	1964	1965	1966
All Countries	100%	+ 5.2	+ 6.6	+ 6.1	+ 1.2	+ 8.0
A. All Western Industrial Countries	74.9	+ 5.0	+ 6.3	+ 7.9	+ 3.1	+ 8.6
E.E.C.[a]	37.2	+ 1.5	+ 2.4	+ 3.2	− 1.4	+ 1.5
E.F.T.A.[b]	21.0	+ 5.0	+ 5.8	+ 7.9	+ 7.2	+ 8.3
U.S.A.	10.7	− 2.2	− 2.6	− 3.3	− 3.5	− 2.0
B. Developing Countries	20.8	− 0.06	+ 0.25	− 1.9	− 1.8	− 0.9
Imports		(10.9)	(10.9)	(13.8)	(15.4)	(16.2)
Exports		(10.8)	(11.1)	(11.9)	(13.6)	(15.3)
C. Eastern Bloc Countries	4.2	+ 0.3	+ 0.03	− 0.01	− 0.2	+ 0.2
D. Ship and aircraft fuel (from all above blocs)	0.1	−	−	−	−	−

Source: *Monthly Report of the Deutsche Bundesbank,* May 1965, pp. 126–127, and July 1967, pp. 78–79.
[a]European Economic Community.
[b]European Free Trade Association.

There is nothing in the structure of German foreign trade to make a (large) excess of exports over imports inevitable since both trade flows depend ultimately on internal economic conditions—as the years 1964–1966 have demonstrated clearly. Nevertheless, the fact that the value of industrial goods—the overwhelmingly dominant part of West German exports—has been rising faster than the value of the foodstuffs and raw materials—which weigh heavily in its imports—makes such a trend likely. Even so, in 1960, the West German exports and imports with the underdeveloped countries (which, as purchasers of industrial goods and sellers of raw materials, should have been most affected by this factor) almost cancelled each other

13. For a geographic breakdown of the trade with the developing countries see Chap. X, note 16.

out. With the countries of Asia, West Germany's balance at the year's end was $114 million, but with those of Africa it was −$19.6 million, and with the Latin American nations −$94.2 million. Nor was the trend from 1961 to 1964 completely constant: in 1962, the foreign-trade export surplus dropped from the 1961 figure of $1.66 billion to $.882 billion. Nonetheless, in 1964, German economists and government officials felt the need to curb the overall trend. Their efforts appear to have been successful, for they were followed during that year by a sharp rise in imports, increased spending abroad by German nationals, and unilateral transfers abroad in the form of debt and indemnity payments. A series of measures discouraged foreign investors and speculators, and at the year's end capital transfers across the West German borders were almost in balance.

Capacity for Economic Aid

A nation's capacity to grant development aid could be determined with greater ease and precision if economic aid were defined, and definable, accurately.[14] But neither aid donors nor recipients have reached an agreement as to what transactions should be termed economic assistance. The OECD Development Assistance Committee's concept of aid covers grants, loans, officially guaranteed credits, contributions in kind as well as reparation payments. The DAC's still broader concept of "flow of financial resources" also includes private direct investment and officially guaranteed private export credits.

On the other hand, Professor Edward S. Mason—to cite another authority from among several—has defined foreign aid in narrower terms, doubtless with some qualitative considerations in mind. He described aid as "a transfer of resources from the government and citizens of one country to those of another on terms easier than those that could be obtained in the capital market. This would exclude foreign private investments and suppliers' credits, unless the terms on which these flows were made available were softened by reason of government schemes guaranteeing repayment or in other ways absorbing part of the risk. It would include, of course, in the private flows, grants, soft loans, and technical assistance from foundations, churches and other charitable institutions."[15]

14. Cf. Organization for Economic Cooperation and Development, *Development Assistance, Efforts and Policies, 1966 Review,* (Paris: OECD, 1966), Chap. 4; Wolfgang G. Friedmann, W. G. Kalmanoff, and R. F. Meagher, *International Financial Aid* (New York: Columbia University Press, 1966), Chap. 3; Jacob J. Kaplan, *The Challenge of Foreign Aid* (New York: Praeger, 1967), Chap. 13; Raymond F. Mikesell, *Public International Lending for Development,* (New York: Random House, 1966), Ch. 2; John Pincus, *Trade, Aid and Development,* (New York: McGraw-Hill Book Co., 1967), Chap. 2; Seymour J. Rubin, *The Conscience of the Rich Nations,* (New York: Harper & Row, 1966), Chap. 4.

15. Edward S. Mason, *Foreign Aid and Foreign Policy,* (New York: Harper & Row, 1964), p. 11.

The DAC definition is more comprehensive than Mason's (which is explicitly opposed to inclusion of hard private investments and suppliers' credit) and, therefore, more useful for an evaluation of West German foreign aid. Moreover, this definition permits inclusion in development assistance of such disputable transactions as reparation payments and consolidation credit, both of which the West Germans count as aid.

A characteristic of the German aid program is that it has found relatively little room for the most aid-like assistance, i.e., grants and grant-like contributions. Despite their gradual expansion, predicated on widening technical assistance, German grants have accounted for a smaller percentage of total aid than has been the case with other Western donors. (See Table XI.)

Table XI. Grants as Percentages of Total Public Development Aid.

Donors	1961	1962	1963	1964	1965	1966
Germany	18	24	33	36	37	23
France	83	78	81	78	82	85
U.K.	48	50	50	48	54	49
U.S.A.	74	74	71	35	37	40

Source: OECD, The Flow of Financial Resources to Countries in the Course of Economic Development (Paris, 1964); computed from Table II–3, p. 22, and OECD, Entwicklungshilfe; Politik und Leistungen: Jahresprüfung (Paris, September 1967), Tables 3–5, pp. 260–265.

On the other hand, bilateral loans, which may be considered as economic aid only with certain qualifications, have predominated in German commitments and have loomed larger in these than in those of other DAC members. And because West German loans have been extended on what appear to be commercial terms and, therefore, at interest rates normally prevailing in the Federal Republic's capital market, it is not difficult to conclude that this aid has been self-serving, extended with minimum strain on the country's economy.[16] It is furthermore debatable whether the Germans mean charity or, more probably, certainty of returns on investment when they emphasize project loans and the tying of procurements which prima facie tend to lower the value of such financial assistance.[17] Nonetheless, it is undeniable that in countries where foreign aid depends on budgetary appropriations—as it does in the Federal Republic—project

16. For additional comment on this see Karel Holbik, "West German Development Aid —The Means and Ends," Quarterly Review of Economics and Business, Vol. 5, No. 4 (Winter 1965), pp. 5–19.

17. The idea that "the purpose of an aid program is not to get something back, at least not something material" appears to be foreign to German efforts, as subsequent chapters of this study demonstrate. Wilson E. Schmidt, "The Economics of Charity: Loans versus Grants," Journal of Political Economy, Vol. LXXII, No. 4 (August, 1964), p. 388.

loans stabilize the flow of aid and help to secure public support for governmental assistance efforts.

In view of the existing inability of nations and international organizations to (1) measure comparable costs of various methods of promoting the development of the emerging nations, and (2) devise acceptable international standards for the evaluation of development assistance granted by the nations of the Atlantic area, it is necessary to retain the present conventional measurement, namely, the target ratios based on either the donor's gross national product or his national income. In terms of these two indicators of a nation's financial ability to grant foreign aid, German performance has not been exemplary (as shown in Table III above) and has followed the general Western trend toward a decline in the relative magnitude of development aid.

Nevertheless, Chart III leaves little doubt that West Germany's rising GNP has made increases in aid possible, especially during recent years of internal economic stagnation mentioned earlier in this chapter. The slump should have made it less costly for Germany to allocate some of its resources to foreign aid, tied as it has been to commercial criteria. But it is also true that the country prefers, and is determined, to expand its trade relations with eastern Europe on the one hand and the United States on the other. Similiar intensification of exchanges with the developing nations has not been advocated by West German exporters.

Another restraining influence on foreign aid has been and will doubtless continue to be exerted by federal finance in general and by the state of the federal budget in particular; as Table XII indicates, it is through the latter that the bulk of West German public development assistance has been financed. In 1966 the following funds (in millions of DM) were earmarked

Table XII.   West German Budgetary Appropriations (in millions of DM).

Source of funds	1963	1964	1965
A. Federal Budget (Ordinary[a] and Extraordinary[b])	985.3	806.5	940.4
B. Budgets of the Länder	20.9	28.7	28.7
C. Special Funds[c]			
1. ERP Counterpart Funds	265.1	200.1	229.7
2. Loans of the Kreditanstalt für Wiederaufbau	300.0	200.0	300.0
Total	1511.3	1235.3	1498.8

Source: Ministry of Economics (Bonn).

[a]Includes aid other than loans (contributions to the United Nations, the EEC Development Fund, etc.).

[b]Includes loans plus subscriptions to the World Bank and the International Development Association. Additional loans are financed from Special Funds.

[c]Special Funds are incorporated in the Extraordinary Budget.

GROSS NATIONAL PRODUCT

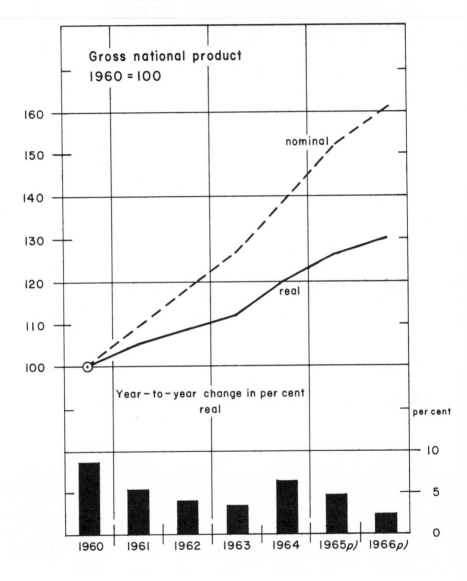

(Reproduced through the courtesy of the Deutsche Bundesbank.)   p = provisional

Chart III

for official development assistance, subject to approval by the *Bundestag*:[18]

I. Estimates for cash payments:

Federal budget	1,681
ERP Special fund	228
Länder budgets	47
Kreditanstalt für Wiederaufbau	200
	2,156

II. Commitment authorizations:

Federal budget	1,528
Länder budgets	6
	1,534

The country's capacity to pursue the aid policy depends inescapably not only on the commitment of the Bonn government to maintain its welfare expenditures but also—and especially—on the cost of the investment called for in its stabilization program and its medium-term fiscal planning. In public finance, the Federal Republic has to deal with new realities, internal as well as international (an exposition of which is beyond the objective of this chapter). One of these new developments consists in budgetary deficits and the federal government's rising indebtedness; this burden of debt can be, and perhaps will have to be, lightened by cuts in spending, already-envisaged increases in (income) taxation, and reduction of preferential tax treatments.

The trend of this evolving fiscal situation is evident in the following tabulation of federal government statistics (in billions of DM); the figures also disclose that West Germany has recently had to adjust to living with an internal debt:[19]

Fiscal Year	Cash Receipts	Cash Expenditures	Balance	Indebtedness (Bonded Loans)
1961	43.7	42.6	+1.1	1.2
1962	48.6	49.9	−1.3	2.7
1963	51.5	54.2	−2.7	4.5
1964	56.8	57.4	−0.7	5.4
1965	61.3	63.2	−1.9	6.3
1966	64.9	67.3	−2.3	6.7

In its concern about the future of its foreign aid, the federal government apparently had good reasons for initiating, in 1964, a campaign designed to

18. Ministry of Economics, *Report on German Development Assistance Policies in 1965* (mimeographed), p. 26.

19. Deutsche Bundesbank, *Monthly Report*, Aug. 1967, pp. 122–123.

induce private business to invest in the developing nations on a larger scale.

While the governments of the West German *Länder* contribute to the effort, their shares are nominal;[20] thus practically the entire cost of that effort is underwritten by the federal government. The appropriated funds, authorized by the budget committee of the Bundestag, are spent primarily by the Ministry for Economic Cooperation. However, the complexity of both aid administration and aid project classification have been responsible for conflicts between several federal departments as they seek to participate in aid distribution. Unavoidably, actual disbursements have not always equalled budgetary appropriations and commitments.

But in spite of the above-mentioned problems of a dynamic economic system, the German economy appears to many to be stable and resourceful enough to support a larger development-aid program. But a program's effectiveness is only partly measured in terms of the donor country's economic capabilities. Foreign aid, to be effective, must stabilize the economy of the developing nations. If it is to be both extensive and popular at home, it must be presented as ultimately beneficial to the donor country as well. In West Germany's case, if development aid results in expanding world markets, its economy—geared for world trade—is bound to benefit. It will be seen from the development-aid policies discussed below that the assistance efforts of the Federal Republic clearly are aimed toward increasing the number of its suppliers and customers in international trade.

West German Analysis of Economic Backwardness

The German decision—governmental as well as private—to use the nation's economic potential in developmental assistance is based on an analysis of what accounts for economic backwardness and how it can be eliminated. This section is devoted to an outline of the analysis.[21]

Like other Western industrialized nations, West Germany realizes that rapid economic development is hindered by the emerging nations' inadequate capacity for internal investment ("absorptive capacity") for which both economic and non-economic factors are responsible. Basically, whatever their other differences, all the underdeveloped countries are faced with

20. Financial demands on the *Länder* and *Länder* indebtedness have also been rising.

21. It is necessary to acknowledge, *after* the underlying research work has been completed, that the theoretical underpinnings of West German development efforts do not differ in any dramatic degree from theoretical views held in other parts of the Western industrialized world. The guiding function of economic theory can be appraised best in the annual reports of the *Kreditanstalt für Wiederaufbau*. From among other works in this field, the following are especially noteworthy: Hans Besters and Ernst E. Boesch, ed., *Entwicklungspolitik, Handbuch und Lexikon* (Stuttgart-Berlin: Kreuz-Verlag, 1966); Von Spindler, *Das wirtschaftliche Wachstum der Entwicklungsländer* (Stuttgart: W. Kohlhammer Verlag, 1963); and Kurt Hesse, *Planungen in Entwicklungsländern* (Berlin: Duncker & Hamblot, 1965).

low average incomes which are, moreover, extremely unevenly distributed. This vicious circle is aggravated by the fact that the poor countries' populations are growing at high rates, and that financial capital is insufficient to finance the capital investment required for broadly based economic growth. These conditions explain low productivity and income formation. Inflation, from which many economically backward nations have been suffering, has not only interfered with their progress, but has also prevented clear understanding and analysis of the underlying developmental difficulties. The well-known stimulating effect of inflationary environments has caused many a country to adopt economic policies that have enhanced the difficulties and burdened primitive economies.

International aid programs have supplied much evidence that these complex problems cannot be solved by either the developing countries alone or by Western nations for them, and that the only hope for improvements consists in cooperation between the two groups of nations. How then can emerging nations contribute to the attainment of the common objective— their own advance?

They can, first of all, change the existing distribution of income by creating small and medium-sized ownership in agriculture and the crafts. So far as present and future (higher) incomes may leave the country via capital flight, they should be prevented from doing so. In many cases it may prove expedient to carry out land reforms (along with irrigation, communication and similar projects) inasmuch as in farming economies the investment and savings rates have frequently been high.

All the developing countries are in need of an efficient banking system as a reservoir of savings and as an institutional arrangement eventually facilitating the organization of a capital market. Local banking systems could be also instrumental in rationally assimilating and relending the capital supplied through foreign aid and investment, thus rendering valuable services to all concerned.

The tax system is another segment of the developing countries' economies which lends itself to reforms. In most of these countries the average burden of income taxes is much lower than that of industrialized nations. While it is true that the problems and scope of taxation in the two groups of countries are hardly comparable, and any general tax increases are difficult to carry out in the poor nations (because of administrative obstacles, illiteracy, corruption of tax collectors, etc.), many of the difficulties in question could be overcome by properly selected methods of taxation. With more savings and tax revenues, the demand for foreign assistance would decrease and the local costs of developmental projects would be easier to meet. As a result, available foreign assistance could be extended to new projects.

If the developing countries gained greater financial power in the areas of banking, taxation, etc., their internal financial stability would be increased, and the crutch of inflationary stimulation could be dropped. They would also be in a position to correct (somewhat) their balances of international payment, and subsequently, to raising their credit standing.

Internal inflation, in many instances protracted, has caused substantial strain on the balance of payments of developing countries. Such a situation has become responsible for discrepancies between the internal and external values of the developing nations' currencies, especially where there is no correction by exchange rate adjustment. Thus external values turn out to be too high and the currencies are overvalued in relation to internal purchasing power; the practical consequence is that the new countries' capacity to borrow is overestimated (with excessive imports and depressed exports being the usual results).[22]

In West German experience, insufficient foreign exchange receipts and inadequate capital formation are—besides low levels of education and training—the principal obstacles to economic progress in poor countries. Balance of payments deficits exert decisive influence on the methods through which developmental efforts are made as international accounts are used to determine the basic criteria of the external assistance sought.

The conclusions and recommendations at which German economists have arrived may be summarized as follows:

1) The developing nations should give priority to combatting inflation. If they succeed in this, their imports and inclination to borrow abroad will decrease while their competitive strength in international markets will rise. They will find existing import restrictions superfluous and may well discourage flight of capital. On the other hand, successful anti-inflationary policy may also favor foreign private investment.

2) Another recommendation is to adopt policies encouraging private investment, especially through the establishment of a banking system and through utilization of existing cost and production advantages. Exploitation of these latter should both render domestic goods more competitive internationally and benefit trade relations among the developing countries.

3) A third recommendation calls for rationalization and qualitative improvement within the traditional productive sectors (be it agriculture, mining or handicraft) with internal rather than external capital. Hand in hand with this suggestion goes the proposal that the developing countries investigate carefully foreign markets for their exports and pursue complementary foreign exchange as well as fiscal policies.

The administrators of West German development aid appear to be of the opinion that it is in the industrialized countries' own interest to help new nations discover and expand their economic advantages even if this should call for appropriate long-term planning and aid on the donors' part. They

22. Cf. Manfred Dittmar, *Inflation in Entwicklungsländern als strukturbedingtes Problem* (Berlin: Duncker & Humblot, 1966), *passim*. To the extent to which developing nations seek to avoid international competition, they frequently adopt excessively one-sided policy of import-substitution thus hampering further their capacity to export.

recommend that Western trade policies be shaped so as to accommodate the emerging nations in all practicable respects, especially if these nations' need for foreign capital could thereby be depressed. Trade preferences and commodity price stabilization should be explored first. While West Germans admit that the present structure of world trade sets definite limits on expansion of commercial relations with the developing countries, they see a constructive move forward in Western willingness to liberalize imports from these countries even if such measures necessitate changes in the production of the industrialized nations. The latter's technological progress is expected both to minimize any sacrifice rendered unavoidable by the proposed "indirect development aid," and to induce the new nations to participate more than hitherto in supplying the industrial countries' markets. This they are already in a position to do in some foodstuffs, textile, leather, ores, etc.

The Germans envision that following the above-mentioned policies will enable the developing countries to get rid of their large balance-of-payments deficits or—more likely—reduce them to the core determined by real development. The resulting genuine financial gaps presumably will be closed more effectively with less external assistance and within shorter periods of time.

West Germany shares with other DAC countries the view that the most appropriate form of aid is a combination of project and program financing with the proportions varying according to the developing country's particular conditions. Although the distinction between these two types of financing is not clear-cut, projects are designed to implement programs. Both call for close coordination of the donor's and the recipient's activities.

The most effective use of limited domestic and foreign financial means can be made through long-term capital projects and comprehensive development plans, both of which are being taken into consideration in negotiations between aid-granting and aid-receiving countries. Regardless of the donor's attitude toward long-term plans as the framework for economic policy, their acceptance in foreign aid can hardly be avoided, especially if they are not excessively ambitious and can be carried out by the recipient country's own administrators.

Germany considers the following prerequisites and criteria of developmental plans to be essential:

1) Adequate knowledge of overall economic data, which includes accurate knowledge of available resources and the country's financial capacity. The Germans have learned that in planning they frequently must substitute estimates for missing statistics concerning population trends, industrial output, harvest results, formation of income, savings accumulation, etc. The developing countries tend to overrate domestic productive capacity and demonstrate undue optimism as regards the inflow of foreign capital. Fre-

quently they underestimate the donor countries' internal problems of raising funds. Inaccuracies in planning have been responsible for misconceived capital projects, insufficient utilization of productive capacity, supply difficulties, inflationary tensions, and balance-of-payments crises.

2) Another requirement is careful harmonization of government financial means with planned objectives, so that anticipated capital expenditures are adequately budgeted for. Development plans must be embodied in budgets. They must not depend on inflationary financing on the one hand or lack coverage through foreign exchange reserves on the other hand. German experience has been that some development plans have started off with internal and external financing gaps with the result that internal inflationary financing has widened the balance-of-payment deficit (which has frequently been shown as "capital aid requirement"). With some types of planning there arises the danger that the plan—because of the impossibility of closing the planned gaps— comes to dead stop midway.

Although West Germany has assisted in solving such developmental problems through participation in multilateral consortia, she has been restricted in her contribution, along with other donor countries, by budgetary appropriations. Thus, it has become necessary for the developing countries themselves to draft and execute their plans in a flexible manner. In the interest of flexible development plans, the Germans have encouraged harmonization of such plans with those of neighboring countries so that all production possibilities can be utilized to the optimum extent and regional orientation of plans achieved. In the German view, regional integration is a requirement especially for the small new nations.

THE PHILOSOPHY OF GERMAN DEVELOPMENT AID

The Basic Vocabulary

The economy described in Chapter II is undoubtedly capable of support-ing a development-aid program, and there is an abundance of official pronouncements which indicate that the West German government con-siders the continuation and probable enlargement of it to be a matter of course. Underlying the country's assistance to the emerging nations is a basic official philosophy which has changed little since the mid-1950's— when developmental aid first became an item in the West German budget— and is conveniently summarized in a statement by the Federal Republic's President, Heinrich Lübke: "The majority of the German people have not forgotten the extremities of war and postwar times, and are ready to return the aid and understanding they found at that time ... But it would be wrong to think that financial contributions alone can suffice. Development aid must also be educational aid and thereby a help toward self-help. It must enable the people of the developing countries to establish a profitable agriculture and efficient trade, but industries only after the necessary conditions have been created. Our task is to spark development and to train people who some day will be able to complete what we have started."[1]

This view of West German foreign aid has remained constant in the pub-lic utterances of Chancellors Erhard and Kiesinger, as well as Ministers Scheel, Schmücker, and Wischnewski—the government spokesmen who have discussed the program most often for the public communications media.[2] The recurring words are *education, cooperation, partnership, self-help,* and *trade,* whether referring to the German aid program by itself or internationally coordinated development efforts.

Although the Cold War tends to dominate foreign-aid discussions in the United States, there are several reasons why its terminology appears less

1. Text in *Twelve Years of German Development Assistance* (Bonn: Druck- und Ver-lagshaus Heinz Möller, 1964), p. 2.

2. After the Erhard administration was succeeded by that of the "Grand Coalition" (CDU/CSU-SPD) in October 1966, under Chancellor Kurt Georg Kiesinger, Federal Min-ister for Economic Affairs Kurt Schmücker became Federal Treasurer and Minister for Economic Cooperation Walter Scheel (FDP) was replaced by Bundestag delegate Hans-Jürgen Wischnewski (SPD). It had been the resignation of the FDP ministers as a group which precipitated the end of the previous CDU/CSU-FDP coalition.

prominently in German discussions of aid to underdeveloped countries. West Germany is, of course, very intimately concerned with countering Communist moves. Its determination to keep East Germany isolated and to make West Berlin as integral a part of West Germany as possible has run as a continuous thread through all foreign-policy moves of the Bonn government for the last fifteen years. But precisely because opposing the moves in Europe of Russia and its East German satellite is the greatest Cold War reality for the Federal Republic, Communist threats in the underdeveloped countries necessarily appear more peripheral. Americans sense immediately any nibbling away at the sphere of U.S. influence in regions where Communist success threatens to expand—as from Cuba into the rest of Latin America, or from North Viet Nam into areas where the United States is committed by treaty to intervene with its own troops. But the Communist threat in the underdeveloped nations is not seen as a direct one to German interests there. The Cold War enters West German discussions of foreign aid most pointedly when the question arises of competing with East Germany for the future good will of developing nations; in practice such competition has seemed real only in Africa and the Near East. It is still shadowy in Latin America and amounts to almost nothing in Asia.

East Germany's trade missions in Africa and the Near East serve the purpose of giving a sort of quasi-recognition to its government. Although under the Hallstein Doctrine West Germany follows the policy of breaking relations when a country gives *diplomatic* recognition to East Germany, this has not affected the proliferation of East German trade missions overseas. In this way the East German government has established a series of beachheads which are quite imposing on paper; in some underdeveloped countries there have been more East German personnel assigned to trade missions in the capital than West Germans stationed in the embassy. For example, in 1960 there were seventeen East German trade representatives in Conakry, Guinea, and a total of three West Germans assigned to the embassy of the Federal Republic; in Damascus, Syria, the ratio was thirty-six to seventeen; and in Khartoum, Sudan, twenty-five to eleven.[3] East Germany has, understandably, used its trade missions for propaganda purposes, playing up Communist solidarity with the colored peoples of all the world and condemning West German "neo-colonialism." Similarly, references to the need for bringing the truth about the Cold War to the peoples of Africa and the Near East frequently occur in discussions of West German aid.[4]

3. H. J. Winckler, *Die Entwicklungsländer* (Berlin: Otto-Suhr-Institut an der Freien Universität Berlin und Landeszentrale für politische Bildungsarbeit Berlin, 1961), p. 45. See also Hans Braker, "Probleme der deutschen Entwicklungshilfe," *Aus Politik und Zeitgeschichte (Das Parlament)*, Aug. 29, 1962.

4. In their own propaganda, the West Germans point to the fact that East Germany has made promises of aid to only eight developing countries while the Federal Republic has supported ninety-four countries. By the end of 1963, the East German *promises* were supposed to have totaled $192 million, but West German *disbursements* as much as $2.37 billion. *Hands Across the Sea*, Bonn: Druck-und Verlagshaus Heinz Möller, p. 12.

Nevertheless, vehemence of any kind is very much out of fashion with German leaders when expressing themselves on international topics other than the oppression of the people in East Germany—still regularly referred to as the Soviet Occupation Zone—or Soviet threats to West Berlin. The following excerpts from an interview with former Minister Scheel bring out the tone of official German reluctance to connect West German development aid with the Cold War, except as it relates immediately to German interests.

Q. "Does this [statement that 'foreign aid policy is a high form of security-politics'] mean that development aid is a part of the East-West cold war?

A. "The Communist countries plan their economic cooperation with the Afro-Asian countries entirely along political lines, and development aid is bound to reflect the resulting tensions to some degree. To avoid any misunderstanding about German development aid, however, I must point out that we do not permit it to be influenced by the East-West conflict.

Q. "Is this also true in regard to the position a country may take in the Berlin question or in connection with the Communist regime in East Berlin?

A. "We cannot overlook the position which a developing country takes in regard to the German question at the UN, or what relations it maintains with the Soviet-occupied zone of Germany . . . Anyone will understand that no Bonn government can afford to grant development aid money, at the expense of its taxpayers, to a country whose policies run against the vital interests of the German people."[5]

Or, in the words of Economic Cooperation Minister Wischnewski: "We will not attach political conditions to our development policies, but we do consider correct the words of Pakistan's President, who said that he who takes something from another puts himself under the moral obligation at least not to stab the man he takes it from in the back. This, I believe, we are quite justified in expecting; no other political conditions are imposed by us."[6]

Some didactic talk of the necessity for influencing world opinion on behalf of a favorable termination of the division of Germany occurs in official West German treatments of development-aid questions. In such statements Bonn reminds the receiving countries that the principles of self-determination and national unity, which they claim for themselves, should be applied

5. "New Style in Foreign Aid: 'Promoting Project Groups Instead of Single Projects,' " German International, Vol. VII, No. 2 (Feb. 1963), pp. 22 and 25; Ernst Majonica, "Deutschland und die dritte Welt," Für Sie gelesen, No. 22 (May 1965), pp. 17–19. (Für Sie gelesen—Collected for You—is a monthly publication of the Ministry for Economic Cooperation, consisting for the most part of articles and book reviews on development aid which have appeared in other periodicals.)

6. "Positive und konstruktive deutsche Entwicklungshilfe," interview on the German Overseas Radio (Deutsche Welle); text in Bulletin, No. 162 (Dec. 29, 1966), p. 1,319.

equally to Germany.[7] Then, too, there are occasional references to the colored voting majority in the United Nations and the imperative to win the allegiance of the non-white underdeveloped world for the final defeat of the Ulbricht regime (presumably through United Nations measures which will lead to free elections for all Germany). But all this has a very abstract and far-off sound to it. The vocabulary of teaching people to help themselves for the greater ultimate good of mankind—as an end in itself—dominates the rationale of development aid as it is presented to the West Germans. This finds clear expression in the proposed addition of development attachés to the Federal Republic's foreign representations, with the same rank as commercial attachés; in itself this change is eloquent evidence of West Germany's primary attention to the long-term purposes and, therefore, to the theoretical conception of developmental assistance.

It has probably already struck the reader that the term "development aid" has been repeatedly used in the preceding sections of this study in places where "foreign aid" would be used in a discussion of the American program. This reflects the term consistently found in German source materials. It is characteristic of the lack of Cold War militance in West German discussions of the foreign-aid program that the term "development aid" *(Entwicklungshilfe)* is much preferred to the more general term "foreign aid" *(Auslandhilfe* or *Auslandshilfe).* Yet the German press regularly refers to American foreign aid with the latter expression,[8] and official German publications in English use "foreign aid" where *Entwicklungshilfe* would probably be used in a corresponding context in German.[9] Although the choice is possibly not intentional, it carries with it an emphasis: *development* aid is not used for weaponry. While U.S. discussion of foreign aid often centers around the effectiveness of military assistance to a given country, the reader of German materials on foreign aid finds the military aspect so minimized that he soon feels that *all* German aid of any consequence to foreign countries is aid for their economic development. Nevertheless, military assistance has been granted to Tanganyika, Nigeria, and the Sudan.

It is frequently pointed out that Germany is a comparative newcomer in the business of assisting developing nations on the road to economic growth. While this is true, it is also true that other Western nations are not exactly old hands at rendering assistance within the framework demanded by the

7. Chancellor Erhard in a stance continued by the Kiesinger Administration openly emphasized the diplomatic function of aid-giving when he announced: "A durable peace in Europe includes a fair solution of the German question. Our relations with foreign nations are influenced by those nations' attitude toward that question. This is true, not least, for development aid." *Hands Across the Sea,* p. 8.

8. For example, *Der Spiegel,* which uses article headings in a fashion almost identical with *Time* magazine, within a short space of time printed two articles on the German aid program under the caption *"Entwicklungshilfe"* (No. 31, July 26, 1961, pp. 17–18, and No. 35, Aug. 23, 1961, p. 30) but an article on American aid to supposed neutral nations—in which only economic, non-military aid was discussed —under *"Auslandshilfe"* (No. 40, Sept. 27, 1961, pp. 78–81).

9. See, for example, West German official English-language publications of statements by Scheel and Schmücker, notes 5 and 16, this chapter.

new politesse. Unlike her Western neighbors, the Federal Republic does not have the background derived from continuous years of colonial experience and has had to experiment considerably in creating development-aid programs and policies. This necessity, however, is coupled with advantages which more than compensate for it. Not only have the Germans had to overcome fewer fixed ideas on the subject, but their lack of a reputation as a colonial power has made their assistance more acceptable to the emerging nations. Local leaders do not associate Germans with colonialist attitudes of superiority, and Bonn can elaborate the principles of its foreign-aid philosophy and effectively employ the vocabulary of equality, independence, and mutual respect. Outside Europe and North America the Germans are not burdened much by memories of Nazism. Then, too, the lack of old ties has made it possible for Bonn to devise an aid policy which, despite the inevitable shortcomings of a comparatively new venture, is not distorted by the need to serve Germany's short-term interests.

To its own people the Bonn government can justify the expense of development aid, as it has done especially since 1964, by pointing out that: (1) it seeks to enhance international economic, political, and social stability; (2) that this policy offers a welcome and unique opportunity to West Germany to play a significant part in international affairs; and (3) last but not least, the ultimate long-run effect of developmental assistance will be to expand the foreign market for West German products. The fact that historically Germans have been Europe-oriented as regards to trade adds to the force of persuasion which Bonn can apply to make the public realize that economic assistance to underdeveloped areas is also in the German national interest.

While figures and percentages to prove the point may vary, it can be shown without difficulty that at least the capital-assistance part of the German foreign-aid program has a pronounced businesslike aspect:

> Of the German development-aid credits financed by public funds, 80 per cent are repayable and interest-bearing. In 1965, approximately 83 per cent and, in 1966, approximately 82 per cent of the credits granted developing countries flowed back in the form of purchase orders to the German economy. In 1965, the developing countries paid DM 230 million [$58.07 million] and, in 1966, DM 250 million [$63.12 million] in interest on German developmental credits.[10]

> Apart from this flow of orders, German industry received additional orders of about a billion marks [$252.5 million] in the past year [1966]. These orders happened to go most of all to industry which produces investment goods, a sector struck particalarly hard by the let-up in broom conditions. The Federal Government will make efforts to promote a project policy that is even more economically beneficial in the future.[11]

10. Minister Wischnewski, "Zahlen der deutschen Entwicklungshilfe; Offener Brief an den Präsidenten des Bundes der Steuerzahler," Bulletin, No. 33 (April 4, 1967), p. 275.

11. Wischnewski, "Aktuelle Probleme der deutschen Entwicklungspolitik," address before the Ausschuss für Entwicklungsländer der Friedrich-Ebert-Stiftung, ibid., No. 58 (June 2, 1967), p. 495.

Evidence of sound business practices in the granting of capital aid (to allay domestic fears of excessive liberality by the Government) necessarily opens the question of whether profitable economic arrangements in a developing country entirely deserve the designation "aid," particularly as these are judged abroad. For example, the Federal Republic was described as a partner to a distinctly "non-aid-like transaction" when in 1958 it agreed to take promissory notes of the Government of India to allow postponement of Indian payments to German contractors working on the Rourkela Steel Works—often-cited example of a successful German capital-aid project (see below, Chap. IX). In this—admittedly exceptional—instance, the issuing of the notes at the "distinctly commercial rate of 6 per cent and an additional fee of 0.3 per cent for service and administrative charges" together with the fact that they were to be repaid in DM within three years, demonstrates the difficulty of counting all credits extended to developing countries as aid.[12]

Policies

Germany spent $7,145 million on development aid between 1956 and 1966.[13] Since 1961, its contribution to development aid has averaged over 7 per cent of the Western world's contributions; this places the Federal Republic fourth behind the United States, France, and Great Britain.

Having invested relatively large sums of money in development-aid projects, namely some 60 per cent of the above total, private sources having furnished the remainder, the Bonn government has naturally come to consider development aid an important feature of its economic and foreign policies. As such, all aspects of development-aid policy are coodinated in the Ministry for Economic Cooperation and the Bundestag. Shortly before retiring as West German Foreign Minister in 1961, the late Heinrich von Brentano gave the following principles as the official guideline governing German development-aid policies:

1. Bonn recognizes the developing countries' right to equality and self-determination, and will therefore refrain from interfering in their internal affairs.

2. German decision on development policies will not be influenced by what the Eastern Bloc does or does not do.

3. The Federal Government fully appreciates the developing countries' desires for closer economic and political cooperation among each other in various areas.

12. Wolfgang G. Friedmann, W. G. Kalmanoff, and R. F. Meagher, *International Financial Aid* (New York: Columbia University Press, 1966), pp. 334–335.

13. OECD, "Report of Sixth High-Level Meeting of the Development Assistance Committee," press release, Paris, July 20, 1967; figure computed from appended tables.

4. Relations with developing countries will be based on the principles of partnership and equality.

5. Assistance will only be given in response to the express wish of the country concerned and in close cooperation with its government.

6. Since economic assistance is given with a view to improving living standards and to promoting economic and social progress, it must not be employed to hamper social evolution in the interest of outdated social systems.

7. German assistance efforts should in the first place be directed toward self-help in the countries concerned.

8. In view of the importance of the human factor, the Federal Government will intensify its help in education and training in the developing countries.[14]

These principles were formulated after the Federal Republic acquired, in 1960, the necessary clarity of purpose for its foreign-aid program and after it had decided, in 1961, to establish the Ministry for Economic Cooperation. At that time the West Germans could already draw on some experience in contacts with the developing nations and involvement in developmental assistance.

Since 1953, the Federal Republic has offered technical education to foreign trainees in Germany and has sent West German consultants abroad. It has also set up guarantees for private export credits and contributed extensively to multilateral developmental finance, the World Bank and the European Economic Community Development Fund in particular. Multilateral aid remained Bonn's principal channel of assistance through 1962 and tended to overshadow the contributions of other major Western donors.[15]

When its own comprehensive aid program with emphasis on bilateral agreements was inaugurated in 1961, the federal government found itself in a more favorable position from which to exhibit to the West German public the boon of this new form of international cooperation. Since then, the above principles have been refined, particularly towards curbing the desire of the emerging nations for prestige projects and finished goods without delay.

The principle given in Von Brentano's list as number seven, self-help as the prime goal, is probably the most basic and least-modified principle of the development-aid program since its inception. It has meant that public funds shoud be used primarily to develop the national infrastructure while private investors are encouraged to develop basic industries compatible with the needs of the individual country. This thought was emphasized by Ludwig Erhard, speaking in 1959 as minister for economic affairs, when

14. "The Principles of German Development Aid," *Germany*, Vol. VI (1961), No. 22, p. 18.

15. As of December 31, 1960, Germany had contributed to the World Bank (IBRD) $698.5 million, which equalled about 20 per cent of all contributions, and made the country one of the four largest shareholders. At that time, West German private investors and the Federal Bank had claims on the World Bank (resulting from floated bonds and notes) amounting to 29 per cent of IBRD's total indebtedness. Otto Donner, "Germany's Part in the World Bank Aid," *ibid.*, No. 21, pp. 29–31.

the scope of the Federal Republic's foreign-aid program had been extensive for only a few years: "In any process of development, the socio-economic overhead capital to be financed by public means must be combined with private initiative. It will be incumbent upon the latter to make a productive and successful effort at the further development of a country's resources. Only in this way can the danger be avoided of national ambition exhausting itself in the setting up of a few giant plants while human labor remains unused. What matters is rather that there should be established numerous small and medium-sized enterprises which will insure a highly diversified, sound and resilient economy and at the same time provide a maximum of employment."[16] West German authorities have never concealed their conviction that development aid is, and should be considered by its recipients, an expedient to help a country overcome its structural economic bottlenecks. Bonn is prepared to stretch out its helping hand in a way similar to that of the Marshall Plan which—as is well known—proved immensely valuable in West Germany's postwar economic recovery.[17] In fact, the Germans are convinced, as were ERP administrators, that their assistance should have the implicit objective of promoting free enterprise institutions to the degree that they have proven themselves beneficial in their own country. Inescapably, this bit of ideology has at times been out of place in the underdeveloped areas, although the German commitment to free enterprise is more empirical and consequently less dogmatic sometimes in its application—notably in Latin America—than that of American planners.

The German emphasis on self-help carries with it a certain degree of compulsion inasmuch as the governments of the recipient countries are expected to prepare those internal conditions under which the aid they receive can be of maximum benefit. This, Bonn believes, can be insured when the recipients offer the maximum of cooperation and assume responsibility for costs of initiated production and plants.

The West German insistence on environmental preparation by the leadership of the underdeveloped countries—to encourage domestic capital formation through appropriate planning, to maintain internal monetary stability, and to pursue such tax policies as will favor the sponsored developmental projects—has found partial expression in intergovernmental contracts. In these, Bonn has avoided explicit restrictions on where in the non-Communist world the capital-aid funds are to be spent; however, the effect of advancing credit tied to purchases in the Federal Republic has been much the same. As anticipated, this procedure has succeeded in gaining greater support for governmental policy among West German industrialists. Less

16. "The Significance of Foreign Aid," speech delivered at the discussion of the World Bank's annual report. Text in *News from the German Embassy*, Vol. III, No. 14 (Oct. 12, 1959), pp. 1–2. The German Minister for Economic Affairs is the *ex officio* governor of the Bank for the Federal Republic.

17. Cf. J. M. Hunck, "How Good is German Foreign Aid?", *German American Trade News*, June 1965, p. 13.

strict criteria have been used in deciding on the geographical distribution of West German development assistance, although the practice has been to extend capital aid through loans while technical assistance is implemented through grants.

German awareness of the need to improve development assistance through international revision of price and tariff policies has been increasing. It is characteristic of the non-dogmatic approach of German development-aid philosophy that Bonn has supported removal of tariffs and domestic taxes by industrial nations on products of developing countries without demanding reciprocal liberalization of foreign trade policies by the developing nations themselves. Specifically, the Foreign Office's department for trade and overseas development, through its head, Hans-Georg Sachs, has consistently advocated the idea, now incorporated into the older General Agreement on Trade and Tariffs (GATT), that developing countries should keep preferential tariffs against industrial nations, as well as among themselves, if they are advantageous to them at their particular stage of economic development.[18] At the same time, the new chapter provides better marketing conditions for the main export goods from developing countries pledging the industrial nations to give priority to the removal of all obstacles to their importation. Here the hope is that prices for products may become stabilized at a level profitable to the exporting country.

In its general principles the philosophy underlying West German foreign aid encounters little serious domestic opposition. In the Bundestag debates which preceded the 1965 vote on appropriations for the development-aid program, a CDU member cited a public opinion poll, according to which 70 per cent of the West German population responded favorably to tax support for the Federal Republic's development-aid program.[19] The Social Democrats, then in opposition, were content to abstain rather than vote against the detailed plan put forth by Minister Scheel. Delegate Wischnewski, the present minister for economic cooperation, who then voiced the SPD's criticisms, based his objections on what was in his view the diffuse and indiscriminate nature of some of the suggested projects, rather than on any principles of development aid espoused by the government. Oddly enough,

18. Hans-Georg Sachs, "The United Nations Conference on Trade and Development," *Germany*, Vol. IX (1964), No. 38, pp. 11–12; and interview with the author, "GATT Milestone for New Countries," *German International*, Vol. IX, No. 4 (April 1965), pp. 22–24. The new chapter of the agreement contains three articles to favor the trade position of developing countries; agreed upon by negotiators and signed at Geneva on February 8, 1965, it will take effect upon ratification by two-thirds of the sixty-four GATT signatories. There is, to be sure, an escape clause, whereby industrial nations may decline to apply the new provisions in pressing circumstances, but even there they are enjoined to settle their differences by negotiations with the developing countries. "Neue GATT-Bestimmungen," *Bulletin*, No. 24 (Feb. 9, 1965), p. 192.

19. "Entwicklungspolitik ist langfristig angelegt: Die Debatten um das Gesundheitswesen und die Entwicklungshilfe während der Haushaltsberatungen im Bundestag," *Bulletin*, No. 38 (March 4, 1965), p. 305. Another West German public opinion poll found 77 per cent of the people in favor of development aid in 1965 as opposed to only 47 per cent in 1963.

the Socialist opposition to Minister Scheel's proposals resembled American conservative opposition in Congress to certain foreign-aid projects of the last fifteen years: money was being spent to help nations whose friendship, to judge by past performances, could not be counted on.[20]

Since its inception, the West German development-aid program has experienced some ups and downs in the country's public opinion. ("Vom Überschwung zum Überdruss bewegt sich nach typisch deutscher Weise auch unser Verhältnis zur Entwicklungshilfe,")[21] Accepted originally with uncritical enthusiasm, the program suffered subsequently from disillusionment when idealized conceptions of underdeveloped areas clashed with reality. It was not only West German desire to find a new international mission for the nation, but also active governmental publicity that prevented the German public from losing all of its interest in this national policy.

The government could have probably avoided some of its own and the people's frustrations with aid, had it not established artificial and, therefore, false analogies between Germany as the recipient of Marshall Plan aid and the emerging nations. The economically backward areas have, of course, none of the technical, economic, nor social ingredients without which the postwar "economic miracle" could not have been worked; nor do they have a corresponding set of values (for the most part) to make an analogy based on the experience of a European people valid.[22]

Foreign Aid and the German International Image

In spite of the refusal of German officials to link their foreign-aid program as rigidly to Cold War strategy as their American counterparts, the similarities in American and West German philosophies of aid for development still greatly outweigh the differences. If notions of cooperation in mutual respect, self-help, technical education, and development or liberalization of international trade furnish to the virtual exclusion of other ideas the slogans of West German aid publicity, the same notions are also very much a part of the concept of foreign aid publicly espoused by all governments of the West and sincerely believed in by large segments of their nationals.

20. *Ibid.* The Social Democrats undoubtedly had Egypt and probably Iraq in mind with their accusation that "in the past those countries have obviously been given first consideration who have kicked us particularly hard" (*Bulletin's* indirect quotation). For the American counterpart of these criticisms, see Eugene W. Castle. *The Great Giveaway: the Realities of Foreign Aid* (Chicago: Henry Regnery, 1957).

21. "In typically German fashion our relationship to development aid also shifts from exhuberance to weariness." Dr. G. A. Sonnenhol, "Grösse und Elend der Entwicklungshilfe," *Für Sie gelesen,* No. 20 (March 1965), p. 1.

22. Andreas Paulsen, "Real Capital and Human Capital in Economic Development," *German Economic Review,* Vol. IV (1966), No. 4, pp. 275–276. The problem is also dealt with by Joan Robinson, *Economic Philosophy* (Chicago: Aldine Publishing Co., 1962); and Gerald M. Meier and Robert E. Baldwin, *Economic Development* (New York: John Wiley, 1957), p. 418.

The role of the Federal Republic as a donor nation with an aid program of its own has, of course, helped it with certain close-at-hand practical problems. Some impact is discernible on Germany's economy from its trade relations with the developing nations, and more undoubtedly is expected. Then, too, Bonn's foreign assistance gives a few teeth to the Hallstein Doctrine: threatened cancellation of diplomatic relations with a country recognizing East Germany implies a simultaneous withdrawal of economic aid. Taking Africa as an example, one sees that East Germany's aid program equals about one per cent of West Germany's, so that the uncommitted African nation has a basic choice between West Germany's aid and the dubious advantage of recognizing East Germany.[23] Except for Zanzibar, which did so before its union with Tanganyika, no African nation has opened formal relations with East Germany.

But in the last analysis, there is a danger in attaching too much importance to factually calculated, practical, "rational" benefits of foreign aid from West Germany's standpoint. Hard proof of the imagined future benefits to the economy of the Federal Republic from greater and more liberalized trade with the developing nations is yet to come. From a political standpoint, the inability of the Hallstein Doctrine, teeth and all, to cope with East German trade missions can be taken to show that it is more effective in appearance than fact. The point here is this: real benefits to a donor nation from its own aid program need not be tangible. Whether or not the African's acceptance of trade missions from Berlin-Pankow implies a *de facto* recognition of East Germany is less important in the mind of many West Germans than the success of his government in thwarting the desire of Walter Ulbricht and his regime for full and open recognition. This sort of feeling can be found on all levels; it is hardly necessary to drive home the point that psychological satisfactions are worth a lot to the people they satisfy.

And what an immense psychological benefit it is for Germans to be treated to journalistic outpourings about factories, dams, and technical schools, all rising from jungles and wastelands as a result of German ingenuity and beneficence! What a pleasant sight those dark-skinned natives in gay pink and gold garments make, as they smile into newsmen's cameras or furrow their brows in rapt attention at the words of pith-helmeted emissaries of culture and technology, who will drain their swamps and water their deserts—without a hint of condescension, of course, but to the end that all may reach a better life! All this is surely an element in the American public's reaction to U.S. foreign aid efforts as well; in fact, it has been the

23. Such a computation is based on payments actually made and reflects the world-wide records of the two parts of Germany through the end of 1964 (West Germany, $6,400,000,000; East Germany, $63,000,000). See chart "Contrast in Development Aid," unsigned article, "East and West—20 Years After" *German International*, Vol. IX, No. 4 (April 1965), p. 11. In promises, of course, the discrepancy is much less. East German credit promises to Africa alone totalled $108,000,000, substantially more than its whole record of payments to *all* developing regions. Chart "Credit Promises to Developing Nations," *ibid.*, p. 14.

staple fare of a good many Sunday supplements for ten years or so. But for Germany, which has struggled with what is now called an "image problem" for two decades with varying success, publicity for the nation's humanitarianism satisfies a special need.

Enlightened self-interest and humanitarianism, whether as an end in itself or as an ego builder, emerge as the components of West German foreign-aid philosophy. It is often impossible to distinguish them in the various public pronouncements on development assistance, where aid must be justified before taxpayers as good business and where national political motives often appear submerged in the rhetoric of "help for self-help." But both elements are very much present, and *in toto* they justify the extensive and diversified West German program of foreign aid.[24]

24. For discussions of the program's rationale, see Walter Scheel, *Konturen einer neuen Welt* (Düsseldorf: Econ-Verlag, 1965), esp. Chapter II, "Von der Entwicklungshilfe zur Entwicklungspolitik"; Dr. Walter Rau, "Warum Entwicklungshilfe?" *Für Sie gelesen*, No. 35 (June 1966), pp. 1–13; and the concluding section of this book.

CATEGORIES OF DEVELOPMENT AID AND ITS ADMINISTRATION

However various the forms in which West German development aid is extended, in comprehensive statistics they are usually divided into bilateral and multilateral transactions, both of which are broken down into public (i.e., government) and private aid as shown in Table XIII.

The bulk of public expenditures is financed through budgets supplemented by budgetary appropriations of the *Länder* (see above Table XIII). Federal appropriations are consolidated in the budget of the Ministry for Economic Cooperation, which, however, does not control further distribution of the funds in question; instead, the ministry channels them to various government departments for direct use. Other sources of government development finance are: the ERP Special Fund (consisting of Marshall Plan counterpart funds), the Development Loan Corporation (Kreditanstalt für Wiederaufbau), the Volkswagen Foundation (disposing of funds which stem from denationalization of the VW Company), and the Industrial Loan. Private aid is financed primarily through industrial investment and the capital market (see Chap. II.) Parenthetically, though, no remarkable success has been achieved in mobilizing the German capital market on behalf of aid to emerging nations. Chapter V takes up some details of the aforementioned methods of financing developmental assistance.

During the 17-year period between 1950 and 1966, West German aid to 95 countries exceeded DM 26 billion (over $6.5 billion) in bilateral transactions and DM 5 billion ($1.25 billion) in multilateral transactions. In very general terms, this distribution of development aid has been governed by the formula, adhered to by West German development planners, "bilateral aid as much as possible, multilateral aid as much as necessary."

While between 1961 and 1964 government payments showed a relative decline, the importance of private aid almost doubled. In 1961 public funds made up 74 per cent of total aid, but in 1964 they equalled only 53 per cent. In contrast, private funds for these years amounted to 26 per cent and 47 per cent, respectively. Nevertheless, by 1966 the earlier ratio was restored with private aid at as low a level as DM 625 million (24 per cent of total aid).

Table XIII. Development Aid Payments[a], 1961–1966 (in millions of DM).

Type of Aid	1961	1962	1963	1964	1965	1966[b]
A. Bilateral Aid	2183	2121	2209	2873	2364	2448
1. Public Funds						
Technical assistance[c]	109	157	288	348	403	432
Capital aid[d] (new loans, net)	887	953	1030	1032	1025	1367
Reparations	320	280	278	250	300	—
2. Private Funds						
Export credits	329	161	287	887	233	150[e]
Investments, reinvested proceeds and other payments	538	570	326	356	403	499
B. Multilateral Aid	1132	407	147	264	457	125
1. Public Funds						
Contributions to U.N. and its agencies	43	41	48	55	—	—
Grants to EEC Development Fund	180	308	—	—	155	149
Quotas in and loans to IBRD, IDA and IFC	920	60	52	−20	—	—
2. Private Funds						
Bonded loans, participations and credits	11	−2	47	229	302	−24.1
Total Development Aid	3315	2528	2356	3137	2822	2573
Public Funds	2459	1799	1697	1666	1884	1948
Private Funds	856	729	659	1471	937	625

Source: Kreditanstalt für Wiederaufbau, *XVII. Jahresbericht (1965)*, p. 25; and *XVII. Jahresbericht (1966)*, p. 24.

[a]Including credits of more than one year.
[b]Provisional figures.
[c]Including other grants and settlements for damage.
[d]Including consolidation loans.
[e]The conspicuous decrease in export credits reflects termination of the program of credits to German shipyards.

Bilateral Assistance

Bilateral *capital aid* is designed to provide funds for projects for which private capital is usually not available, whereas bilateral *technical assistance* is to teach the new nations technical, economic and organizational know-how. Table XIV leaves no doubt that capital aid calls for relatively larger amounts, although it is recognized that in the long-run, technical assistance may be the more effective and important type of aid. This, by the way, also explains why the Germans began their development-aid policy through technical assistance. Unexplained remains the continued lack of coordination between the two principal kinds of bilateral aid.

The funds allocated to capital aid are a direct reflection of German emphasis on, and priority given to, project assistance, i.e., financial support of specific undertakings. Bonn appears to be convinced that infrastructural projects especially will not be undertaken by private business and depend, therefore, on official aid. And yet it is infrastructure that has—in the government view—the capacity to implement production diversification in the developing countries. Infrastructure stimulates investment, provides employment opportunities and promotes economic growth. The Germans realize, too, that the new nations have to rely on foreign assistance inasmuch as their financial means (foreign exchange) are too limited to enable these countries to acquire the needed infrastructural projects.

However, capital aid loans are not made available by the Federal Republic on particularly easy terms, although credit terms for infrastructure (DM 2,146 million in 1964) are softer than those for production ("commercial") purposes (DM 2,147 million in 1964).[1] For infrastructural projects (such as roads, railroads, canals) current interest rates vary from 1 to 2 per cent. For business enterprises these rates may be as much as 5-1/2 per cent.

In general, bilateral capital aid implements the principles underlying West Germany's development assistance (see above, Chap. III), which means that the recipient governments: (1) are responsible for an orderly management of the projects; (2) are expected not to interfere with the use of (German) transport facilities and personnel; (3) are to assume local costs of carrying out the projects; and (4) are obligated to repay loans in German marks (DM). Because of both international competition among suppliers and pressures exerted on Bonn by German business groups, an increasing proportion (80 per cent) of West German loans have been "tied"; i.e., borrowing countries have had to spend the loaned funds in the Federal Republic. Some feel that this feature of German capital aid has in a way compelled the underdeveloped areas to consider primarily those projects for which the Germans are prepared to provide funds and equipment. The importance of this point is further magnified by the fact that as a matter of principle it is the developing countries that are to submit project proposals, which German authorities, theoretically, are not supposed to do. Unquestionably, tying of credit has reduced internal German resistance to development aid.

The harder credit terms applied to production loans have been justified on the German side by expected yields which, it is argued, must compare favorably with conventional market returns. It is also contended that tighter credit terms prevent borrowers from buying nonessential imports, and that diversity in projects should find expression in diversity of credit terms. The recent trend toward lengthening loan periods so as to make the terms more attractive has been brought about by the criticism that the shorter periods imposed too heavy a burden on some borrowers. For until 1965, the thought

---

1. The DM 2,146 millions for infrastructural projects were distributed as follows: transport and communications, DM 1,102 millions; irrigation, DM 693 millions; public utilities, DM 351 millions. From the production loans, manufacturing received DM 1,796 millions, agriculture and mining DM 351 millions. Kreditanstalt für Wiederaufbau, *Annual Report*, 1964, p. 55.

that the number of economically sound projects approved for government credits should be increased was scarcely challenged in the Bundestag. This is no longer the case, as the Ministry for Economic Cooperation noted in March 1965: "In the days before the Near East crisis there was talk from many places: 'Give credits to as many developing countries as possible, for only on the basis of close economic cooperation will respect for our national interest thrive.' Now, since the Federal Republic of Germany is harvesting ingratitude where it expects understanding, the demand is being reversed with: 'Don't give them to all those countries, but only to those who prove to be our friends.' "[2]

While giving no direct answer to the difficult questions connected with long-term credit planning that are raised by having a recipient country turn hostile in its foreign policy measures, the same statement went on to indicate that the Bonn government plans no change in its policy of granting credits. Outlining the strictly economic criteria used for assessing applications for credits, the statement makes it clear that political and social questions are theoretically relevant only as they relate to the proposed project's desirability or feasibility. There was no reference to any governmental desire to increase the number of credit takers for the moment.

Despite gradual easing of credit terms, German loans appear to be extended at higher average interest rates, with shorter maturities and grace periods than those of the other large Western lenders.[3] The loan contracts concluded under the 1965 bilateral capital assistance stipulated an interest rate of 3.7 per cent, maturities of 20.2 years, and grace periods of 5.3 years.[4]

The Federal Republic's commitment to project assistance on the one hand and to encouragment of small enterprise on the other hand has accounted for two noteworthy aspects of the country's development aid effort: (1) preference for areas with operational development plans (such as those of India and Pakistan); and (2) granting of credit through development banks in twelve emerging nations. The latter channeling of credit has enabled the development banks to promote small and medium-sized firms in trade, industries and agriculture; to mobilize domestic funds; to stimulate the initiative of local private entrepreneurs; and to build up efficient banking systems. The Germans have supplied only the foreign exchange called for by the new investments, anticipating that additional financial means would be provided locally. Occasionally, Germany's credit has been combined with other foreign sources, such as World Bank loans.

By the end of 1966, the funds advanced by the Federal Republic in forty-

2. "Entwicklungshilfe ist keine Giesskannen-Politik: Der Weg zum Kapitalhilfe-Kredit ist genau festgelegt," *Bulletin,* No. 50 (March 20 1965), p. 403.

3. For some comparative details on this, see Holbik, "West German Development Aid."

4. Ministry of Economics, *Report on German Development Assistance Policies in 1965,* p. 19. These terms of lending were not influenced by the 1965 DAC recommendation that its members soften the existing conditions.

seven loans (totaling DM 622 million) to twenty-one development banks in Asia, Africa, and Latin America testified to the high value which the Germans attach to project selection and loan administration carried out by these banks. The loans have a maturity of twenty years and—while untied— have been used to purchase West German goods to as high a proportion as 85 per cent.[5]

Table XIV summarizes West German capital and technical assistance and illustrates the diversity of projects supported.

Encouragement of Private Participation in Development Aid

It has long been a policy of the German Federal Republic to encourage private enterprise to take over a larger share of the aid program. This policy is motivated by the government's desire both to hold down the tax drain on the federal budget and to create a more favorable impression of the private enterprise system in the developing countries through the example of German-sponsored firms and private organizations at work there. After all, the whole concept of foreign aid, German as well as American, is ideologically tied in with the development of a strong property-holding middle class: "A privately owned business in a developing country—if possible, one with local partners—will, if successful, be an excellent advertisement for the private enterprise system and will help counteract the growing tendency towards government-controlled economy in these countries."[6] Bonn is aware that continued extensive government assistance entails considerable disadvantages, and further, that official capital aid is but a substitute for a worldwide market economy and the free flow of goods and capital which go along with it.

From the standpoint of the developing countries themselves too, private investment retains all the advantages of government aid, enabling increased employment of indigenous personnel, more local facilities for technical training, a rise in gross national product with resulting higher tax revenues, and the introduction of foreign exchange to finance investments. At the same time, since private investment—unlike government aid with its concentration on infrastructure—is geared to the production of goods within a relatively short period of time, it can improve a developing country's balance of payments position by facilitating export increases and import decreases before the grandiose government-sponsored economic and social changes have been felt.

5. Total investment resulting from the Federal Republic's seed money is perhaps six times as large, according to German estimates. The 35 loans granted by the end of 1965 gave rise to 563 credit transactions of the development banks. Kreditanstalt für Wiederaufbau, XVII. Jahresbericht (1965), pp. 75 and 78.

6. Jochen Holzer, "Easing the Way for Private Investment in Developing Countries," Germany, Vol. IX (1964), No. 37, p. 20.

Table XIV. Capital Aid and Technical Assistance, 1965

Type of Project	Number of Projects		
	Capital Aid	Technical Assistance	Total
1. Industry	35	—	35
iron and steel	5	—	5
textile	8	—	8
cement works and brickworks	6	—	6
others	16	—	16
2. Mining	7	—	7
3. Transport	59	17	76
railways	10	5	15
roads	16	—	16
bridges and tunnels	10	—	10
other projects (such as supply of ships, airplanes, etc.)	13	—	13
harbors	10	—	10
4. Telecommunications (radio, posts, etc.)	7	7	14
5. Land cultivation	8	—	8
6. Mills and silos	2	—	2
grain mills	1	—	1
oil mills	1	—	1
7. Irrigation	21	5	26
irrigation	7	—	7
water supply	10	—	10
drainage	1	—	1
sewage treatment	3	—	3
8. Dams	8	—	8
9. Power projects (chiefly industrial diesels and power plants)	8	—	8
10. Electrification	9	—	9
11. Hospitals and clinics	6	400	406
12. Housing	6	38	44
13. Development banks	26	—	26
14. Co-operatives	2	—	2
15. Other capital aid (chiefly commodity aid)	41	—	41
16. Schools (establishment, equipment)	—	353	353
trade schools	—	222	222
agricultural and other schools	—	131	131
elementary and secondary schools	—	212	212
	(number of persons)		
17. Trainees	—	8900	212
18. Social projects	—	69	69
19. Model institutes (workshops, pilot plants, pilot farms	—	177	177
20. Planners, consultants, research services	—	529	529
21. Seminars, evening and day courses	—	284	284
22. Other projects	—	22	22

Source: *Hands Across the Sea* (Bonn: Druck- und Verlagshaus Heinz Möller), p. 26.

But it is one thing to outline advantages from a national or international standpoint and an entirely different one to find individual investors in large quantity. Objections felt by the German government to be at the heart of its citizens' reluctance to invest abroad are all reducible to skepticism about the high risks which investors encounter in countries with primitive economic conditions, persistent inflationary pressures, and shaky governments often characterized by collectivist leanings.[7] The same hesitation, to be sure, is found among American investors, but for Germans there are more restraining factors: the violent disruption of twentieth century German trade in two world wars with its mass confiscations of German overseas holdings, has tainted the whole idea of investment risks abroad for many investors. Then there is the irresistible competition of investment at home, which entails minimal risks. Moreover, there are attractive investment opportunities in the European Common Market area and in other industrialized nations.

The low rate of investment in developing countries discernible in Table XIII stands in marked contrast to the steady growth of total investment holdings by Germans, which approached a market value of DM 7,812 million in June 1965; of this sum, DM 2,478 million is invested in emerging nations. (Between January 1962 and June 1965, the flow of private capital to industrialized nations rose by 126 per cent, to underdeveloped nations by 65 per cent.) In a speech to representatives of German industry in March 1965, President Lübke voiced his discouragment at the lag in German investments abroad and emphasized his government's willingness to offset the risks of investment in developing countries. The three approaches which he cited— tax-relief measures, federal guarantees, and the work of the German Development Company— are the staples of the Federal Republic's gradually developed campaign to promote privately sponsorship of enterprises in Asia, Africa, and Latin America.[8]

The Development Assistance Tax Law (Entwicklungshilfe-Steuergesetz), which took effect on January 1, 1964, provides tax relief for German investors in two principal ways. First, the government assesses such foreign investments at 85 per cent of their market value and allows the investor to permanently write off 15 per cent of the otherwise taxable profits accruing from them. In addition, the investor may set aside a temporarily tax-free reserve totalling up to 50 per cent of the remaining profits, in order to offset losses or meager returns in the first few years after an investment.

7. Cf. Dr. R. Meimberg, "Jenseits der Entwicklungshilfe," *Frankfurter Allgemeine Zeitung*, Jan. 23, 1965, p. 5; Dr. Matthias Schmitt, "Ein Schritt ins Ungewisse," *ibid.*, Oct. 23, 1965; "Die Deutsche Entwicklungshilfe," *Neue Zürcher Zeitung*, Aug. 17, 1965, Dr. Matthias Schmitt, *Entwicklungshilfe als unternehmerische Aufgabe* (Frankfurt: Fritz Knapp Verlag, 1965), *passim*. In 1965, German private investments in the developing countries totaled DM 449 million and consisted of direct investment (DM 279 million), portfolio investment (DM 33 million), and reinvested profits (DM 137 million).

8. Heinrich Lübke, "Mehr Investitionen im Ausland notwendig," *Bulletin*, No. 51 (March 23, 1965), p. 405.

This reserve sum need not be put back on paper as taxable assets, that is, as profits earned, until six years from the date of purchase, and then this is done in six equal installments over the next six years. The Ministry for Economic Cooperation calculated that under this law the Federal Finance Office would assume about 33 per cent of investment costs in the year of purchase, with 25 per cent to be repaid six to eleven years later and 8 per cent to be kept by the investor until he would have sold these holdings, at which time the money received in the transaction would be fully taxable.[9] In its present form, the law allows exemptions only if the capital transferred to the developing country is spent for machines and buildings. This restriction was undoubtedly intended to prevent abuses in the purchase of paper securities or materials less related to industrial development processes by the company operating overseas. But in 1964, Minister Scheel complained that the narrowness of this provision tended to negate much of the effect which the Development Assistance Tax Law was supposed to achieve; in particular, he noted "the trade establishments are excluded in this law from the beneficial tax measures, not legally, to be sure, but as a matter of fact."[10] This practical exclusion follows naturally enough from the very limited needs for machines and new buildings in the marketing process. More than a year after the Ministry for Economic Cooperation expressed a desire for expanding the tax-relief coverage, no changes in it had been made; but the ministry's compromise recommendation that at least capital used for purchasing manufacturing supplies and merchandise be made subject to the same tax exemptions was taken under study by the Bundestag.[11] The tax loss for 1964 which resulted from the law as it stands has been estimated at $16 million, which will be offset by repayments of by far the larger part after six years. Proponents of expanding its coverage have insisted that the additional tax loss incurred would be "insignificant."[12]

The West German government provides guarantees for German firms trading with or operating in developing countries chiefly through export-credit protection and treaties with recipient nations. In 1963, the guaranteed portion of export credits was raised as indicated in Table XV.

The tying of governmental capital assistance to orders which must be placed in West Germany by recipient nations should, in the course of the next few years, greatly decrease the need for credits extended overseas by

9. Bundesministerium für wirtschaftliche Zusammenarbeit, "Das Entwicklungshilfe-Steuergesetz: Anreiz und Starthilfe für deutsche Privatinvestitionen," *Bulletin*, No. 25 (Feb. 10, 1965), p. 196. An English publication of the same ministry, *Report on Development Assistance Efforts in 1963*, printed as "Enclosure to letter dated 23-3-1964," treats these rather complicated tax regulations, pp. 7–8.

10. "Entwicklungspolitik im Wandel," press release by the Bundesministerium für wirtschaftliche Zusammenarbeit of speech given in Bremen, Feb. 14, 1964, pp. 5–6.

11. Bundesministerium für wirtschaftliche Zusammenarbeit, "Das Entwicklungshilfe-Steuergesetz," p. 196.

12. Scheel, "Entwicklungspolitik im Wandel," p. 6.

German exporters and subsequently make this kind of guarantee proportionately less relevant to the Federal Republic's total aid program.

Table XV. Maximum Percentages of Government Guarantees for Export Credits to Developing Countries

Type of risk	Before 3/16/63	Effective 3/16/63
Economic, including nonfulfillment of payment obligations by governmental contracting parties	70	80
Political: interdiction of payment, moratorium, conversion, and transfer	80	85
Remaining political	80	90
Manufacturing	80	85

Source: Der Bundesminister für wirtschaftliche Zusammenarbeit, *Report on Development Assistance Efforts in 1963*, adapted from p. 8.

Entirely different types of guarantees, preventive rather than compensatory in nature, are contained in bilateral agreements with governments of recipient countries. In February 1965, the federal Ministry of Economic Cooperation announced the conclusion of twenty-five such agreements, which go by the name of "investment-encouragement treaties" *(Investitionsförderungsverträge)*: "These treaties secure the required legal protection for German foreign investments and are regarded as a necessary supplement to the German measures of encouragement for private investments in developing countries. In particular, the following principles have been agreed upon in the treaties: (a) reasonable, just, and non-discriminatory treatment of capital investments; (b) guarantee of the transfer of profits and of payments following sale; (c) protection against arbitrary dispossession; and (d) arbitration-committee clause."[13]

The German Development Company (Deutsche Entwicklungsgesellschaft) is a government-sponsored organization founded in 1964 to aid in establishing or expanding medium-sized enterprises in the underdeveloped world. It supports ventures which seem potentially profitable but which cannot be locally financed. It does not support government-owned or operated enterprises, although the investment of a limited amount of local government funds is acceptable when necessary; it has generally steered away from infrastructure projects in favor of such businesses as textile mills, construction-material manufacturing plants, and food-processing works. The main task of the company is confined to the encouragement of

---

13. Das Bundesministerium für wirtschaftliche Zusammenarbeit, "Investitionsförderungsverträge mit Entwicklungsländern," *Bulletin*, No. 30 (Feb. 18, 1965), p. 243.

private participation in its projects, for its holdings may make up only one fifth to one-half of the total stock in any one business, with the remainder necessarily supplied by private capital overseas. Such official governmental association as a business partner in development projects has proven an effective stimulus, although necessarily on a small scale. The Development Company's participation funds—$18.75 million in total capital, to be invested over three years in annual installments of $6.25 million—are rapidly being used up as more private investors support its projects. (Fifty-eight projects at the end of 1965 ranged from a powdered tea company in Ceylon to a leather sandal company in Nigeria.) The company hopes to be able to use some of the profits gained in its established businesses and possibly to withdraw its participation from successful operations in order to help finance new ones. But this is a future goal, dependent on the willingness of the Bonn government to raise the company's funds out of tax revenues.[14]

The minister for economic cooperation has set the desirable degree of private participation in the development program at 50 per cent, rather than the prevailing 25 per cent; but it is evident from the foregoing that this will be a long time in coming. Partly offsetting the relative indifference of private investors, noncommercial private organizations deserve mention, and the West German government has acknowledged their efforts as developmental spade work. In the 1964 federal budget, an allotment title "Support for plans of developmental importance advanced by private German sponsors in underdeveloped countries," appeared for the first time. The modest funds allocated under it have been furthering projects of churches, trade unions, universities, and similar organizations, in which economic profit from aid projects is not a driving force. Minister Scheel, in assuring these private agencies cooperation in every respect, noted that many educational and social development projects require more flexibility and a greater variety of experience in specialized fields than government agencies can supply. The government's support of these agencies is naturally more passive from a policy standpoint than its encouragement of private business undertakings. It is generally assumed in Germany (and probably elsewhere in the West) that projects undertaken by churches, labor unions, and universities are—by virtue of the nature of their sponsorship—both sufficiently benevolent and progressive to require no governmental policy directives, except perhaps to avoid duplicated or otherwise wasted efforts. The West German government sees these operations as creating basic conditions for development, which do not so much complement the government's official projects as precede them. In Minister Scheel's hopeful words: "Governmental organs are responsible for development policy.

---

14. Lübke, "Mehr Investitionen," p. 405; and "How to Make Five Marks out of One," unsigned article, *German International*, Vol. IX, No. 4 (April 1965), pp. 25–26.

The cooperation of private forces creates realities by which government policy, too, will find its direction."[15]

Multilateral Assistance

Table XIII above indicates clearly not only that, in comparison with 1961, German multilateral aid has decreased drastically in recent years, but also that the volume of total aid has fluctuated as a result of changes in the country's contribution to international aid-giving organizations. The ratio between multilateral and bilateral aid will hardly ever be 1:2 again, as it was in 1961 when the Germans were more or less obligated to purchase DM 848 millions' worth of World Bank debentures. During the 1950's, before the Federal Republic inaugurated her own bilateral aid program, she found it easier to finance multilateral aid.

By the end of 1965, multilateral payments totaled DM 3,308 million ($827 million), of which DM 762 million were available (interest-free) to the World Bank (IBRD) and its sister organizations, the International Finance Corporation and the International Development Agency. On the other hand, the World Bank borrowed in West Germany a total of DM 2.85 billion at an interest rate of 3.5 to 5 per cent.

Germany's total contribution to the United Nations and several of its specialized agencies (e.g., the Food and Agriculture Organization, the International Labor Organization, and the World Health Organization) amounted to DM 289 million at the end of 1965. Payments to the EEC Development Fund, corresponding to 35 per cent of the fund's total receipts, fulfilled the Federal Republic's obligation to the first fund as early as 1962 and totaled DM 816 million. (In the second fund—1963–1968—West Germany's share will come to 34 per cent or DM 984 million.)[16]

The Germans do not hesitate to admit that their contributions to the World Bank have proved profitable; some of the country's producers of heavy industrial equipment have received substantial orders based on the bank's loans. The United Nations, too, has drawn on a valuable German resource, using the services of hundreds of German experts. But the Federal Republic's participation in the EEC Development Fund has been both less rewarding and somewhat disappointing; German business has not received the proportion of contracts from EEC's affiliated African countries equal to Bonn's financial contribution. In fact, West Germany received only 3 per cent of such contracts. Understandably, in areas with tradition-

15. "Im Geiste menschlicher Solidarität," speech before representatives of seventy-five private organizations, June 26, 1964, *Bulletin*, No. 109 (July 10, 1964), pp. 1,033–1,034. See also unsigned article immediately preceding text of speech: "Privatorganisationen— Partner in der Entwicklungshilfe."

16. *Hands Across the Sea*, pp. 32–34; "Der Europäische Entwicklungsfonds," *Entwicklungspolitik*, Sept. 27, 1965, pp. 3–6.

ally strong French influence (West and Central Africa), the prospects for German enterprise have not been bright. (See below, Chap. VII.)

In general, Germans discount the effectiveness of aid-giving through multilateral channels and believe that international institutions and aid interfere with the proper and desirable close relationship between donors and aid-recipients; this is especially so if a relationship is expected by Bonn to have political and cultural ramifications.[17]

Other noteworthy disadvantages of multilateral assistance, of which the Germans are acutely conscious, rest on the fact that (1) certain international organizations are regarded as American simply because their headquarters are located in the United States; the U.S. thus frequently gets credit for financial support given by other member nations; (2) Germany is not sufficiently represented in the administrative bodies of such organizations; and (3) there exist irreconcilable differences among members of international institutions as to how development funds should be distributed.

The Bonn government is furthermore convinced that budgetary appropriations from the Bundestag are easier to obtain when identifiable German-financed projects rather than multilateral (anonymous) cooperative ventures are at stake. Nevertheless, the Germans are prepared to adapt their bilateral aid to a larger multilateral conception, especially when sponsored by the DAC. Some coordination of West Germany's assistance with that of other OECD member nations has taken place under the DAC's and the World Bank's auspices in consortia concerned with development aid to India, Pakistan, Turkey, and Greece.

Administration of Development Aid

The proverbially strong German sense for organization notwithstanding, the organization of the Federal Republic's development aid is extremely complicated and characterized by redundant authorities—largely because of excessive decentralization. To some extent, the unwieldy aid machinery can be explained by the principle (touched upon in Chap. II) that West Germany prefers to grant aid in response to foreign request rather than through its own initiative. In one serious attempt to count all German aid sources, over 250 participating organizations were listed.[18]

The efforts of many of these agencies are competitive.[19] This could be avoided if the Ministry for Economic Cooperation were not only free to coordinate the multitude of aid sources, but also did not have to compete

17. Cf. Hermann Niggemeyer, "Wer hilft, muss richtig helfen," *Frankfurter Allgemeine Zeitung,* Sept. 7, 1961, p. 16.

18. Günther von Lojewski, "Die Konkurrenz der Hilfsbereitschaft—Über 250 Organisationen teilen sich in der Bundesrepublik in die Aufgaben der Entwicklungshilfe," *ibid.,* Dec. 2, 1964.

19. Fritz Ullrich Fack, "Mehr Kompetenzen für Minister Scheel," *ibid.,* Oct. 10, 1964.

for influence with both the Ministry of Economics and the Foreign Office. It is possible that some of the disillusionment of the German people with development aid has been caused by the undisguised jurisdictional conflicts or what the Germans call *Kompetenzwirrwarr.*"

Apart from the federal government, which dominates aid-giving (because it is the most bountiful source), the other contributors of public aid are the executive and administrative organs of the individual German states (Landesregierungen and Landesbehörden). These established in 1960 a special commission (Landeskommission für Entwicklungshilfe) in Stuttgart to assist individual states in putting their modest resources to the best use. In addition: many states grant aid directly in the form of scholarships and other forms of educational assistance.

Private development aid consists of contributions which are either altruistic in nature and purpose or are motivated by self-interest. To the latter group of donors belong, for example, the Federal Association of German Industry (Bundesverband der deutschen Industrie), the Assembly of German Industry and Commerce (Der Deutsche Industrie- und Handelstag), the Banana Institute (Das Bananen-Institut), clearly interested in importation of bananas, the Association for Africa (Afrika-Verein) and the German-Iranian Chamber of Commerce—to name just a few of the private organizations. Labor unions, too, have set up their development-aid program (e.g., We Help, Wir Helfen), as has the German Red Cross and the Federal Medical Chamber (Bundesärztekammer).

Outstanding work in development assistance has been done by both the Protestant and Catholic churches through their respective organizations, Bread for the World (Brot für die Welt) and Misereor.[20] However, there are many other Christian groups which have aroused interest in the emerging nations. Some 160 scientific and research institutes sponsor activities in behalf of the same objective, in addition to stimulating cultural contacts.

On the federal level, cooperation between a dozen of more or less directly involved ministries and some government agencies including, among others, the Federal Bank (Bundesbank) and the Development Loan Corporation (Kreditanstalt für Wiederaufbau), is the responsibility of the Inter-Ministerial Committee for Development. Since 1961, the Ministry for Economic Cooperation has succeeded in streamlining West German development-aid programs "for which nobody and everybody seemed to be responsible before its establishment." The ministry is in charge of planning and implementing all technical-assistance projects, although it only

20. By June 1964, Brot für die Welt collected DM 97 million and established 453 projects in many countries providing them with indispensable medical and social services. Misereor collected DM 264 million and sponsored some 3,000 projects, many of them designed to teach the underdeveloped world new industrial skills and agricultural methods. Together the church organizations engaged the services of almost 2,500 professionals (including doctors, engineers, consultants, etc.) *Für Sie gelesen,* No. 22 (May 1965) and No. 23 (June 1965). Both of the above named organizations receive federal subsidies (DM 73 million in 1965).

plans capital-aid projects. Implementation of the latter is the responsibility of the Ministry of Economics.

The Ministry for Economic Cooperation operates through four executive agencies:

1. The German Institute for Developing Countries (Deutsche Stiftung für Entwicklungsländer), where experts from the developing countries can exchange views and establish contacts with German specialists. The Institute maintains centers in various German cities and sponsors seminars.

2. The German Development Company (Deutsche Gesellschaft für wirtschaftliche Zusammenarbeit) provides funds for investment in small and medium-sized firms in the backward areas, with a German company of comparable size as a third partner.

3. The German Development Service (Deutscher Entwicklungsdienst) is based on the idea of the U.S. Peace Corps. The service recruits young people skilled in various trades and operates a school in Berlin to train volunteers.

4. The German Institute for Development Policy (Deutsches Institut für Entwicklungspolitik) offers one-year courses in problems of development for German graduate students who are to form an elite of German development specialists. This Institute intends to overcome the scarcity of these experts.

Among other government agencies is the above-mentioned Development Loan Corporation extending capital aid loans (for more on this see Chapter V), and the German Company for the Furtherance of Developing Countries (Deutsche Förderungsgesellschaft für Entwicklungsländer); together the two comprise the Federal Office for Manufacturing Industry (Bundesamt für gewerbliche Wirtschaft), responsible for selection of German experts going overseas under the technical assistance program. The Carl-Duisberg-Gesellschaft is an independent organization supervising training of foreigners in Germany and looking after German trainees overseas. German Academic Exchange Service (Deutscher Akademischer Austauschdienst) assists students selected by German embassies in developing countries.[21]

21. For current reports on German accomplishments in development aid see *Partnerschaft* (Inter Nationes, Bonn) and *Entwicklungspolitik* (Ministry for Economic Cooperation). A detailed account of the institutional aspects of West German aid appears in John White, *German Aid* (London: The Overseas Development Institute, Ltd., 1965).

DEVELOPMENT AID AT WORK

Capital Assistance

As Table XIII (Chap. IV) reveals, bilateral capital aid constitutes the most important source of German development aid, in spite of inevitable annual changes:

Official bilateral capital aid as percentage of total aid

1961	27
1962	38
1963	44
1964	33
1965	35
1966	53

Profiting from experience which has confirmed the intimate interdependence of capital investment and technical assistance ("know-how"), the West German government has begun to place greater emphasis on the social aspects of its financial commitments. One purpose of this emphasis is to overcome difficulties traceable to human factors— such as German experts' sometimes inadequate command of the aid-recipients' languages and their lack of familiarity with local customs. Experience has taught the Germans, too, that thorough technical and economic analyses of contemplated investments not only ensure the success of capital-aid projects but also prove time-saving. These and other empirical findings have resulted in the recent adoption of new methods of credit extension which render developmental loans more effective on the one hand, and attract private capital (German or international) on the other. Support given to development banks (see Chap. IV) has also been instrumental in increasing the effectiveness of capital assistance.[1]

As of the end of 1965, total general advance commitments *(Regierungszusagen or Regierungsabkommen)* of West German official capital aid

1. For more on this see "Overseas Banking" in *Hands Across the Sea*, and *Deutsche Entwicklungspolitik im Jahre 1965*, Sonderdruck im Auftrag des Bundesministeriums für wirtschaftliche Zusammenarbeit, p. 16.

amounted to DM 9,166 million. However, loans actually granted through the Development (alternatively, Reconstruction) Loan Corporation and the German Development Company totaled only DM 6,989 million or 76 per cent of the whole sum. Considering German preference for sound development projects, the difference of DM 2,177 million is understandable; moreover, it is typical of the credit-granting process. Yet even out of the authorized amount *(Kreditverträge)* no more than DM 4,800 million or 68 per cent had been paid out to recipients.[2]

The discrepancy between authorized and disbursed credit (referred to frequently as "pipeline") results from the fact that (1) loaned funds are released in accordance with the sponsored projects' actual progress; (2) some projects lack sufficient preparation; (3) unforeseen changes occur in the realization of investment plans; (4) political instabilities, e.g., governmental changes in the developing countries, intervene; and last but not least, (5) delays take place in the coordination of interrelated projects. The OECD has held pipeline impediments partly responsible for the fact that government flows from West Germany (along with those from the United States, Great Britain, and France) have not increased since 1961 in accordance with expectations.[3]

Geographically, the general advance commitments of DM 9.2 billion have been distributed as follows:[4]

Asia	58 per cent (19 countries)
Africa	20 per cent (34 countries)
Europe	15 per cent (4 countries)
Latin America	7 per cent (10 countries)

Inasmuch as both official long-term capital aid and export financing are administered by the Development Loan Corporation, the latter's activities provide a reliable clue to West Germany's bilateral capital assistance program in addition to bearing witness to some of Bonn's development-aid policies.[5] Table XVI summarizes the corporation's transactions for the past six years. To these statistics it is useful to add that "export financing" is nearly the same as the commercial credit serving German producers and the economy; the remarkable decline in "non-tied loans" after 1961 may be

2. *Ibid.,* p. 18.

3. OECD, "What is Happening to Development Assistance?" press release, Paris, Oct. 11, 1966, p. 2; Willard Thorp, "Introductory Statement," DAC meeting, July 19–20, 1967.

4. *Deutsche Entwicklungspolitik . . . 1965,* p. 18.

5. The Reconstruction Loan Corporation—Kreditanstalt für Wiederaufbau (henceforth KW)—was originally founded to oversee expenditures of Marshall Plan funds and subsequently guided much of the government financing for postwar German reconstruction. In 1961 it took over the function of a foreign development bank, retaining its original name and Frankfurt am Main headquarters. The domestic long-term loans which the KW continues to grant have in recent years made up between one-fifth and one-third of its total commitments. Between 60 to 73 per cent of the KW's resources have been "public" (stemming from federal appropriations); some of the KW's own funds have been acquired in the capital market through the issue of securities.

explained by balance-of-payments difficulties experienced by the emerging nations.

Table XVI. The KW's Foreign Business, 1961–1965 (in millions of DM).

Type of Loan	1961	1962	1963	1964	1965	1966
A. Capital-Aid Loans	889	1265	1858	924	1179	1312
B. Export Financing	183	637	412	670	475	416
1. Loans to foreign purchasers	78	225	284	336	310	240
2. Loans to German exporters	104	413	128	334	165	176
C. Non-tied loans	628	69	290	52	201	—
D. Loans for establishing projects and participation abroad	9	12	7	10	18	16
Total	1707	1983	2567	1655	1874	1744

Source: Kreditanstalt für Wiederaufbau, *Annual Reports, 1962–1966.*

Table XVII shows the use to which the Development Loan Corporation's "foreign" funds of DM 1,874 million (see Table XVI) were put in 1965 on four continents. While this table makes abundantly clear that export fi-

Table XVII.   The KW's Foreign Loans Committed in 1965 (in millions of DM).

Type of Loan	Europe	Asia	Africa	Latin America	%
A. Capital-Aid Loans	50	678	209	243	63
1. Project Loans	—	493	199	243	50
2. Non-project Loans	50	185	10	—	13
B. Export Financing	211	163	13	85	25
1. Loans to Foreign Purchasers	167	106	8	29	17
2. Loans to German Exporters[a]	44	56	5	56	9
C. Non-tied Loans	40	—	71	90	11
D. Loans for Establishing Projects and Participation Abroad	5	8	4	2	1
Total	305	849	296	420	100

Source: Kreditanstalt für Wiederaufbau, *German Loans to Developing Countries, Africa and Asia,* 1965, pp. 5 and 21. This table shows positions as of September 1964.
[a]Omitted are DM 3.7 million loaned to German exporters for use in Australia.

nancing has contributed most to West Germany's trade with a few European countries, and that Latin American nations have been the primary beneficiaries of non-tied loans, it also shows that 74 per cent of project loans have been extended to Asian and African nations. How West German government funds are employed in these two areas is evident from the following tabulation:[6]

Types of Projects	Asia	Africa
A. Infrastructure		
1. Power production and supply	1	4
2. Water supply	1	4
3. Transport	14	18
4. Communication	6	—
5. Health service	1	1
B. Direct production		
1. Agriculture	1	7
2. Irrigation	4	3
3. Mining	1	—
4. Industry	25	4

As will be shown in later chapters, the proportions of infrastructural and industrial projects vary widely from region to region. In 1965, two-thirds of Development Loan Corporation credits awarded to projects were given for "direct production."

Requests for capital assistance pass through many hands, but most applications can be completely processed within ten months. First, the developing country submits its application, either on its own or at the suggestion of a German agency. If the Foreign Office and the Ministries for Finance, Economic Affairs, and Economic Cooperation give it their preliminary approval, it is submitted to a blue-ribbon committee of economic organizations, the "Task Force for Developing Countries" (Arbeitsgemeinschaft Entwicklungsländer) for an opinion on the project's feasibility. The opinions of the ministries consulted and those of the task force are forwarded to the Interministerial Review Committee for Capital Assistance (Interministerieller Referentenausschuss für Kapitalhilfe), which makes the real yes-or-no decision on the project. If this body approves it, research on optimum ways for carrying out the project is conducted, usually at the sites of construction suggested by the KW's economists and technologists; the Development Loan Corporation then returns the results of its investigations to the Interministerial Review Committee, which must restate its affirmation of the request for capital assistance on the basis of the corporation's reports. If it does so, the Development Loan Corporation will then fix the duration, grace period, interest rate, and amortization terms of the project.

Finally, the Development Loan Corporation is instructed to complete a contract. After it is signed, regular payments begin according to a schedule, not to the government of the country which made the request, but rather to the producers and suppliers of needed goods and services. The Development Loan Corporation remains responsible for interest payments and amortiza-

6. Kreditanstalt für Wiederaufbau, German Loans to Developing Countries, Africa and Asia, 1965, pp. 5 and 21. The tabulation shows positions as of September 1964.

tion as well as for the expenditure of funds according to the contract. Supervision has doubtless been facilitated by the assignment of over 80 per cent of the payments to German firms for materials ordered, so that only a small portion of the funds is lent outside the Federal Republic.[7]

Technical Assistance

"Technical assistance, in the official definition, is 'help toward self-help' chiefly through the teaching of know-how."[8] And indeed the terms "self-help" (Selbsthilfe) and "know-how" (retained in German as "know-how") appear repeatedly in official West German presentations of the total aid program. Probably no thought is dearer either to German or American officials connected with foreign aid than the notion that, by imparting technical information to the hungry, ignorant, and politically volatile nations and would-be nations of the world, the West can enable them to become aware and affluent supporters of a stable socio-political order.[9]

In contrast to capital, technical assistance—whether bilateral, multilateral or private—is normally a gift: goods and services, particularly those of German experts and teachers, go to the developing country, with no attempt made by anyone to prove that the funds spent will return even in part to the Federal Republic. The following exchange occurred in the interview with former Minister Scheel on the politics of development aid:

Q. But there are development monies which are lost, aren't there?
A. The federal government spends many millions every year on its so-called technical aid program. This is money which is used, for example, for the construction of vocational schools, hospitals and certain infrastructural projects. The money spent for this could be regarded as 'lost.'[10]

7. Steps in the credit-granting process are given according to the Ministry for Economic Cooperation's defense of its procedures at the time of the Near East crisis in German foreign relations of the spring of 1965. "Entwicklungshilfe ist keine Giesskannen-Politik: Der Weg zum Kapitalhilfe-Kredit ist genau festgelegt," Bulletin, No. 50 (March 20, 1965), pp. 403–404 (see above, Chap. IV). An earlier description of the system is Wilhelm Hankel's "How Does German Capital Assistance Work?" Germany, Vol. VIII (1963), No. 35, pp. 18–21.

8. "Technical Assistance," unsigned article in Twelve Years of German Development Assistance (Bonn: Druck- und Verlagshaus Heinz Möller, 1964), p. 12. In one of his public lectures, Minister Scheel made this quotable point: "Unsere Entwicklungshilfe ist Hilfe zur Selbsthilfe. Ähnlich wie der Strom beim Motor. Der Strom liefert den zündenden Funken, die Leistung aber muss der Motor selbst vollbringen." ("Our aid for development is help for self-help, resembling electric current in the case of a gasoline motor. The current delivers the igniting spark, but the real work has to be done by the motor itself.") For a comprehensive analysis of the Federal Republic's technical assistance see Ferdinand Kopp, Unsere Welt im Umbruch (Bonn: Eichholz-Verlag GmbH., 1965), pp. 34–47.

9. Cf. Fritz Baade, . . . denn sie sollen satt werden, (Oldenburg: Gerhard Stalling Verlag, 1964), especially Chap. I.

10. "New Style in Foreign Aid: 'Promoting Project Groups Instead of Single Projects,' " interview in German International, Vol. VII, No. 2 (Feb. 1963), p. 27.

Of course, few in the liberal, Judaeo-Christian West would consider funds expended for health, education, and welfare as "lost." Probably because technical assistance is seen as a donation, West Germany insists on retaining more of the initiative in starting projects than it does in capital assistance. Earlier technical assistance measures were based primarily on the wishes of the governments of developing nations; now the Federal Republic determines projects on the basis of its own estimate of the recipient's need. Projects are coordinated with capital aid and with other parts of the overall development program in the country.

But it is difficult to speak of technical assistance without mentioning the government's general educational assistance, which supplements the individual projects. There are some bookkeeping problems involved: education, including that of foreign students, has its own fiscal headings; some of the money is not spent on technical assistance by the federal government, but through non-government bodies; the federal government is relieved of some of the expenses, particularly for scholarships to study in Germany which are granted by the individual states (Länder) to students from developing countries.

Another look at Table XII confirms that, absolutely, official technical assistance has increased steadily; namely, from DM 109 million in 1961 to DM 432 million in 1966. A continuous rise can be observed in relative comparisons as well: while in 1961 this form of German development aid equaled 3 per cent of total aid, it made up as much as 17 per cent in 1966. Recipients of technical aid were thirty-six African countries, twenty-five Asian countries, twenty-four Latin American countries, and nine European countries. In 1965, technical assistance consisted of the following principal components which added up to DM 338.4 million:[11]

I. Technical training centers, model institutions, advisors, experts, etc.[12]	DM 106.1 million
II. Training of skilled personnel	
a. under federal government sponsorship	DM 17.8 million
b. Under sponsorship of the Länder governments	DM 13.0 million
III. Educational programs, especially for higher education, sponsored by the Länder governments	DM 5.3 million
Ditto, sponsored by the Federal Foreign Office	DM 102.1 million
IV. Social assistance (to improve social legislation and administration through thirty-five centers in eight developing countries)	DM 2.1 million

11. Deutsche Entwicklungspolitik . . . 1965, pp. 6–7; for previous years see Jochen Holzer, "Principles, Form and Scopes of Technical Assistance," Germany, Vol. IX (1964), No. 38, p. 22.

12. A comprehensive account of the reasons why technical assistance, including social and cultural aid, has become one of the principal instruments of West German development policy, appears in "Technical Assistance, Focal Point of German Development Policy," Der Volkswirt (1963), Special Supplement No. 38.

V. Personal assistance to Germans assigned to the
emerging nations   DM   3.1 million
    German Institute for Development Policy   DM   1.1 million
VI. German Institute for Developing Countries   DM   7.6 million
VII. German Development Service[13]   DM   7.5 million
VIII. Development assistance programs of churches and
other private organizations[14]   DM 72.7 million

Leading beneficiaries of the above funds were the five economic sectors
listed below. Comparison with 1964 demonstrates both rational flexibility in
resource allocation and the special attention being given by the Federal
Republic to agricultural projects.

Percentage of aid received

	1965	1964
Industries and crafts	30.3	51.4
Agriculture and forestry	28.0	21.9
Information services	12.7	6.3
Transportation	4.8	1.9
Health services	4.4	5.9
	80.2	87.4

Among their top technical assistance projects the West Germans include:

Country   *Project*

A. Schools and Training Centers

India	Technical Institute, Madras
Egypt	Polytechnical College Cairo-Helwan
Ethiopia	Technical Department at University of Addis Ababa
Turkey	Technical Institute, Izmir
Afghanistan	Three Technical and two Trade Schools at Kabul
Iran	Trade Schools at Teheran and Taebris

B. Pilot Plants and Model Installations

Indonesia	Pilot Plant, Rayon
Egypt	Institute for Norms and Standards
India	Agricultural Advisory Office at Mandhi
Tanganyika	Institute for Water Development and Agricultural Techniques at Ifakara
Turkey	Pilot Farm Tahir Ova

13. Although the German Development Service received 22,000 applications by 1965, only 450 volunteers perform their duties in 16 developing countries. Of the 450 persons 180 are in Africa, 150 in Asia and 120 in Latin America. *Deutsche Entwicklungspolitik* ... *1965*, p. 13.
14. Cf. Chap. IV.

Country	Project
Ethiopia	Bahar Dar Hospital
Libya	Extension of Broadcasting Sytem (two stations, studio equipment, German experts)

C. Consulting

Thailand	Investigations into Natural Resources
Kenya	Agricultural, veterinary and cooperative experts for Kenya's Settlement Program
Liberia	Group of experts for forest inventory
	Town planning for Monrovia
Afghanistan	Group of consultants for Planning Ministry
	Geological and hydrometrical services
Greece	Investigations into brown coal deposits of Ptolemais and Megalopolis
	Study for use of Aliakmon River

On the whole, model institutions in the form of farms, villages, experimental stations, sprinkler irrigation plants, slaughterhouses, and sawmills have been most significant. Public health services concentrate on preventive medicine and emphasize mobile clinics rather than large hospitals poorly suited to the requirements of developing nations. Some of these models have no doubt been intended chiefly as symbols of West Germany's good will—similar to the private American "Project Hope"—rather than as instruments for raising the local level of technological development. But, all in all, a hard headed business approach predominates, and the trend is toward even more realism. Foremost among current efforts is an attempt to gear education to a level appropriate to the stage of economic development of the student's own country. Prestigious displays of inappropriate sophisticated equipment are out. In the stately phrasing of the Ministry for Economic Cooperation:

> Projects must be started on a technical level which can also be attained by the initiative of the population of the recipient country itself in the light of its economic development. However, the realization of this principle often meets with difficulties because the governments of the developing countries frequently tend to regard only projects with the most up-to-date technical equipment as important for their development. In order to prevent that the model facilities fail to achieve the intended effect of being imitated and in order to avoid that they become islands of superior technology with no impact on their surroundings, only such projects will be promoted in the future whose dimensions and equipment will permit an 'imitation' by the exercise of the recipient country itself.[15]

15. Der Bundesminister für wirtschaftliche Zusammenarbeit, *Report on Development Assistance Efforts in 1963*, p. 14. Minister Scheel's keen awareness of the close connection between technology and specilized training led him to coin the phrase "Keine Mark ohne Mann," as another guide for the Federal Republic's developmental policy.

More General Educational Aid

Technical assistance is largely education, and until quite recently it has meant specific job preparation. But even slightly specialized training is not the first educational step in the West today; and it seems doubtful that developing countries can profit from projects designed to teach more progressive, efficient modes of production and public administration—those levers by which their peoples are to achieve economic advancement—without a greater diffusion of basic education through their masses. Over the last few years, the Ministry for Economic Cooperation has had serious second thoughts about the effectiveness of technical-assistance projects as conceived so far. First, there is the question of limiting the grandiose designs of local authorities who sometimes want more complex installations than indigenous personnel can operate. And there is also the need to "condition" the countryside, so that large numbers of people will gain from modest and appropriate technical-assistance projects. A recent review of technical-assistance policies released by the ministry's Scientific Advisory Board (Wissenschaftlicher Beirat) disclosed two basic defects in current ideas of what technical assistance should be: (1) planners have tended to overlook gaps in fundamental education needed for the absorption of technical training; and (2) they have often failed to take into account the absence of attitudes necessary to industrial enterprise in developing countries.[16]

The need for general preliminary education is a rather obvious one, and the extent to which it has been ignored thus far is traceable to an over-optimistic search for tempting shortcuts by both donor and recipient lands. By this time, however, scarcely any doubt remains that unless primary schools can teach reading, writing, and arithmetic on a serious basis to huge numbers of potential workers in the underdeveloped regions, there will be a shortage of competent construction workers, repairmen, machine operators, and the rest of the skilled army on which a complicated industrial economy depends. The problem of accommodating functional illiterates in the United States economy is severe enough, even though assembly-line production has given seemingly mindless, rote actions the dignity of industrial employment. But in an economy at the early stages of its development, industry has not yet reached the level of providing the simple, specialized screw-turning, lever-pulling operations on a large scale; the artisan who has enough basic education to read notes or gauges and who can transfer basic principles in measurement and assembly from one job situation to another

16. Printed as "Bildungshilfe—Gutachen: Grundsätze für eine Bildungshilfe der Bundesrepublik Deutschland and die Entwicklungsländer" in three Bulletin installments: Vol I, No. 127 (July 24, 1965), pp. 1,028–1,031; Vol. II, No. 128 (July 27, 1965), pp. 1,037–1,040; and Vol. III, No. 129 (July 28, 1965), pp. 1,046–1,048. See also Bildungshilfe für Entwicklungsländer (Stuttgart: Deutsche Verlags—Anstalt, 1963; Schriftenreihe der Friedrich Naumann—Stiftung zur Politik und Zeitgeschichte No. 6), passim.

is the man who is needed. Without fundamental learning and a cultivated ability to apply principles flexibly, the imitation of operations in a technical-assistance project becomes a mere aping of a given set of actions. Presumably the institution of free, compulsory education for at least six years will help, and governments of developing countries do seem generally reconciled to the fact that mass basic education must precede real technological advancement. Budgetary problems may intervene, but there are no voices of theoretical opposition in Germany or the developing countries. Adult primary education with courses of at least several months, organized outside the regular school system and taught by indigenous teachers and German advisors, is another measure advocated by the Advisory Board. These courses are particularly necessary for the next decade, as primary education will have no effect on the present working force.[17]

The behavioral deficiencies are harder to define, and more difficult to remedy. People in a developing country do not always make the connection —for Germans so evident and necessary—between hope for a higher standard of living and the need to get up early five or six days a week, appear at an appointed time and place, and begin carrying out directions exactly and promptly. In short, the whole set of notions about working hard and saving your money to get ahead has been very difficult to transplant from the industrial West. In many primitive societies, hard, prolonged, even partly physical work is often considered such an abomination that the suggestion that it leads to greener pastures is rejected out of hand. Even in parts of the underdeveloped world, such as Iran and India, where education has enjoyed time-honored respect, it is thought of as freeing the individual from the boorish necessities of the workaday world; a system which seems to reward the grubby applier of practical skills in the material world and to punish the devotee of pure liberal arts by ignoring him is clearly perverted.

All this as it is reported by unhappy evaluators of educational aid has a vaguely familiar sound: it has not been so long since the same laments were heard in Europe on the first dim appearance of the ethics of capitalism: "For it happeneth often that those of the basest sort, yea the very skum of the people, do scrape together great wealth, as those that apply themselves to filthy artes, and illiberal occupations, never sparing the toilsome and careful wearing out of their lives, but with an intolerable saving, defrauding themselves of the comforts of life, thereby to increase their substance. Contrariwise the honest citizens, and those that are liberally brought uppe, oftentimes fall to povertie, either (as it often happenth) by adverse fortune, or els that being wholly addicted to noble and liberall studies, they neglect the increasing of their wealth."[18] Of course, we have learned to think differently, by and large. But even now neither Germans nor Americans have any

17. Ibid., II, p. 1,037. The same tendency is evident within UNESCO. See above, Chap. I.

18. Cardinal Gasparo Contarini, The Commonwealth and Government of Venice [1543], transl. Lewes Lewkenor (London, 1599), Book I, p. 17 (STC microfilm, 205).

right to astonishment at the underdeveloped world's insistence on clinging to the notion that work with the mind is exalting and work with the hands more or less degrading. After all, it underlies the firm habit of the German workman—famous for pride in his craftsmanship—who regularly carries his lunch to his place of work in a briefcase. The equally irrational American notion says that the brown paper lunch bag of the $70.00-a-week office worker is somehow more respectable than the blue lunchbox of the $140.00-a-week cabinetmaker who made his status-giving desk.

In the less-developed countries the prejudices against the often grimy jobs most urgently needed for national economic development are necessarily far more ingrained than in the West of today. Religious tabus, rigid caste or class traditions, and a climate often inconducive to exertion reinforce them and add to the problems of the would-be educator, who must really start by remolding his students' mental sets toward useful employment. "Teaching and learning must not be confined to matters of knowledge and skills. Behavior, attitudes, and manners of cooperation must be learned simultaneously, for example: discipline, concentration, exactness, initiative, consciousness of responsibility, inclination to competitiveness, planning ahead, and teamwork."[19] This is a big order. A man can acquire technical information in great bulk and feel no intrusion upon his personality or upon his relationship to society; but when faced with such demands as these, he is really being asked nothing less than to change his whole personality. Most difficult of all, while remaining a member of a traditionalist society, he must somehow realize that his whole pattern of attitudes in what is now presented as the most important part of his daily life— routine employment—is defective. And he must realize this without resentment toward those who desire to improve him through what he can only feel to be the imposition of countless restrictions and requirements.

More fundamental education here is not, in itself, the answer to this problem. Germans have been particularly distressed to see money for basic schools in developing countries spent to procure clerkish teachers who continue to instill the same aversion to useful, partly physical labor. Nor does secondary or even advanced education necessarily provide a solution. Far too often the old mental set accompanies a student throughout his education, so that institutions of higher learning in developing countries are still capable of turning out that anomaly to the German and American: "the engineer who refuses to pick up a screwdriver."[20]

Something, of course, can be gained in this respect by confronting trainees or students from a developing region with the total experience of living in a land where they must imbibe the spirit of modern industrialism (including its soot and grease components) and observe how initial demands of hard, regular work come to be connected with rewards of well-being and satisfac-

19. "Bildungshilfe–Gutachten," I, p. 1,029.
20. *Ibid.*, II, p. 1,039.

tion for the diligent. After all, even socialist Germans mentally associate work and rewards: why shouldn't uncommitted foreigners do so if they are given a glimpse of the big picture? The West Germans have invited thousands of trainees and students to come to the Federal Republic for such experience in a new environment and have investigated ways of helping them learn better. In Berlin, the government-financed German Foundation for Developing Countries, has been sponsoring seminars and conventions where timely problems relating to economic development can be studied and debated; in 1963 alone, the foundation had fourteen seminars and three international conventions, attended by 337 visitors from developing countries. Two subsidiaries were established in 1964, an agricultural center in Munich and the Institute for Development Policy in Berlin, to broaden the capabilities of educational programs under which trainees and students receive instruction in the Federal Republic. In industry the need for labor of all kinds throughout West Germany has stimulated the interest of private employers in these programs: in 1963, 2,448 students trained at German firms under federal government grants; 1,050 under grants from the German states; and some 12,000 under private industrial sponsorship.[21]

In spite of the fairly large numbers of trainees and the evident willingness of private industry to use still more, the training of development-country personnel in West German factories is not yet generally considered a success. Many trainees from a tradition-directed society have great difficulty in adapting to the regimen of German industrial life; others, having made the transition, have little desire to return home. Some employers have compounded the problem by recruiting the best of the trainees assigned to them for permanent employment.

A similar kind of problem is encountered in giving German university training to students from developing countries. The language barrier, lack of sound preliminary education—sometimes in spite of their governments' certificates to the contrary—financial problems, and other aspects of the need for dealing with a totally strange environment have caused many students to leave the universities before the completion of their study programs. The Ministry for Economic Cooperation began to review, during the summer of 1964, at Bundestag prompting, the special problems faced by students from developing countries at German schools; it is hoped that the system can be tightened up to prevent waste of funds and humiliated foreign students.[22]

21. Werner Lamby, "German Development Aid in 1963," Germany, Vol. IX (1964), No. 38, pp. 14–15. There were also 584 government-sponsored trainees in a variety of non-industrial programs, including 88 in agriculture and 20 in administration. "Fortbildung von Angehörigen der Entwicklungsländer in der Bundesrepublik," Jahresbericht des Bundesminsteriums für wirtschaftliche Zusammenarbeit–1963, p. 17. During the period 1956–1965, about 10,200 skilled workers from underdeveloped areas received advanced training in the Federal Republic. The Bulletin, Press and Information Office of the German Federal Republic, Bonn, Sept. 13, 1966, p. 1.

22. Das Bundesministerium für wirtschaftliche Zusammenarbeit, "Das Studium der Studenten aus Entwicklungsländern," Bulletin, No. 132 (Aug. 26, 1964), p. 1,238.

The Scientific Advisory Board's recent suggestions point to a revision of present emphasis on both trainee work and university study in the Federal Republic. It holds that trainees should be sponsored for employment only when they will learn skills of immediate use in the modestly developed industries of their native country. When possible, those trainees who are eventually to return as instructors should be more carefully informed as to the reasonable limits of progress that they can expect to experience in their own countries, in order that they may be prevented from being jolted into resignation or from coming into excessive conflict with older persons of authority when confronted with the very gradually developing economy at home.[23] University students, in its opinion, should study for their first degree at institutions in their own country whenever possible, sometimes under German instructors and making use of German scholarship support and other aid to the institution at which they study. Study at institutions in other developing countries where the curriculum is geared to solving problems analogous to those of their own nations should be facilitated with German government funds. Undergraduate students who for some special reason desire admission to West German universities must be tested and tutored far more than has been the case thus far; German universities have in the past prided themselves on letting all students do as they please.[24]

Sending Experts Abroad

If there are to be fewer participants from developing countries in on-the-job training and university study within West Germany under stricter regulations, while technical assistance and general educational aid as a whole are to be expanded, then the remaining alternatives are sending increased numbers of Germans to developing countries to supervise training there and providing aid in funds and teaching materials to institutions in developing countries. There is little doubt any longer that these are easily the most effective steps to be taken in improving the technical assistance program. But raising the number of experts abroad is difficult. As of 1963 a total of 345 German experts had been sent to developing countries as planners and advisors. About 100 of these were advisors to trade and industry, aiding in the establishment of small and medium-sized enterprises. The others dealt with a variety of areas, such as agriculture, fishery, forestry, transport, general economics, health, communications, and postal and information services.[25]

Previous attempts to recruit much larger numbers of advisors or instruc-

23. "Bildungshilfe-Gutachten," II, p. 1,031.

24. For those students whose backgrounds or abilities are unequal to completing a program of studies, and who, in spite of careful selection occasionally cannot be identified until a year or so has passed, the board now recommends a face-saving "certificate"; the time each student spends in West Germany is at least acknowledged. *Ibid.*, III, p. 1,047.

25. "Technical Assistance," unsigned article, *Germany*, Vol. VIII (1963), No. 35, p. 31.

tors have been hindered partly by the difficulty of finding engineers and technologists in needed fields who like consulting or teaching—preferably in English, French, or Spanish, as the regional requirements demand—and partly by the unwillingness of their firms to have them leave for a year or so. Contrary to popular belief, the general shortage of labor in West Germany, where recently more than 1,200,000 foreign workers have found jobs, is as acute in the highly developed branches of industry requiring specialists as on the assembly lines and in work crews. The fact that many Germans with technical training have emigrated to other industrial countries in the last decade does not indicate a surfeit of people like them at home; it has simply made the situation worse. Further, where day laborers can be imported by the trainload from countries with chronic unemployment, such as Italy and Greece, this is not true of engineers and technologists. Prior to the establishment of the Ministry for Economic Cooperation, the Economic Ministry's Scientific Advisory Board determined more than five years ago that for instructional aid to be effective, a large reserve of qualified specialists would have to be built up.[26] In the intervening years, however, the demand for technologists at home has retained its force to the point where talk of a reserve seems to have less basis in reality than ever. A press release by the ministry in 1963 stressed the need for economizing with technical advisory personnel by temporarily joining forces with consulting firms and agencies operating in the developing world to form "advisory bases" in individual regions.[27]

In recruiting professional teaching personnel with technical specialties, the prospects seem a bit brighter. Academicians generally are more used to the idea of plying their trade for short periods abroad than are engineers; professors from Germany have been avid participants in exchange programs to which teaching in developing countries bear some resemblance.[28] The practice of treating each academic year as a complete entity in itself makes getting into and out of institutional assignments easy in a way for which industry provides no analogy. Teachers are in short supply in Germany too, but most of them are employees of the government, which has

---

26. Wissenschaftlicher Beirat beim Bundeswirtschaftsministerium, report issued upon completion of a series of meetings on Jan. 23, 1960, *Probleme einer rationellen Wirtschaftshilfe an die Entwicklungsländer unter besonderer Berücksichtigung der von der Bundesrepublik zu treffenden Massnahmen*, p. 20.

27. Klaus Billerbeck, Policy Coordinator (*Grundsatz-Referent*), Ministry for Economic Cooperation, "Instrumente der deutschen Entwicklungspolitik und der Beitrag deutscher Ingenieurfirmen," press release, March 21, 1963, p. 8.

28. As yet, to be sure, reciprocal programs with developing countries have hardly been possible. According to the German Academic Exchange Service (*Deutscher Akademischer Austauschdienst*), only Indonesia and Mexico among the underdeveloped countries furnished partners on the university level in the 1964 exchanges. "Austausch von 132 Professoren mit 13 Ländern: Kontinuierlich ausgeweitetes Austauschprogram . . .," *Bulletin*, No. 80 (May 7, 1965), p. 639. But the number of German applicants for temporary teaching posts abroad has been higher than existing exchange programs can accommodate. Cf. "Entwicklungshilfe: Die Steppe ruft," *Der Spiegel*, Vol. XV, No. 35 (Aug. 23, 1961), p. 30.

been investigating ways to give them extra motivation for accepting assignments in underdeveloped countries. Inducements include: generous allowances for travel expenses and for expenses in relocating upon returning home; pension benefits; and, most recently, the establishment of permanent chairs in economic development and its related fields at German universities, for which teachers returning from Asia, Africa, and South America would be best qualified.[29] The Scientific Advisory Board is hopeful of good results from academic "partnerships" between single institutions in Germany and in developing countries. "Partnerships" is admittedly a euphemism here: the goal described is that of having German schools and research establishments support like institutions in pursuing their work according to the latest methods, by providing scholarship money and funds for research projects. German provision of as much in teaching and research materials as can profitably be used in underdeveloped countries can perhaps best be overseen on such an institution-to-institution basis; here the sums of money required of the Federal Republic are not burdensome in any event. There are, of course, special problems concerned with using German teaching materials, whether books for universities or tools for technical schools: translations of reading matter and substitutions or adaptations of equipment must doubtless be made frequently. Still, the demands of universities in developing countries are finite, and German governmental resources seem equal to meeting them.[30]

The Institute for Development Policy is attempting to make what volunteer personnel is available from industry or academic life more effective by providing classes for German experts, such as economists, businessmen, lawyers, farmers, sociologists, and geographers. Each student receives one year of specialized training for development tasks in the political, economic, and social problems related to them. He also studies the development-aid programs of Germany, other nations, and international organizations, along with statistics and planning techniques; he is made familiar with regional geography and cultural relations. Graduates of the program then assume positions in German agencies dealing with development aid, or in industry, international agencies, and voluntary organizations with operations in developing countries.[31]

29. As a first step, the University of Cologne was commissioned to teach "Developmental Policy and Regional Developmental Planning" as a subject. Das Bundesministerium für wirtschaftliche Zusammenarbeit, "Lehrauftrag für Entwicklungspolitik und regionale Entwicklungsplanung," Bulletin, No. 79 (May 6, 1965), p. 630.

30. "Bildungshilfe-Gutachten," I, p. 1,031 and II, pp. 1,039–1,040. Special research has been conducted over a number of years to decide upon the best materials for trade schools in developing countries. Das Bundesministerium für wirtschaftliche Zusammenarbeit, "Lehrmaterial für Gewerbeschulen in Entwicklungsländern," Bulletin, No. 134 (Sept. 1, 1964), pp. 1,258–1,259.

31. "Partnership Criteria in Development Policy," Germany, Vol. IX (1964), No. 37, p. 11; for numerous accounts of the experiences which German experts have had abroad see Dr. Norbert Zimmer, ed., Deutsche in Entwicklungsländern, (Hofheim/Ts.: Verlag des Auslands-Kurier, 1966. Schriften des Auslands-Kurier, Band 3), passim.

The German Peace Corps

You have committed yourselves to a great task, a task on which our world's future quite decisively depends. You, too, want to aid in stopping ignorance, sickness, and hunger from overshadowing the life of whole peoples. But you must not now go about your work with the feeling that you are superior to those who need you. The people who are waiting for you can keenly sense your attitude. Show them that you feel like their partners. Take hold with your hands and teach less by explanation than by example! In those very lands in which physical work does not enjoy complete recognition you can, through your own labor, arouse a willingness to work.[32]

With a few more such words of admonition and encouragement President Lübke took leave of the first volunteers from the then year-old German Development Service (*Deutscher Entwicklungsdienst*—DED) who had completed training for overseas assignments. The DED, an analogue to the U.S. Peace Corps, had been founded on June 24, 1963, symbolically enough in the presence of President Kennedy during his visit to Germany. The short excerpt from President Lübke's speech above contains almost the whole rationale of the organization. Following the Peace Corps closely in a policy of putting young people—usually less than experts by domestic standards —to work on aid projects overseas, it hopes to demonstrate Germany's lack of arrogance at being the donor rather than the recipient of assistance and the dignity which Germans desire to attach to largely physical labor. With the Peace Corps it also shares the idea that informal, personal contacts can aid both in gaining the good will of the developing peoples and— through reports of stimulating experiences always more exciting on a personal level—in awakening more interest in foreign aid among the German people at home.

Along with public denials of the glamorous and romantic attractions to be found within it, both the Peace Corps and the Development Service make frank appeals to the missionary, crusading spirit of young people searching for an answer to the question: "After our own prosperity, what?" Both organizations, in spite of professions of modesty, see themselves grasping "the opportunity to mobilize the idealism which all free peoples have within themselves."[33] Although neither the Peace Corps nor the DED are supposed to have any militant Cold War tie-in, both have been spoken of as competitive instruments for overcoming not only hunger and need but the Communist enemy: "Although Communism is repulsive to all of

32. "Soldaten des Friedens," speech of the West German President at the Villa Hammerschmidt (Presidential residence), July 15, 1965, *Bulletin*, No. 117 (July 24, 1964), p. 1,113.

33. President John F. Kennedy, speech on the occasion of the founding the DED at the Villa Hammerschmidt, June 24, 1963; German text, " 'Ich gratuliere dem deutschen Volk,' " *Bulletin*, No. 108 (June 25, 1963), p. 963.

us, we must nonetheless admit that it has found it possible to acquire a certain devotion to itself in many regions of the world. We must prove that we can bring people to the point where they are far more attached to our free ideals and prove that these can present a far greater attraction than Communism."[34]

In structure, the DED is quite different from the Peace Corps. It stems from the initiative of the Conference of Development Helpers (Gesprächs-kreis Entwicklungshelfer), formed in February 1961 by forty-four private organizations with an interest in foreign-aid work; some of the member organizations date back to the 1940's. Early in 1962, together with the Ministry for Economic Cooperation, the Conference worked out a program called "Learning and Helping Overseas" (Lernen und Helfen in Übersee) for sending young Germans abroad to work on aid projects under joint private-and-state sponsorship. In December 1962, the same union of forty-four private organizations registered Learning and Helping Overseas as a permanent non-profit organization. Then in 1963 the German Development Service was founded as a corporation, with Learning and Helping Overseas supplying a rather symbolic thousand marks as 5 per cent of the investment capital and the West German government holding the remaining 95 per cent.[35] As the Federal Republic's competent organ for foreign-aid policy, the Ministry for Economic Cooperation retains ultimate control of the DED and, of course, economic responsibility for its obligations. In fact, the total original capital could not begin to finance the DED's administration, let alone its aid projects, and the government allocates funds for its serious expenses. Still, the DED has its own director and officially relies upon Learning and Helping Overseas as its advisory body. The question of who has authority over the members working on foreign projects could have become a rather sensitive one: in order to avoid clashes with representatives of more established agencies and to help the young people retain the feeling that they are working creatively, the DED planned from the outset to send volunteers—at least at first—to work only on projects which were already established and supervised by persons who were "well known and reliable-seeming" to the DED's sponsors, i.e., friendly to the idea of the Development Service.[36]

Early applications for the DED were so numerous—1,500 in its first three months—that its officials could afford to be highly selective from the start. They have selected recruits according to the demands of specific projects

34. Ibid.

35. Das Bundesministerium für wirtschaftliche Zusammenarbeit, Lernen und Helfen in Übersee, press release (Bonn, Oct. 1963), pp. 5–6.

36. Prof. Friedrich Karl Vialon, Executive Under-Secretary in the Ministry for Economic Cooperation, speech at Bad Godesberg, June 24, 1963, "Der Deutsche Entwicklungsdienst im Rahmen der Entwicklungspolitik: Schaffung einer gemeinnutzigen Gesellschaft mit dem Bund als Hauptgesellschafter," Bulletin, No. 120 (July 11, 1963), pp. 1,078–1,079.

after a careful screening of their documents—application form, certificates and transcripts, autobiographies, and references—followed by interviews and tests for particular assignments within the project. After the final group is chosen, training begins; subjects resemble those taught in the Institute for Development Policy: economic, political, health, and educational problems of developing countries; but they are taught for a briefer and more intense period of eight weeks with sixty course hours a week. There is more emphasis on language training and preparation for free-time activities: the general curriculum includes "sports and leisure education." A detailed, practical course follows: four to eight weeks in which group members train for their special tasks. Job preparation is necessarily varied, since DED members may be put to work on almost any undertaking which brings them into contact with residents of a developing country on a coworker level and which promises to make a reasonable contribution to the nation's development. On their projects they may work as farmers or artisans; they may help with clinics and community development projects; or they may give instruction, particularly in vocational schools and adult education programs.[37]

After their formal send-off by President Lübke and a two-week leave at home, the first graduates of Development Service training left Germany in August 1964, to work on a slum-clearance project in Dar-es-Salaam, capital of Tanganyika (later Tanzania). A second group of fifteen was scheduled to depart for work in an automobile factory in Tripoli, Libya, soon afterwards; a third contingent of fourteen was slated for a variety of teaching posts in Kabul, Afghanistan. All had signed the contract required by the DED to remain at work on their projects for a period of almost two years.[38]

The Development Service has been accused of making a colorless impression for itself because of a seeming absence of spontaneity in its undertakings, an avoidance of publicity during its first year, and its lack of involvement with newsworthy personalities. This is the unavoidable result of constant contrasts of the DED with U.S. Peace Corps, which has been pictured with particular enthusiasm in the German press as extremely quick to place volunteers in needed projects and has retained personal

---

37. Das Bundesministerium für wirtschaftliche Zusammenarbeit, *Lernen und Helfen in Übersee*, p. 8 and "Der Dienst deutscher Entwicklungshelfer: Die ersten Freiwilligen reisen aus—Zweck und Aufgaben des DED," unsigned article, *Bulletin*, No. 128 (Aug. 18, 1964), pp. 1,207–1,208.

38. Members are paid a minimal salary which is determined by conditions in the host land. They are given $151.13 for clothes and equipment before their trip, and, after completion of their term of service, they receive $50.38 for each full month on the job. They are granted two-and-a-half days vacation per month overseas, which is to be taken at any time in the host land during the first year; leave time for the second year is saved until completion of project obligations and may be spent in the host land or on the trip home if the volunteer so desires. *Ibid.*, p. 1,208. See also Walter Scheel, "Ein neues Stadium des Entwicklungsdienstes," speech at the Villa Hammerschmidt, July 15, 1964, *Bulletin*, No. 117 (July 24, 1964), p. 1,114.

color from the lasting, youth-inspiring image of President Kennedy.[39] Still, the German Development Service is new, and such occasional disparagement from the press has not discouraged it. Applications are still heavy at its headquarters in Bad Godesberg, and its officials claim the weight of public opinion is behind their organization's efforts.

39. For example, in winding up for a question in an interview with Axel Freiherr von dem Busche, who took over the management of the DED in 1964, a reporter for the magazine *Deutsche Jugend* (German Youth) noted how "the German Development Service has seemed, at least on the outside, to be an impersonal institution almost like an administrative organ." Text of interview printed as "Die Position des Deutschen Entwicklungsdienstes," *Bulletin*, No. 131 (Aug. 25, 1964), pp. 1,233–1,234.

THE ARAB WORLD AND ISRAEL

German assistance to the Near East has been enormously complicated by the animosity between Israel and the Arab countries. German aid to Israel, granted under several federal laws and a treaty with Israel, reached almost seven million dollars by the end of April 1965; the federal government has agreed to pay another four-and-a-half million dollars to Israel under present commitments.[1] West Germany pays these sums to Israel as restitution with no restrictions upon their use. Thus they are not development aid funds in the usual sense, although much of this West German money has gone into development projects. There is some question as to whether Israel, with the high degree of education diffused through its population and its success in applying technology to increasing productivity and raising the living standard of its people, should be called an "underdeveloped" country.[2] The Germans have in fact expressed the opinion that their latest commitments to Israel, negotiated in 1966, constitute "economic" aid and should go by this name, leaving open the question of how much desire to make restitution and how much unencumbered development-aid motivation were responsible for extending them; "economic aid" has been granted as a rule to more developed countries.

From the standpoint of international politics, German financial assistance to Israel has been quite successful: it has demonstrated West Germany's desire to make good whatever can be made good in German-Jewish relations. While neither Israel nor the Federal Republic has pressed the point, there can be little doubt that the German contributions were an important factor in leading the Israeli government to pursue a more friendly course toward the Federal Republic; no doubt it influenced Israel's favor-

1. "Novelle zum Wiedergutmachungsgesetz," *Bulletin*, No. 99 (June 10, 1965), p. 795.
2. To be sure, almost any country is "underdeveloped" in the sense of "having regions which are not as productive as they might be." But such a definition of "underdeveloped," which would also apply to the U.S. and U.S.S.R. and West Germany, as well as to Israel, is too broad to be useful. Since in general practice the term is employed as a euphemism for "backward and needing outside aid to become less so," it clearly implies the inability of a country to overcome general cultural obstacles to the developmental process by itself.

able response to the West German proposal for establishing full diplomatic relations between the two countries in the spring of 1965.[3]

In the Arab world, on the other hand, the net effect, economic and political, of the German foreign-aid program is not at all clear. While individual projects have been successful there, some questions about whether they have really bettered West Germany's relationship with the recipient countries—particularly when they are taken together as a bloc—remain unanswered. After all, German-Arab relations were decent enough in 1950. Now, seventeen years later, in spite of aid totalling well over a quarter of a billion dollars, German ties to the Arab world are under a considerable strain. How long the present difficulties will last, of course, remains to be seen.

Capital Assistance to Arab Countries

Irrigation projects have been the most striking West German undertakings in the Arab world. To Libya, the Sudan, Egypt and Syria, West Germany has extended credits for expensive dams intended to raise agricultural productivity while providing electricity for nascent industries. For example, the Federal Republic is providing more than a third of the funds for the $50-million Roseires Dam in the Sudan through the Reconstruction Loan Corporation in cooperation with the Sudanese government, the World Bank, and the International Development Association.[4] The German government has also extended credits for industrial and transportation projects in Arab countries; but because overcoming the general water shortage remains the most urgent problem in Arab agriculture, Bonn has placed less emphasis on capital agricultural projects in Arab states than in other parts of the underdeveloped world (notably Latin America).[5] Nonetheless, West German technical-assistance projects have included considerable quantities of advisory aid in agriculture.

As of December 31, 1964, West Germany had granted the capital-assistance credits shown in Table XVIII. The relatively large shares of German capital credits received by Egypt and Syria are evident here. The Euphrates Dam in Syria, toward which the Federal Republic pledged a loan

3. For the still unsettled German-Israeli relations see Otto Diepholz, "Kein Entwicklungsland wie andere," *Frankfurter Allgemeine Zeitung,* April 1, 1966, p. 2.

4. Kreditanstalt für Wiederaufbau, *Deutsche Kredite für Entwicklungsländer: Afrika und Asien* (Frankfurt am Main, 1964), p. 4.

5. Specifically, the following projects have been supported by German project loans: in Jordan, the port of Aqaba; in Egypt, a dry dock at Alexandria, an electricity grid with power and transformer stations, bridges across the Nile, river ships on the Nile; in Tunisia, three dams (for irrigation), a textile factory, a high-tension line, the fishing harbor at Mahdia, the Melitta airport; in Algeria, pipe lines for irrigation projects, farm equipment, the harbor of Annaba; in Morocco, the chemical industry based on phosphates, port and other transportation facilities. *Annual Reports* of the Kreditanstalt für Wiederaufbau, 1962–1965, and Bundesministerium für wirtschaftliche Zusammenarbeit, *Entwicklungspolitik,* Ausgabe I/8, May 25, 1965.

of $87 million in 1963, is envisioned as providing water to make 500,000 acres agriculturally productive. When completed, it should easily be the most impressive irrigation and power-generating installation in Western Asia for some time to come, although political controversy has recently impeded work on it. Egypt alone received almost 25 per cent of West German capital aid to Arab countries through 1964; Syria, which was merged with Egypt from February 1958 until September 1961 in the United Arab Republic, has received over 35 per cent. Projects financed by the Federal Republic are nearer completion in Egypt and Syria than elsewhere in the Arab world. Six large-scale industrial, power, irrigation, and transportation projects are already producing results in these two countries, whereas only Tunisia among the other Arab countries has more than one project backed by West Germany in operation; in three of the remaining five Arab recipient states, capital-aid projects are scarcely past the planning stage. West German loans, of which the Egyptians have availed themselves to carry on industrialization, have unavoidably added to that country's international indebtedness. This burden caused President Nasser to state that he would not permit the interest service to "drain the economy's life blood." In a way this statement lent support to former Minister Scheel's admission, made in another connection, that "the last thing to expect is permanent thanks. This is even more true for peoples than it is for individuals."[6] On the other hand, grateful Tunisians have named one street in their capital "Rue d'Allemagne."

Table XVIII.   West German Capital Assistance to Arab States (in millions of U.S. dollars).

Algeria	17.6
Jordan	12.7
Morocco	22.7
Sudan	31.1
Syria	88.1
Tunisia	15.1
United Arab Republic (Egypt)	57.9
Yemen	2.5
Total	247.8

Source: Derived from chart, "Außenhandel der Bundesrepublik Deutschland mit den Ländern der arabischen Welt," *Bulletin,* No. 47 (March 17, 1965), p. 374.

In 1965, Near East countries were also granted non-project loans. Israel received DM 75 million for general-development needs while Morocco and Tunisia were to use DM 20 million each to improve their international reserves positions.[7]

6. Siegfried Sterner, "Sünden der Entwicklungspolitik," *Frankfurter Allgemeine Zeitung,* March 3, 1965, p. 21.

7. Kreditanstalt für Wiederaufbau, *XVII. Jahresbericht, Geschäftsjahr 1965,* pp. 79 and 82.

Technical Assistance to Arab Countries

West German technical assistance has been somewhat more evenly distributed among the Arab countries than capital assistance, although again Egypt and Syria together have received some 40 per cent of the assistance given to this region. Almost every type of German technical assistance is represented in the Arab world, although the proportionate weight varies greatly from country to country. For example, in Morocco, model installations and training centers for artisans have been emphasized: these include a metal workers' school in Nador and a center for training with agricultural machinery in Rabat. In Tunisia, emphasis has been more agricultural, with aid provided for a cotton institute, a model dairy farm, an experimental station for sugar beets, and a mobile veterinary station. In Algeria, where public-health problems appeared to be the most pressing ones immediately after the country's independence (July 3, 1962), the first German technical-assistance efforts were medical. An independence gift of four Volkswagen ambulances and an X-ray diagnostic apparatus was followed by the dispatch of German doctors, a mobile dispensary, and medical supplies of all kinds. Subsequently, the West Germans equipped an agricultural model installation at Milliana.[8] In Saudi-Arabia, where the leadership has been noticeably hesitant about introducing innovations which will have ultimate socio-political consequences, the Federal Republic has confined its technical assistance to cooperation with the Saudi-Arabian government in establishing trade schools.[9]

Probably the most impressive German educational project in the Arab countries has been the Polytechnical Institute in Cairo–Heluan, now near completion. German and Egyptian teachers have also been cooperating for some years at the Institute for Technical Education in Cairo, a school which now enjoys an excellent reputation. German funds have also aided the Institute for Trade-School Teachers in Cairo–Heluan and the Center for Precision Mechanics in Cairo. Also, in Egypt, West German technical aid has set up or furthered such varied enterprises as the Petroleum Institute in Suez, an institute for meteorology and materials testing in Cairo, a criminal detection laboratory, a photographic laboratory, and a research center for schistosomiasis. Then, too, West German Government has sent advisors

8. "Technische Zusammenarbeit mit Entwicklungsländern: Ein Überblick über Massnahmen im Mittelmeerraum und in Nahost," unsigned article, *Bulletin*, No. 226 (Dec. 21, 1963), pp. 2,019–2,021. Encouraged by initial successes in Tunisia, the Federal Republic plans to continue agricultural advisory aid there and to expand its technical assistance efforts with emphasis on communications, particularly radio and motion pictures. Bundesministerium für wirtschaftliche Zusammenarbeit, "Deutsch-tunesische Zusammenarbeit," *Bulletin*, No. 123 (July 20, 1965), p. 994.

9. Der Bundesminister für Wirtschaft, "Deutsch-saudi-arabische Zusammenarbeit," *Bulletin*, No. 124 (Aug. 7, 1964), p. 1,179.

to Egypt to aid projects ranging from harbor construction to the organization of a savings-bank system.[10]

**Table XIX.   West German Technical Assistance to Arab States
(in millions of U.S. dollars).**

Algeria	2.1
Iraq	2.6
Jordan	4.8
Lebanon	1.6
Libya	3.4
Morocco	2.9
Saudi-Arabia	.08
Sudan	5.3
Syria	4.7
Tunisia	3.5
United Arab Republic (Egypt)	17.6
Yemen	3.4
Total	51.98

Source: Derived from chart, "Außenhandel der Bundesrepublik Deutschland mit den Ländern der arabischen Welt," *Bulletin,* No. 47 (March 17, 1965), p. 374.

As of March 1965, the Federal Republic had sent 210 experts to Arab countries; of these, 50 went to Egypt alone. At the same time, 4,283 Arab students were studying in West Germany, with the largest contingents from Egypt (1,153), Syria (1,200), and Iraq (795). Many of these students were sponsored by the Federal government or the German states. In addition, 762 technical trainees came to West Germany during 1965; 3,469 had previously completed training in the Federal Republic at a cost of well over seven million dollars from German public funds.[11]

Germany and the Arab-Israeli Conflict

But in spite of these considerable injections of West German aid to the Arab world, recent improvements in German relationships with Israel have been enough to sour the official Arab view of the Federal Republic. To be sure, Germany initially enjoyed more good will among Arabs than other European powers, but this had been very expensive for Germany's standing elsewhere in the world. For, besides Germany's lack of colonial associations in the areas in which Arab states had been controlled from Europe, the Federal Republic was unique among Western nations in having no diplomatic relations with Israel and in sharing with the Arabs a world-wide reputation for enmity toward Jews. In this connection, Arab leaders

10. "Technische Zusammenarbeit mit Entwicklungsländern: Ein Überblick"; "Die deutsche Hilfe für die VAR [Vereinigte Arabische Republik—United Arab Republic]," unsigned article, *Bulletin,* No. 32 (Feb. 20, 1965), p. 253.

11. "4283 arabische Studenten in der Bundesrepublik," unsigned article, *Bulletin,* No. 49 (March 19, 1965), p. 389.

tended to overlook the fact that German lack of relations with Israel was due solely to Israeli unwillingness to have them; it was no secret that the Bonn government was engaging in a massive aid program to Israel (in the form of restitution payments) with a view toward eventually establishing formal relations.

Stories of escaped Nazis being fondly received in the Arab world and of apolitical German businessmen occasionally greeted there with a "Heil Hitler!" have been painful to the West German government from the outset. But in spite of earlier Eastern allegations to the contrary, there is no evidence to indicate that West German officials, when dealing with Arab countries, have ever purposely capitalized on Germany's past anti-Semitism. Nonetheless, when the Federal Republic finally succeeded in gaining Israeli assent to full diplomatic relations in the spring of 1965, Arab leaders acted as if Germany were somehow breaking faith with them. They were particularly incensed by West Germany's implied willingness to keep German scientists from aiding Arab countries in the development of missile bases.[12] In West Germany, Egypt's President Nasser was blamed for the sudden worsening of Arab-German relations because of his invitation to Walter Ulbricht for a state visit in the U.A.R. and his announcement of the opening of a consulate in East Berlin. These actions aroused great resentment in West Germany but changed nothing; rather, they further encouraged the Israelis and West Germans to normalize relations between their countries.[13]

German public reaction to such apparent Arab ingratitude as was manifested in demonstrations against West German diplomatic installations in Iraq and Yemen at the time of the Israeli–West German–Egyptian embroilment was sufficient to call into question the whole concept of foreign aid as practiced by the Federal government. Nonetheless, West Germany took no steps against any Arab states beyond a demand for compensation for damages and punishment for the perpetrators of the demonstration. Still the Bonn Government felt constrained to announce that no reprisals would be taken: "It is a matter of course to the Federal Government and to the inhabitants of the Federal Republic that all Arabs who conform to the rules of hospitality will in the future as before be received and treated as guests in accordance with the traditions of German-Arab relations. No property

12. Former Chancellor Erhard's published letter to Premier Levi Eshkol of Israel contains a statement which clearly refers to Germans at work on such projects in Arab countries: "In recent months many of the German scientists, technicians and experts who were working on military projects outside NATO have returned to Germany. The Federal Government has reason to assume that some of the experts who remained abroad, particularly those engaged in rocket construction, also intend to return to Germany in the near future. The German authorities take legal action against any person or persons who, without permission, seek to entice German nationals to take up scientific, technical or expert activities in the military field abroad." English text of this letter, dated May 12, 1965, and Eshkol's reply in News from the German Embassy, Vol. IX, No. 8 (May 18, 1965).

13. Dr. Eugen Gerstenmaier, President of the Bundestag, radio interview printed as "Sitzung des Bundestags in Berlin: Zur Entwicklung in Nahost—Eine unfruchtbare Alternative," Bulletin, No. 48 (March 18, 1965), pp. 381–382.

that the Arab states or their citizens may have in the Federal Republic is endangered; nor is it being exposed to any hostile demonstrations. Arab students and technical trainees continue to receive the same aid they have received so far."[14]

Even when the Arab League decided that its member states should break diplomatic relations with the Federal Republic and ten of them did so, West Germany refrained from taking counter measures. By the end of 1965, Bonn seemed to have justified its confidence that it could ride out its Near East crisis without drastic changes in aid policy toward the Arab world. In reducing tensions with Arab states, Germany's trade with them has probably been as important a factor as its aid: in 1964, the Federal Republic imported three-quarters of its oil from the Arab world (40 per cent from Libya alone). In Algeria, President Boumedienne, shortly after he took office, expressed a preference for the Western countries, including the Federal Republic, as trading partners. Even in the U.A.R., the leading country in organizing Arab expressions of hostility toward Germany in 1965, some care was taken not to disrupt commercial and travel contacts with the Federal Republic too suddenly. Egypt's $75 million favorable balance of trade with West Germany in 1964 undoubtedly played some part here as has the profitable German tourist trade in Egypt during recent years: an estimated 35,000 West German tourists visited Egypt during 1965—10,000 more than during the pervious year. Over a third of the 1,900 Egyptians with professional experience sent to Europe in 1964 for further training came to West Germany; a report in the last quarter of 1965 gave no indication of any decrease.[15] Both German tourism in Egypt and the training of Egyptians in West Germany declined in 1966 and 1967 however.

As a concession to Arab feelings, West Germany stopped its shipments of arms to Israel in 1965. The short Arab-Israeli War in June 1967 changed Germany's relationship to both sides scarcely at all. At the time of the crisis, the Soviet delegate to the United Nations Security Council charged that West Germany had increased its weapons shipments to Israel several months before; and *Izvestia* lamented predictably that the Federal Republic had "cranked up the machinery of Israeli aggression."[16] Equally predictably, West Germany denied the charge, insisting on its total commitment to non-intervention in the crisis and on the finality of its 1965 cessation of arms shipments. Arab officials have not seriously pressed the issue. In fact, Foreign Minister Willy Brandt stated in September 1967 that the posi-

14. Karl Günther von Hase, Director of the Press and Information Office, "Unentschuldbare Ausschreitungen gegen deutsche Botschaft in Irak," *Bulletin*, No. 47 (March 17, 1965), p. 373.

15. *Handelsblatt* (Düsseldorf), Oct. 6, 1965; article translated as "Arabian West Wind: Contracts with Arab World Still Lively," the *German Tribune*, No. 185 (Oct. 16, 1965), p. 2.

16. Klaus Schütz, Deputy Foreign Minister, interview, *Bulletin*, No. 66 (June 23, 1967), gives citation, Soviet and East German charges, and the West German response, pp. 566–567.

tion of the Federal Republic in its attempts to restore diplomatic relations with all Arab states had not been adversely affected by the June crisis.[17]

All in all, it seems likely that German-Arab relations will retain some scars of the Arabs' 1965 attempts to make the Germans choose between having diplomatic ties with them and the Israelis. Germans responsible for approving aid to Arab countries will, no doubt, be less optimistic about obtaining Arab support in international political quarrels from now on as a result of the aid. But there is no indication at the moment that Germany's special Near Eastern problems will cause it to revise its policies of aid to that region.

17. Interview, *Bulletin,* No. 96 (Sept. 8, 1967), pp. 831–832.

EAST AND WEST AFRICA

In Africa south of the Sahara, German capital and technical assistance efforts have not suffered through any such painful choices between hostile ethnic groups as West German officials have been subject to in the Arab-Israeli area. The prospect of West Germany's being drawn into the conflict between white and black Africans in Rhodesia, Angola, or South Africa appears remote; if Germany should eventually be caught in the middle of such controversy, it would certainly be less badly pinched than other European powers. The political unrest brought about by tribal rivalries and resentment of the white man in Africa does, of course, present an implicit threat to the German program. But from several standpoints, twentieth-century history has placed Germans in a much better position to deal on amicable terms with Africans than most other Europeans. They realize, however, that the African continent has traditionally been something of a British and French preserve.

Germany's psychologically advantageous situation in Africa stems, ironically enough, from its defeat in World War I and from the heavily punitive peace treaty which followed. For Germany had become a considerable colonial power in the late nineteenth century and until World War I held the provinces of Cameroon, German East Africa (Tanganyika, now merged with Zanzibar in Tanzania), and German Southwest Africa (each of a respectable size by African territorial standards), along with the smaller colony of Togo; and Germany held her colonies in no more popular a role of white master than England, France, or Portugal. But as part of the Treaty of Versailles, Germany surrendered all of its overseas holdings, including the African colonies. This was beneficial to Germany in short-run economic terms, since only one of its African colonies was ever self-supporting at any one time—Togo at one point, later German East Africa. But it was even more beneficial in long-run political and economic terms, since the Germans were spared the burden of a probably inevitable series of conflicts in their colonies, and Africans never had to fight, or even ask, Germany for independence.

A certain, thinly concealed pleasure in this fact emerges in German official writings on development aid; they refer to the Federal Republic as more acceptable from a public-relations standpoint in the underdeveloped world, particularly Africa, than its NATO allies. For example, implicitly stating Germany's loss of her colonies as though she had really never had colonies—which is, of course, true if one thinks of the Federal Republic— a 1961 CDU/CSU statement on development aid refers casually to West Germany's "non-colonial past."[1] A bit of the Who-would-have-thought-it-in-1946? tone, common enough in partisan political writings in West Germany, shimmers through the following lines from this document: "We are asked in certain cases by the great powers of the West to intensify our public-relations work in those places where we, as artless and unencumbered speakers for the Free World, can stimulate a better response than the psychologically often impeded United States or the former colonial powers."[2] Minister Scheel has said rather much the same thing in slightly more diplomatic language: "The German Federal Republic now finds itself in a special position: in the last forty-five years we have not stood over anyone as colonial lords. We have no special spheres of interest but are interested in a healthy and quick economic build-up in all developing regions to an equal extent. In the development of the African continent, which has a very close tie to Europe not only because of its geographical position but also because of its cultural bonds, we have a special share."[3]

The statement that Germans have a special share in Africa's development partly because of cultural links which involve Germany more than other European countries strikes an American first as perhaps an empty formalism to be dropped for the sake of politeness in the presence of African dignitaries visiting in Germany, as sheer fantasy, or as a mild slip of the tongue. But it is none of these. The Federal government has taken some pains to give real substance to the claim of German cultural links to Africa: a list of early German sojourners in Africa whose reports reflect intense interest and considerable respect for things African can be assembled: it features such scholarly personages as Gustav Nachtigall, the German traveler, administrator, and author of *Sahara and Sudan*, who as the Kaiser's commissioner in German Southwest Africa annexed Togo and Cameroon; Leo Frobenius, a late nineteenth-century ethnologist and explorer became

---

1. Diskussionskreis Entwicklungshilfe der CDU/CSU Fraktion des Deutschen Bundestages, *Die Entwicklungsländer und unsere Hilfe* (Bonn: Presse- und Informationsdienste der Christlich Demokratischen Union Deutschlands Verlagsgesellschaft mbH., 2nd ed., 1961), p. 132.

2. *Ibid.*, p. 134.

3. Bundesministerium für wirtschaftliche Zusammenarbeit, "Entwicklungshilfe für Afrika," press release of speech at the opening of the second German "Africa Week," Oct. 18, 1962, p. 3. With minor alterations in phrasing, Minister Scheel inserted the same sentences into a later speech, which emphasized the role of the EEC in Africa, "Wirtschaftliche Zusammenarbeit mit Afrika," press release of lecture on "African Research Day" of the Geographical Society (Gesellschaft für Erdkunde) in Berlin on April 4, 1963, pp. 3–4, and into his book, *Konturen einer neuen Welt* (Düsseldorf: Econ-Verlag, 1965), p. 73.

an authority on prehistoric African art. Even German nineteenth-century philology is put to use here: Heinrich Barth's six-year (1849–1855) stay in Africa which resulted in a series of dictionaries of the languages spoken in central Africa attests to the deadly seriousness of German scholars in their study of Africans.[4] To Africans who have been sensitive to European contempt toward the black savagery long assumed to be the dominant fact of African life, the thought that German scholarship can show a serious and respectful century of study of Africana is probably quite appealing.[5]

To be sure, the historical luster of the German image in Africa should not be exaggerated. Africans have a plethora of real and imagined reasons to distrust anything smacking of the white man's power and influence, and Germans are not only unmistakeably white but are more vulnerable in some ways than the French and British because of old racist pronouncements placing Africans as a subhuman species in the Nationalist Socialist anthropological hierarchy. Eastern propagandists have been quick to attack the Germans on this point, although how conscious Africans and their leaders are of the whole Nazi episode in world history remains an uncertain variable.[6]

Capital Assistance to Non-Arab Africa

In spite of Germany's stated special interest in Africa,[7] the fact remains that—however much African leaders may resent being told that they are "not ready" for a desired objective—most African states do not have sufficient trained personnel resources to turn German or other capital into going industrial operations. The uncertain political situation prevailing in many new African states has been an additional inhibiting factor for otherwise interested German companies and investors. Consequently, West German bilateral capital assistance to non-Arab African states often appears to be on a very small, trial, or symbolic basis, when contrasted with that given other regions. For example, the German iron and steel industry has a few

4. President Heinrich Lübke, "Besonderer Anteil der Deutschen an Afrika," *Bulletin*, No. 46 (March 16, 1965), p. 365.

5. There are many examples of a desire to have African cultural history given full faith and credit in the works of contemporary African writers. See Basil Davidson, "Africa: the Face behind the Mask," *Horizon*, Vol. V, No. 4 (March 1963), pp. 38–59; "Who's Underdeveloped?" Vol. V. No. 3 (Jan. 1963), pp. 116–117.

6. The problem of National Socialist racist propaganda, its echoes in the developing world, and Communist exploitation of it are discussed by H. J. Winckler, *Die Entwicklungsländer* (Berlin: Otto-Suhr-Institut an der Freien Universität Berlin, rev. ed., 1961), pp. 43–45.

7. This interest found also expression in President Lübke's two visits to several African countries in 1962 and 1966, which probably did not fail to strengthen Bonn's position vis-à-vis East Germany. Cf. Klaus Natorp, "Würde und Geld," *Frankfurter Allgemeine Zeitung*, March 21, 1966, p. 1.

holdings of 5 per cent or so in mines in Sierra Leone, Gabon, and Guinea; but only two German companies have bought controlling interest in African firms (both in Liberia) or own equipment used in African mining operations. As for the steel rolling mills, which the Federal Republic has backed in such profusion in India, Brazil, Egypt, and elsewhere—let alone the integrated iron and steel plants, of which Germany risked setting up two in India and has even considered building in such far-off and unlikely places as Burma and South Viet Nam—none of these have been attempted in Africa.[8]

West German firms have been quick to seize the initiative in organizing part of the South American automobile industry and have substantial holdings in four Brazilian and five Argentina plants; in both Egypt and Turkey German truck and bus factories have been in operation for some time. But the lack of the preconditions for appreciable motor traffic between the Sahara and the more-developed regions at the southern tip of the continent has meant that West German capital assistance to Sub-Saharan Africa in this industry has been limited to loans to local governments for importing cars, trucks, and busses from Germany, and by occasional gifts of vehicles. An assembly plant for trucks, operated by a Cologne-based company in Leopoldville, whose directors profess some hope of converting or expanding it into a manufacturing installation, is the sole exception.[9]

German capital assistance to most of Africa has thus far made its greatest progress in agricultural undertakings and in very rudimentary infrastructural projects, chiefly in the area of communications. For example, in Guinea Federal Republic loans made possible the purchase of some $4.27 millions' worth of tracks and rolling stock; the Germans were subsequently satisfied enough with the results to authorize $7.56 million more to expand the national railway system there.[10] But in the same country, according to an American source, a "West German slaughterhouse . . . kills no more than one steer a month, though its capacity is 40 tons of beef a day";[11] and West German firms have no capital participation whatsoever in industrial construction projects in Guinea.

In the Congo (Kinshasa) West Germany has also invested in infrastructural improvements; in 1964 a loan of $3.7 million was approved which was used the following year to finance two bridges. Recently West Germany granted the Congo credits for $2.52 million "as an expression of the faith which the Federal Government has in the further development of the

8. Similar hesitancy and caution has been displayed in banking. In Africa, as well as in other parts of the world, German banks have limited themselves to the establishment of representative offices and have been reluctant to set up branches or subsidiaries.

9. *German International*, brochure compiled from articles printed during 1963–1964, entitled *Twelve Years of German Development Assistance*, pp. 79–82.

10. Auswärtiges Amt der Bundesrepublik Deutschland, "Kapitalhilfe für Guinea," *Bulletin*, No. 98 (June 9, 1965), p. 792.

11. "Guinea: A Reason to Worry," *Time*, Jan. 7, 1966, p. 27.

Congo."[12] Part of this is to go into expanding communications, especially radio and telegraph services, while the remainder will be used to establish a factory for producing starch from cassava. West Germany rather hopefully takes its own increase in imports from the Congo as a sign of growing Congolese economic competence, justifying its application for foreign-aid grants. Elsewhere, Bonn finds Kenya's report of having exceeded its goal for the first year of its multi-year plan as evidence of a "very satisfactory state of cooperation with Kenya" and speaks positively of that country's new plans for land-clearing and hydrology projects, for which the Kenya government seeks further aid from the Federal Republic.[13]

In other examples of capital assistance, the Germans aided Togo in 1963 with a loan of $13.35 million for harbor construction at Lomé, and Tanganyika with loans amounting to $5.15 million for the partial financing of projects recommended by the agricultural advisors within that country.[14] By 1964, $2.5 million of the latter sum had been earmarked for ground-cultivation machinery and the equipping of two flour mills, two milling-machine plants, two breweries, and two harvesting-machine plants. Some $1.45 million went for shares in the Tanganyika Development Company, which was also expected to back further agricultural projects. With another loan of $2.26 million West Germany helped to finance a railroad line from Mikumi to Kidatu.[15]

In Ethiopia, as of early 1963, the German capital assistance program seemed to have little to do with directly advancing either the industrial development of the country or its infrastructure. Of a total of $5.79 million appropriated, $2.52 million went toward founding the Ethiopian Development Bank, the same amount was projected for the Duke of Harrar Memorial Hospital, and the remaining $.75 million had not been allocated. A listing of German government-sponsored civil-engineering projects up to that year also included the "Emperor's Palace,"[16] something of a puzzler for those trying to classify all German development aid into "capital" and "technical" by the stricter definition of either term. The Ministry for Economic Cooperation noted that credit guarantees had been approved by the West German government for almost $20 million but that these had not been utilized, since interested firms, Krupp among others, had not been able to conceive of economically feasible projects in spite of occasional

12. Bundesministerium für wirtschaftliche Zusammenarbeit, "Verstärkter Handel mit der Republik Kongo," *Bulletin*, No. 140 (Aug. 18, 1965), p. 1,130.

13. Bundesministerium für wirtschaftliche Zusammenarbeit, "Kenia auf gutem Wege," *Bulletin*, No. 133 (Aug. 4, 1965), p. 1,078.

14. Bundesministerium für wirtschaftliche Zusammenarbeit, "Entwicklungsförderung der Bundesrepublik in Togo," press release, Bonn, February 16, 1963, and Entwicklungsförderung der Bundesrepublik in Tanganjika," press release, Bonn, March 1, 1963.

15. *Twelve Years of German Development Assistance*, pp. 38–40.

16. *Ibid.*, pp. 31–32.

visits by their representatives.[17] Regarding hope for infrastructural improvement and major industrial progress, the ministry's report was quite pessimistic: "Misdirected developmental measures are evident in plant buildings begun but never completed, communication and supply networks fallen into disuse, and modern machines and apparati lying unused. A poorly functioning and inscrutable administration rounds out the picture... Multi-year plans are imported and never carried out; young, colored experts refuse to work anywhere but in their Ministry, and discouraged white advisors assert that nothing can be realized in this country. Often the 'false suggestions' of foreign advisors are made responsible for the prevailing conditions."[18]

All in all, German capital assistance efforts in non-Arab African countries are characterized by considerable caution; they are responsible for a few noteworthy successes, but even the more optimistic official reports are largely confined to hope and generalities.[19] In this part of the world, technical assistance is probably more to the point, since the effectiveness of capital assistance is most impeded at present by that lack of general education and special skills in the population which it is the task of technical assistance to remedy.

Technical Assistance

Unlike capital assistance, technical assistance can be effective at any level of technology even in a recipient country where the promise of industrial profit is still remote. Except in the Portuguese provinces, Spanish Guinea, and Gambia, West Germany has pilot installations and training centers in every country of sub-Saharan Africa. Project emphasis has almost always centered around communications, agricultural models, and training in the use of basic tools required in handicrafts and small industries. Apart from the rather special case of Ethiopia, there is little variety from country to country in the examples of technical assistance.

In Tanzania, West German technical assistance has concentrated on agriculture and the encouragement of future small industry. As early as March 1963, Bonn had appropriated over five million dollars for improve-

17. Through the World Bank and bilateral technical assistance (engineering consultants), Bonn contributes to the Awash River projects consisting of two dams and a power plant.

18. Bundesministerium für wirtschaftliche Zusammenarbeit, "Entwicklungsförderung der Bundesrepublik in Äthiopien," press release, Bonn, March 1, 1963, pp. 2–3.

19. The limited scope of West German capital aid notwithstanding, the following African countries have received financial assistance: Cameroon, both Congos, Dahomey, Ethiopia, Gabon, Ghana, Guinea, Ivory Coast, Kenya, Liberia, Madagascar, Malawi, Mali, Niger Republic, Nigeria, Rwanda, Senegal, Sierra Leone, Somalia, South Africa, Tanzania, Togo, Uganda. For detailed information, see: Kreditanstalt für Wiederaufbau, *Annual Reports*, and *Hands Across the Sea*.

ment of agricultural production and processing methods in what was then Tanganyika. Subsequently, the Federal Republic backed the purchase of two and-a-half million dollars' worth of ground-cultivation machinery, along with the erection of two model flour mills, two installations to demonstrate milling machinery, two for harvesting machines, one for dairy machinery, and one for brewery equipment. More recently, technical assistance funds provided for an experimental and training center for water and soil technology; a veterinary research institute in Dar es Salaam; a school for game-protection studies, partly to train game wardens; and for dispatching advisors in the field of wild-animal protection and utilization.

In the industrial field, West Germany has sent teachers and materials for technical schools and backed the Management Training Institute in Dar es Salaam, which plans to turn out business administrators. It was to Dar es Salaam, too, that the first contingent of the "German Peace Corps" was assigned in the summer of 1964.[20] Increases are also planned in the number of Tanzanian trainees brought to the Federal Republic. To aid with economic planning, the Germans sent a commission to survey developmental possibilities, and, separately, a number of economic advisors: one to work with the government in general, one to serve as chief advisor to the President, and three to help with questions of construction and city administration in Dar es Salaam. German consulting engineering firms have made plans for chemical factories in Tanzania, although no dates or figures are yet available with regard to financing. In communications, the Federal Republic has undertaken the expansion of the Tanzania Broacasting System and has sent experts to train radio technicians. For the country's public health services Bonn has donated an X-ray diagnostic apparatus and thirty specially equipped ambulances and has enabled six medical assistants to train in West Germany.[21]

As part of her technical assistance to Togo, West Germany has furnished a model installation for stock raising; it has sent personnel to the agricultural school at Tové, to educational institutions for young farmers, and to work with the settlement advisory service in accordance with plans suggested by Sylvanus Olympio, President of Togo, who was subsequently assassinated. The Federal Republic has equipped three model villages in Togo and sent advisors and experts in hydrology, agriculture, and small industry. Particular emphasis has gone into bringing the Togo fishing industry up to date: an expert and demonstration equipment have been dispatched to train fishermen with new types of boats and catching devices and to help with the modernization of fish-processing. German advisors, paid with technical-assistance funds, also helped in planning the Lomé

20. See above, Chap. V.

21. "Entwicklungsförderung der Bundesrepublik für Tanganjika"; *Twelve Years, passim.* It has been contended that West German generosity in Tanzania was motivated by competition with East Germany. Cf. Natorp, "Würde und Geld."

Harbor extensions mentioned in the preceding section financed by German capital assistance. Then, too, German consulting engineers have planned textile and paper mills in Togo. The federal government has sent advisors to help with the telephone and other communications systems; also to aid internal communications, West Germany built a hundred-kilowatt transmitter in Lomé at a cost of $578,000, equipped the state printing office at Lomé, and sent a printing expert to help run the latter. Some $450,000 was spent to establish a trade school at Sokode, and students from the school are regularly sent as trainees to the Federal Republic. Advisors and planners have also been sent to help with general economic problems and the special fields of insurance and city planning. For its public health services, Togo received X-ray equipment from the Federal Republic as an independence gift in 1960; since then West Germany has donated hospital equipment, an institute for hygiene in Lomé, and has sent German surgeons and physicians to Lomé and other cities in Togo.[22]

Ethiopia furnishes an example of more grandiose German technical-assistance plans than any other country on the African continent except Egypt, in spite of the pessimism voiced by the Ministry for Economic Cooperation concerning Ethiopia's receptivity to "imported" plans. As of March 1962, the Federal Republic had allocated $4.2 million in technical-assistance funds. Of this total, some of the main allocations were: $477,000 for equipment and teaching personnel for the technological division of the University of Addis Ababa; $150,000 for sending experts in railroading, local administration, tourism, foresting, and television; and $126,000 for trainees.[23] Later, in 1963, a consulting engineering firm, the Batelle Institute of Frankfurt, cooperated with Professor Max Guther of the Darmstadt Technological Institute to plan a project at Bahar on Lake Tana; the plan was to turn a village of 2,000 inhabitants into a city of 300,000. The core of the new development was to be a textile plant with 200,000 spindles and 400 looms that would employ 2,300 Ethiopians (according to *German International*). Twenty thousand tons of cotton-seed were estimated as an annual by-product of the plant; from these, oil could be extracted in other factories, "and the more thoroughly the project was investigated the more employment opportunities opened up. The final plan, with the textile mill as the point of departure, provides for cattle farms, slaughter-houses, dairies, a meat cannery, a soap factory, a gelatine factory, a tannery, a casein plant, a starch factory, a factory producing varnishes and paints, a margarine factory, a brewery, a coffee-roasting plant, several brickyards, and a stone quarry."[24]

The German Federal Republic, which paid $252,000 for individual

22. "Entwicklungsförderung der Bundesrepublik für Togo"; *Twelve Years, passim;* Bundesministerium für Gesundheitswesen, "Technische Hilfe für Togo," *Bulletin,* No. 56 (March 30, 1965), p. 450.

23. "Entwicklungsförderung der Bundesrepublik in Äthiopien," p. 2.

24. *Twelve Years,* p. 19.

project studies of the consulting engineering firm, decided to allocate $756,000 for the model seed-oil installation envisaged in the plan. And so, in 1963, *German International* referred to Ethiopia as "a model case" for likely success and gave as a statement of fact that in the postulated city of 300,000 "detailed projects have been worked out to assure adequate living conditions to every newcomer."[25] In 1967, according to the German government, these plans were gradually being put into effect; if this optimistic estimation is in time borne out, the undertaking will certainly be a monumental credit to German technical assistance.

Germany, Africa, and the Common Market

International assistance from European countries to Africa has been proportionately greater than to other continents, in large part because of the ex-colonial relationships between Common Market countries and the newly independent African ones. The uninterrupted European presence in Africa has enabled the Federal Republic, as a member of the European Economic Community, to support a large number of cooperative projects and sometimes to work together on projects with another member state, usually France. To be sure, from a strictly economic standpoint, it would be more advantageous for German enterprises to work alone in the old French African dominions; German agreement to work in partnership with the French in Africa often amounts to an economic concession in return for easier access to regions where political-historical factors give the former colonial power experience and psychological advantages.

Within the last few years the Common Market has made efforts to increase its assistance to African states with the adoption of lowered tariffs on African products and a coordinated aid program of the member states. The Yaounde Agreement, which went into effect on June 1, 1964, was directed toward ultimately doing away with all tariffs and quantitative restrictions between any of the African states linked in the Association of African States and Madagascar (AASM) and the Common Market countries. The agreement provided for substantial tariff reductions on the part of the European signatories immediately; of particular importance were its tariff reductions on the following products: coffee, lowered from 16 per cent to 9.6 per cent; tea, from 18 per cent to 0; cocoa, from 9 per cent to 5.4 per cent; and tropical woods, from 5–10 per cent to 0. All quantitative restrictions were to be reduced by 15 per cent of the new, lowered ceiling until they disappeared. Until 1967, the agreement allowed certain limited exceptions for states with existing international economic treaty agreements, and the familiar escape clause of such treaties (whereby temporary

25. *Ibid.*

deviation from the agreement is permitted a nation faced with pressing economic difficulties) is included in it. However, the principle of maximum free trade among the signatories is confirmed. These terms represent a considerable economic sacrifice in revenues for West Germany, for the Federal Republic imports from the AASM states have increased over the preceding four years both absolutely and relative to the other EEC countries. Because it offers economic incentive to develop production of goods which unencumbered world market prices will support, German participation in the specified tariff reductions can be seen as a new series of grants in development aid.

Table XX.   Trade Increases, 1960–1964 in EEC-AASM Trade and GFR-AASM Trade (in millions of U.S. dollars).

Import from or export to AASM states	1960				1964			
	EEC		Federal Republic		EEC		Federal Republic	
	Import	*Export*	*Import*	*Export*	*Import*	*Export*	*Import*	*Export*
Cameroon	92	51	9	3	140	82	18	6
Chad	9	9	—	—	17	15	1	1
Central African Republic	8	9	—	—	16	18	—	1
Congo (Brazzaville)	8	34	—	—	34	46	17	4
Congo (Kinshasa)	395	101	45	16	318	115	37	24
Dahomey	15	17	—	—	13	23	1	3
Gabon	38	17	—	—	86	32	16	3
Ivory Coast	102	83	—	—	218	162	42	10
Malagasy Republic	58	66	3	3	67	94	4	6
Mali	6	11	—	—	3	14	0	1
Mauritania	1	7	—	—	38	12	14	2
Niger	12	7	—	—	23	17	0	1
Rwanda/Burundi	1	3	—	—	7	9	0	2
Senegal	98	113	—	—	123	129	5	7
Somalia	19	10	—	—	16	18	0	2
Togo	13	17	—	2	26	17	3	4
Upper Volta	—	6	—	—	3	18	—	—
Totals	875	561	57	24	1,148	821	158	77

Source: Derived from chart compiled on the basis of EEC Statistical Office information in *Bulletin,* No. 148 (Sept. 3, 1965), p. 1,197.

Besides the indirect development aid provided by the reduction of tariffs on African products, the European Economic Community has a direct-aid program of its own, financed by contributions of member states to the EEC Development Fund. Since the Treaty of Rome, the EEC's charter document, does not give the Common Market as an organization the power to assess funds for development purposes, the amounts of contributions from member states have been worked out in a series of compromises with the proviso that no apportionment scheme is to be construed as setting a precedent. During the first five years of the Common Market, West Germany contributed some $200 million to the Development Fund; the shares of member states from 1964 through 1969 according to the five-year apportionment plan agreed upon are shown in Table XXI.

Table XXI.   Apportionment of Payments to the EEC Development Fund, 1964–1969 (in millions of U.S. dollars).

Belgium	69
Federal Republic of Germany	246.5
France	246.5
Italy	100
Luxembourg	2
Netherlands	66
Total	730

Source: Derived from statistics in "Afrika und die EWG," *Bulletin,* No. 148 (Sept. 3, 1965), pp. 1,195–1,198; and Walter Scheel, "Wirtschaftliche Zusammenarbeit mit Afrika," press release, Bonn, April 19, 1963. The latter, written before apportionment negotiations for the coming five years were complete, gives a somewhat higher total of $800 million (pp. 8–11).

The member countries of the Association of African States and Madagascar are to benefit from the EEC Development Fund in receiving both capital and technical assistance. A special committee of government representatives from the EEC member-nations examines applications for aid with a view toward having the projects financed by loans from the fund rather than grants whenever possible. But the more unusual part of the program for AASM states financed by the EEC Development Fund is "production aid" in the form of non-repayable subsidies to enable them to diversify their economies—dependence on single crops has always been an economic evil in Africa. Granted in decreasing amounts until 1969, it is hoped that the subsidies will allow AASM states to put new products on the world market at competitive prices by the cut-off-date. "Production aid" is also intended to cushion the shock resulting from the withdrawal of prices high above those of world-market prices which several Common Market countries, most notably France, have been granting to their former African colonies.[26]

Obviously the willingness of other Common Market countries to invest substantially in African development projects has made West German marks go further there. But there is, of course, a reverse side to the advantage of being able to work together with European countries having old historical ties in Africa. For it has generally proven true that in the former colonies of Africa, companies from the ex-mother countries are on hand to take first choice of those projects which are seen as most likely to become self-supporting. In the former German colonies, which have been in other hands for the past forty years, the German government finds no such con-

26. Walter Scheel, "Wirtschaftliche Zusammenarbeit mit Afrika," press release, Bonn, April 19, 1963.

centrations of German companies as the French, English, or Belgian governments can use as nuclei in their old territories.[27]

Former Minister Scheel pointed out regretfully on one occasion that in
spite of the fact that Germany contributed 35 per cent of the money used
in the EEC Development Fund, less than 3 per cent of the civil engineering
contracts were awarded to German firms. Civil engineering projects of the
type required in Africa, particularly the rapid building of solid housing
developments and durable road systems, have been a German specialty
since World War II. West Germans justly pride themselves on an ability to
improvise in new construction situations and to get along, if need be, with
minimal funds. They feel cheated of their fair share in projects financed by
the EEC Development Fund. Mr. Scheel explained the anomaly of German
firms' failing to get a proportionate share of the contracts in question by
a general reference to the historical ties of other EEC Member States and
more specifically to the fact "that many of these projects were too small
to interest any firm which was not already active in the country in question."[28] Since current construction emphasis is on larger numbers of smaller
construction projects rather than, as initially, on a few large ones, it is
doubtful that this situation in Africa will improve from the German standpoint.

27. One of the former German areas, Southwest Africa, remains under South African
administration, and German-based development projects there are negligible. It is true
that the West German press and government offices are apt to use German undertakings
in the three remaining German former colonies—Cameroon, Tanzania, and Togo—as
examples of what West Germany is doing in Africa more often than they refer to
operations in, for example, Uganda or Mozambique; but this is no real reflection of
German resources in these countries. Probably the strongest showing of German-
backed engineering strength has been in Nigeria, where to date West Germany has
constructed two railroad lines, two ports, nineteen roads and highways, twenty-one
bridges (including a road-bridge over the Ibo River at Etinan), and many smaller projects.

28. *Twelve Years*, p. 28. The fact that British and French construction firms obtain
about four to five times as many orders as do German firms is further explained by
(1) the more intimate knowledge which Britain and France have of the legal, banking,
social, and psychological conditions of the new nations, and (2) the mutual attraction
of both the sterling and franc monetary areas (from which as hard a currency as the
DM can scarcely benefit). Cf. *Hands Across the Sea*, p. 42.

LATIN AMERICA

Three principal differences distinguish the German effort in Latin America from that in other parts of the underdeveloped world: (1) an open desire to have development aid influence domestic struggles for socio-economic power; (2) a political-psychological cushion of almost uninterrupted good relations for over a century; and (3) massive private investment, whether measured in absolute quantities or in comparison with government support.

Toward a Quiet Revolution

While among Arabs and sub-Saharan Africans, Germans have made only scattered public allusions to the need for a Julius Nyerere, a Haile Selassie, or an Ahmed Ben Bella to undertake a sweeping reorganization of the social structure of his land in order to make government loans more effective, democracy more real, and private investment more welcome, they have been far less restrained in calling for changes in the power structure of Latin American countries.[1] In so doing, their assumption is that short-sighted ruling cliques in Latin America have selfishly retarded the advance of peoples under them through inequitable tax systems, failure to make education accessible to large numbers, and intolerance toward legitimate political opposition. The putative result is that Latin America has been held back by forces from within far more than by factors of climate, lack of natural resources, foreign subjugation, and over-population, which are most often called upon to explain the lack of advancement in other regions. While West German policy statements on Latin America regularly stress economic immobility as the chief obstacle to be overcome, they also make occasional mention of great developmental discrepancies among the regions of single countries there, as causing tension and unrest to a degree that threatens economic progress:

1. The scathing criticism of Ethiopia's handling of aid for development (cited above in Chap. VII), does not fit in with broader West German pronouncements on Ethiopia, which tend to be replete with praise for the Emperor and his administration and—in contrast with analogous statements regarding Latin American countries—do not recognize willful internal resistance to economic progress.

102

Thus in most of the [Latin American] countries the task at hand is to overcome this condition of tension, i.e., to strive for active regional policies, and, of course, the task at hand is also to pursue a policy for the progress of society (fortschrittliche Gesellschaftspolitik)—to use, for once, a more comprehensive term than simply 'social policy' (Sozialpolitik).[2] We explained this quite openly, and in so doing called attention to the example of the Federal Republic, which now has social and political stability because a policy for the progress of society and a policy to safeguard social interests were pursued during its years of economic construction. We made it very clear that for this reason—because we regard this as a precondition—in order to back a healthy economic development the Federal Government will finance only those projects which serve a broad stratum of the population and in no case those which would serve only a small group.[3]

In another statement clarifying German development policy in Latin America, Minister Scheel went a step further in pointing to the absolute necessity of a middle class, conscious of its responsibilities, for economic progress in the recipient countries—a necessity almost entirely lacking there. Given the desire of the Federal Republic to make its aid effective, it follows from these statements that German policy in the underdeveloped world, more openly in Latin America than elsewhere, is to support a hopefully nascent middle class in its movement to gain power.

To Americans, easily the nastiest word used in connection with our relations with Latin America over the last half century has been "intervention." To give moral support to a class within a country so that it may gain power and, hopefully, responsibility, is certainly intervention on a grand scale. To be sure, the Alliance for Progress appears to have been conceived with exactly this end in mind, but American second thoughts about the propagandistic reaction to "attaching strings" to loans and grants in order to hasten desired internal socio-political changes have arisen. Experience has shown that economic interference, while certainly preferable to military intervention, can cause resentment of a strong nation's attempt to exert pressure on a weaker one; as a result U.S. policy statements now tend to blur the aim of backing middle-class interests against others. But the Germans show comparatively little fear that their intentions here will be taken amiss. They assume that, since the advancement of the middle class is practically synonymous with the interest of the people to any clearthinking citizen of the Free World, there can be no reasonable objection to a quiet revolution whereby a middle class rises to ascendancy with the help of outside aid. This view appears to ignore the simultaneous assertions that Germans are not interested in reshaping the social structure of recipient nations or influencing their policies, apart from the proviso that the govern-

2. The term Sozialpolitik often occurs in German political homilies with the very unrevolutionary connotation of "a policy to safeguard the interests of society as a whole." Cf. F. L. Ehlert, "Lateinamerika will mehr Entwicklungskredite," Frankfurter Allgemeine Zeitung, April 16, 1966.

3. Minister Scheel upon his return from a trip through Latin America in 1962, "Bewährte Partnerschaft im neuen Stil," press release, Bad Godesberg, Sept. 10, 1962, p. 7.

ment in power shall neither recognize East Germany nor work to under-mine the independence of West Berlin. On the whole, Germans have been led to believe that the leadership of Latin American countries desire such a revolution; hence their intervention will amount to nothing more drastic than giving support to what the best minds in the countries concerned are planning anyway. And since the question of the specific steps that the Federal Republic will take to back social change in Latin America is answered in terms of support for only those projects which will help the broad multitude, even those who make a distinction between the middle-class and the working-class can scarcely be disturbed by the prospect of such intervention.

While Germans have been encouraged to believe that they are helping to back the right kind of quiet revolution in Colombia, Ecuador, Peru, and Brazil, Chile's President Eduardo Frei has outdone others in extending to West Germany a veritable invitation to intervene on behalf of his "Revolu-tion in Freedom." During his 1965 visit to Germany, Frei quite openly called on the Germans to help him overcome domestic opposition to his pro-gram. In Berlin, for example, he expounded at some length on how his people have pledged themselves to reject "domination by the powerful and the rich" and made a plea for "open and real recognition of the fact that by far the greatest part of humanity lives under disadvantageous con-ditions, not only because of its cultural, political, and economic backward-ness, but also because the present-day structure of scientific, technological, and economic progress inclines toward putting the fate of the entire world and the life of mankind into the hands of a minority of men."[4]

An important clue to the willingness of the Bonn government to embrace wholeheartedly a movement such as Frei's is the nature of the enemies pictured as holding up progress in Latin America. Who make up this name-less, faceless group into whose hands modern technology tends to put enough wealth and power to allow them to dominate whole populations? Before looking for an answer, it might be well to note that Frei identified himself with West Berlin's struggle to maintain itself while surrounded by hostile forces, and that in general the Communists in South America have been critical of the West German foreign-aid effort; this fact has allayed German suspicions that, in opposing plutocratic minority rule in South America, they are undertaking steps desired by the Communists. But the sinister powers in Latin America under attack are the owners of mines and haciendas, who are encumbered abroad with such a collective reputation for ruthlessness and selfishness—as symbols of inequity and decadence to liberals and simply unknown quantities to conservatives—that it is politi-cally quite safe to attack them in any European or North American country. As if the need for meeting this totally disreputable kind of opposition were not enough, the specters of future Perons or Castros loom on the horizon

4. Speech in Berlin, July 20, 1965, printed with speech of Mayor Brandt as "Zur Verständigung der Völker," *Bulletin*, No. 125 (July 22, 1965), p. 1,010.

if Europeans should fail to respond with sufficient aid: "Allow me, Mr. President, to point out that Europe has very special obligations in our [Latin] America. For if, as I have repeatedly emphasized, Europe should fail to impart strength to democratic values through its active cooperation with the peoples of Latin America—in order to secure not only freedom but daily bread—then misery and desperation will drive these peoples into the arms of a radicalism which they reject at the bottom of their hearts."[5]

Bonds of the Christian Occident

German officials responsible for aid to underdeveloped countries find in Latin America an appealing lack of the emotional and dangerous racial or ethnic group rivalry which has produced difficulties for the German program in the Near East and remains a threat in Africa. The Latin American conflicts between native Indians and the Spanish-speaking population or between [east] Indians and Negroes seem not to be of analogous dimension; even when they are quite serious, as in British Guiana, there is no propensity to drag in the Germans. Latin America is the one part of the underdeveloped world where German and local statesmen can publicly and without embarrassment praise advances made toward "bringing the ways of life of both peoples, supported by Christian-occidental traditions, closer together."[6] Then, too, in spite of the presence of Castro's Cuba in the Caribbean, German development efforts in Latin America are much less threatened by a military confrontation of Western and Communist forces than those in Asia.

The results of German immigration in Latin America have been felt for more than a century. With a few notable exceptions, Germans in Latin America tended not to be quite so completely absorbed in the local populations as in North America. Their total numbers remained modest, however, and no rivalry emerged to bring hostility upon them in their roles of farmers, teachers, or even military careerists. Although the Germans frequently refer to their South American settlements as "colonies," the connotation has almost always been ethnic and seldom political.[7]

5. Frei's speech of July 19, 1965, at a state dinner, printed together with that of President Lübke as "Herzliche Freundschaft mit Chile," *Bulletin*, No. 124 (July 21, 1965), pp. 1,002–1,003. Cf. Erik Verg, "Mañana ist es zu spät," *Für Sie gelesen*, No. 24 (July, 1965), pp. 1–6.

6. "Herzliche Freundschaft," p. 1,002.

7. Even allowing for the fact that immigration statistics for the nineteenth century are inadequate, there is hardly any possibility that the total number of German settlers in Latin America before 1900 exceeded 150,000. A fairly consistent 95 per cent of German emigrants before 1900 settled in the United States, where they were generally absorbed beyond recognition of their original nationality within two generations; in contrast, German emigrants elsewhere were found to keep their formal national identity much longer. "Auswanderung," *Brockhaus Konversations-Lexikon*, (14th ed.; Leipzig, 1901). In the speeches cited above, Chile's President Frei paid tribute to the indomitable industry of German immigrants in Chile which, President Lübke noted, were "joined in fruitful combination with the specific talents of the Chilean people. German pedagogues, scientists, farmers, and, in particular, trainers of the Chilean Army, so rich in its traditions, all have a part in this." "Herzliche Freundschaft," p. 1,001.

Nor did the two world wars, which in North America so thoroughly undermined good feelings toward Germans as a group, do much damage to the German image in Latin America. In fact, the long-term psychological effect of the Germans having been opponents of the United States, which Latin American nationalists regard with more suspicion than the traditional European colonial powers, may have cancelled out residues of the rather nominal opposition of most Latin American countries to Germany in the last stages of World War II. Some contention remains, to be sure, about German property seized during World War II, and the government of the Federal Republic has occasionally pointed to a settlement of outstanding claims as a prerequisite for extensive development aid; but courts in some of the countries concerned, particularly Colombia and Ecuador, more recently Chile, have handed down decisions quite satisfactory to German interests, while most of the other countries maintain an at least theoretically open mind toward compromising differences.[8]

When German and Latin American officials discuss development projects, a tangible point of affinity is their common attitude toward capitalism: roughly, that it can do wonders and should be allowed to, but that it is hardly to be valued for its own sake; free enterprise presents itself as a means of realizing a goal under the auspices of a democratic government, the goal of an organic society in which every citizen prospers through developing his talents freely—but in which the government must keep a watchful eye on those who otherwise might exploit the workers and peasants. Relatively few articulate Germans and Latin Americans of any generation look back nostalgically to a golden age of unlimited free enterprise, since marred by the erosion of individual freedoms under an officiously expanding government. Germany's postwar recovery from desolation to prosperity and world importance in fifteen years is a much closer example of the kind of accomplishment Latin American statesmen might envision for their countries than any experience of another Western country. Because of its level of mass education and supply of skilled labor, postwar Germany hardly would qualify as an underdeveloped country in the usual sense; still, the rapid overcoming of seemingly insuperable economic obstacles without recourse to dictatorship can be taken as an inspiration for current Latin American reformers: "This example shows in the final analysis that when a people possesses neither house nor hearth, nor factories, nor great natural resources, but possesses instead a talent for organization, will to work, and an enlightened leadership stratum, it can then call the basic elements for ascendency its own."[9]

8. "Bewährte Partnerschaft im neuen Stil," p. 6; also reprint of his radio speech in series "Politik aus erster Hand" (Bayerischer Rundfunk), Sept. 12, 1962, p. 4.

9. "Herzliche Freundschaft," p. 1,002.

Private Investment and Capital Assistance

The history of good relations between Latin America and Germany, with the Germans' feeling that Latin Americans are more akin to them than are other populations of the developing world—a feeling which the phraseology of Christian-occidental traditions articulates with passable respectability in a world which has, for the moment, sworn off extolling racial heritage and bonds—largely explains the preference of German businessmen for Latin American investments. Previously established industrial enclaves there, too, as around Sao Paulo, Brazil, undoubtedly enhance the investment climate, in making the chance of profits in Latin America within the fore-seeable future seem more real than in Africa and most of Asia.

When contrasted with that in Asia and Africa, the mass of German private capital invested in Latin America is striking: From 1950 to 1960, West German private enterprise invested over $250 million in Latin American countries, against some $55.5 million in Africa and $37.5 in Asia.[10] As of 1963, German private investments in Latin America amounted to 60 per cent of those in all underdeveloped regions and 25 per cent of *all* German foreign investments. By the end of 1964, Brazil alone employed $209 million in direct private investment from West Germany.[11]

In the first thirteen-year period from 1950 to 1963 alone, the Federal Government approved $136 million in capital assistance credits to Latin America, and proportional commitments have followed in the years since then. Most of the governmental credits have served infrastructural needs, particularly—in view of the tendency in Latin America for agricultural regions to be in much more dire need than urban ones—land-reclaiming and fertilization ventures, such as the $54 million approved by 1967 for irrigating 387,000 acres of potential farmland in the Tinajones Project in Peru.[12] In Brazil the Federal Republic has concentrated its capital assistance credits on projects for developing the electrical industry, particularly in the north-eastern sections of the country, which abound in unutilized ore deposits. More recently, Chile has received a very diversified series of capital-aid injections to back projects ranging from furnishing eighteen hospitals with the most modern equipment to an extensive program of residential construction. At the same time, throughout Latin America, West Germany is

10. "Politik aus erster Hand," p. 3. For details see *Hands Across the Sea, passim.*

11. "Die Bundesrepublik und Lateinamerika," *Bulletin,* No. 147 (Sept. 30, 1964), p. 1,361, and "Über 7, 8 Mrd. DM Direktinvestitionen im Ausland," *Bulletin,* No. 5 (Jan. 12, 1966), p. 36.

12. "Deutsche Kapitalhilfe für Peru," *Bulletin,* No. 112 (July 16, 1964), p. 1,072; "Das grösste deutsche Entwicklungsvorhaben; Das Bewässerungsprojekt von Tinajones," *Frankfurter Allgemeine Zeitung,* April 21, 1967.

also backing large numbers of loans to develop industrial production of consumer goods in regions suffering from chronic unemployment.[13]

Technical Assistance

Germany has been giving Latin America a rough annual average of 20 per cent of its total technical assistance. Most of the funds are allotted for projects controlled entirely or in part by the Ministry for Economic Cooperation, but church-sponsored educational projects have also received considerable backing: appropriations for the latter in Latin America were scheduled to reach slightly over $8.3 million for the 1965–1966 period. Within West Germany, the Foundation for Developing Countries receives each year large delegations of Latin American participants in specialized seminars; for example, in 1964 there were 305 Latin American participants in seminars which focused on national and international marketing and economic publicity.[14]

The German Development Service has been active in Latin America since its inception, although the fact that economic conditions there are generally more advanced than in Asia and Africa has meant that Latin American countries have frequently requested a proportionately large number of experienced specialists to supervise economic reorganization and relocation rather than the basic spade work emphasized elsewhere. Where possible, the Ministry for Economic Cooperation has met these requirements, as in sending four experts to Mexico to work with the Mexican State Developing and Planning Institute on reorganizing the chemical, petroleum, iron, and steel processing plants with a view toward establishing small- and middle-sized factory centers.[15] But the extent to which these high-level demands can be met is severely limited by Germany's own short supply of technical experts.

German training centers in Latin America supply the whole range of essential industrial and agricultural skills needed for economic progress. Some of the undertakings are cooperative ones, as is the agricultural settlement begun under Swiss auspices in the Brazilian state of Alagoas, in which

13. "Die Bundesrepublik und Lateinamerika," p. 1,361; Kreditanstalt für Wiederaufbau, XVII. Jahresbericht: Geschäftsjahr 1965 (Frankfurt am Main, 1966), pp. 74, 76. In addition to specific project loans and some untied financial assistance (such as balance-of-payments credits to Chile and Brazil), Bonn has been relatively generous in granting credit to German exporters delivering, for example, a copper-refining plant to Chile, a smelting plant and cement factory to Peru, water pipes to Ecuador, and various installations to Colombia and Mexico. The development banks of Paraguay, Brazil, Chile, and Mexico have also received West German loans. Kreditanstalt für Wiederaufbau, Annual Reports.

14. Kreditanstalt für Wiederaufbau, XVII. Jahresbericht, 74, 76.

15. "Berater für Mexiko," Bulletin, No. 162 (Nov. 4, 1964), p. 1,498.

600 farm families from areas suffering continual drought have been resettled and trained to farm new holdings in an 85,000-acre area.[16]

In cooperative projects with Latin American universities, the Germans have shown a particular interest in promoting forestry along with the related field of wood processing. West German economists have emphasized this branch of agriculture with its industrial ramifications as particularly vital to the developing countries; surprisingly, these countries had to import nearly half a billion dollars' worth of wood products in 1960 and will need to import nearly four billion dollars' worth in 1975, unless local production is drastically increased.[17] In Latin America, where forests abound, there is obviously a chance to make a productive opportunity of immediate demand and close availability of the raw materials to fill it. In helping the University of Bogotá establish a forestry department, the Ministry for Economic Cooperation has assisted with a model forestry and lumber installation in Carare-Opon, Colombia, and has dispatched experts to give instruction particularly on the utilization of tropical woods and on fighting erosion.[18] In Argentina the ministry is also supporting the expansion of a forestry department at the University of Córdoba in Santiago del Estoro; here, however, the project is more under the control of the local university: the German participation is in the form of one advisor, a donation for teaching materials, and a supply of scientific equipment for a number of institutes and a field station.[19]

Also, within the framework of technical assistance in Latin America, the Ministry for Economic Cooperation has financially aided the expansion of elementary and secondary schools begun by German communities to enable them to admit increasing numbers of non-German pupils. Of these schools the most significant is the German School in Bogotá, Colombia, which in the late fifties, expanded to accommodate 1,200 pupils, two-thirds of whom were native Colombian children. By 1962, its excess of applications was so great that 500 had to be rejected. Because this school is not free, but rather expensive to attend by local standards, its popularity has been cited a number of times by the ministry as an example of the eagerness for learning on the part of a young generation in Latin America and as concrete evidence of the enthusiastic local response that increased German technical assistance efforts can hope to meet.[20]

16. "Hilfe für landwirtschaftliche Siedlung in Brasilien," *Bulletin*, No. 127 (Aug. 14, 1964), p. 1,198.

17. "Zur Ausweitung der Holzerzeugung," *Bulletin*, No. 6 (Jan. 13, 1966), p. 45.

18. "Deutsch-Kolombanische Zusammenarbeit," *Bulletin*, No. 143 (Sept. 22, 1964), p. 1,330.

19. "Bildungshilfe für Argentinien," *Bulletin*, No. 160 (Oct. 30, 1964), p. 1,483.

20. "Bewährte Partnerschaft," pp. 7–8; "Politik aus erster Hand," p. 5. Cf. Rolf Seelmann-Eggebert, "Pindorama in Brasilien," *Frankfurter Allgemeine Zeitung*, July 30, 1966.

A Few Special Problems

In line with its more recent policies for the whole developing world, the Federal Republic has tended more and more to tie its loans in Latin America to specific projects which are approved in all essentials when the loan itself is approved, rather than to grant credits to Latin American governments for projects to be decided on later. In fact, unhappy experiences in Latin America with loans made within too general a framework probably was decisive in shifting overall policy toward advance project commitments. The most significant such early German "framework" loan of some $50 million was approved for Brazil before 1962; as it turned out, there were several disagreements over the projects to be used to fill out this total, accompanied by manifest dissatisfaction on the part of the Brazilians that there was so little in their country to show for such large approval. In 1965, $2.3 million was approved for hospital equipment in Guanabara, $280,000 for the same purpose in Alagoas, $4.19 million for a power station, and $10.1 for overland cables and accessories to boost the Brazilian electrical industry.[21] These projects, however, brought the fulfilled percentage up to only one-third of the "framework" approval.

Although in contrast with that in other developing areas, German private investment is very heavy, it is still not nearly as great as either the Ministry for Economic Development or most Latin American governments would like to see. Unlike other developing regions, Latin America is faced with the problem that profits realized on capital investments often find their way abroad rather than into expanding or improving domestic undertakings.[22] German officials believe that apprehension about the continued exportability of profits, coupled with fear of expropriation or excessive local taxation, has dampened the enthusiasm of private investors for increasing their holdings in Latin America in any proportion to opportunities for profitable investments there. They continue to express hope that agreements for the protection of foreign capital in Latin American countries and those to avoid double taxation or profits will help overcome private reluctance to continue investments in Latin America; but, with the exception of Brazil, Latin American countries have not shown notable gains in this respect in recent years.[23]

21. "Darlehensverträge mit Brasilien," *Bulletin*, No. 125 (July 22, 1965), p. 1,016.

22. The Ministry for Economic Cooperation reported discussions in 1962 with Latin American leaders on "the problem of capital expatriated from the Latin American countries, which experts estimate to be about $10 billion. This problem is naturally a result of the political difficulties and the unstable political situation in several countries, and only from there can a solution be forthcoming." "Bewährte Partnerschaft im neuen Stil," p. 8. Two years later Minister Scheel noted with regret the *decrease* in willingness on the part of the German private economic sector to continue making investments in Latin America. "Die Bundesrepublik und Lateinamerika," p. 1,361.

23. "Über 7, 8 Mrd. DM Direktinvestitionen im Ausland," *Bulletin*, No. 5 (Jan. 12, 1966), p. 36. The attractions of Brazil's chemical and electronics industries have put it second only to Switzerland as an investment country for West Germans.

Apprehension in Latin American countries about the possible effects of the European Economic Community has somewhat clouded the picture of German–Latin American economic relations recently. Specifically, Latin Americans have expressed fear that their coffee crop, already sensitive to violent price fluctuations on the world market, will be exported to Europe less and less as the Common Market countries promote the importation of coffee from former colonies in Africa, which will enjoy lower (or no) import duties and which will circulate within the EEC countries with minimal national taxes levied on it.

The Germans have produced figures to show the emptiness of such fears: from the founding of the EEC in 1957 to 1965 Latin America's exports to the EEC countries increased in real value by 59 per cent, considerably more than Latin America's general average of 36 per cent for increased exports during that period.[24] As for coffee and the EEC, during roughly the same period, Latin America increased its coffee exports to all EEC countries, including those with coffee-producing former colonies, from 53.4 per cent of all coffee imported by EEC countries to 59.7 per cent in 1960 and some 62.0 per cent in 1961.[25] But this does not change the fact that total Latin American exports constitute a smaller percentage of German imports than they did before Germany joined the Common Market. In 1959, 9.6 per cent of West German imports came from Latin America; at the end of 1965 this figure was down to 7.5 per cent. German exports to Latin America, which in 1959 were 7.5 per cent of all German exports, fell to 4.7 per cent of this total during the same period. Federal Treasurer Kurt Schmücker unhesitantly attributes a large part of both drops to increased trade among the Common Market nations.[26]

The Germans insist on the ultimate harmony of interests among the EEC countries and Latin America with reference to the predicted chain of events: more European economic efficiency, more money in the hands of European consumers, rising standard of living, larger demand for imports from outside European countries. They have also given every encouragement to the formation of a Latin American free-trade zone.[27] In so doing, their double motivation is to make German development aid in Latin America more effective and—since the Germans presumably would not promote the formation of a free-trade zone which they would have to remain outside of if free-trade zones really were damaging to the long-term interests of outsiders—to help remove the cause of resentment in Latin America over the Common Market.

24. President Lübke, Address before Mexican Congress, Nov. 24, 1966; text in *Bulletin*, No. 152 (Nov. 30, 1966), pp. 1,222–1,224.

25. "Die Bundesrepublik und Lateinamerika," p. 1,361 and "Bewährte Partnerschaft," pp. 8–9.

26. "Südamerika als Wirtschaftspartner Deutschlands," *Bulletin*, No. 74 (June 3, 1966), pp. 581–582.

27. Chile's President Frei is one of the most articulate Latin American backers of this idea. "Ein Land aufstrebender Zukunft," speech before representatives of German industry and finance, July 21, 1965, *Bulletin*, No. 126 (July 23, 1965), p. 1,021.

IX

INDIA AND THE FAR EAST

While the greatest proportion of West German technical assistance has gone to Africa, and the largest part by far of private investment from the Federal Republic in the developing world has found its way to Latin America, it is in Asia that Germany has invested the biggest portion of its capital assistance. Through the end of 1963, Asia absorbed 56.5 per cent of the total.[1] Before 1961, half of German technical assistance went to Asia; the present portion is only a third of the worldwide German effort. In Asia, as in Africa and Latin America, Bonn's development-aid policy has opened the door for many of the country's industrial giants, such as the AEG electro combine, Bayer, Julius Berger AG, Demag, Ferrostaal, Höchst, Hochtief, Krupp, and Mannesmann and Siemens, to name a few. German assistance in Asia, both capital and technical, has concentrated from the first on India; nonetheless there is no German-supported project in India that does not have an analogous undertaking in some other Asian country.

The Far East

Capital assistance in the Far East has focused slightly more on communications than in Latin America and Africa; and technical assistance has dealt somewhat less with agricultural pursuits than with trade education. Considerable West German aid has gone to advance the level of medical practice in the Far East; these projects have aspects of both technical and capital aid.

In South Viet-Nam, West German technical assistance has progressed from supporting a department in the Cao Thang Technical School to expanding and transforming this department into the core of a whole new school on the edge of Saigon; the Federal Republic has promised to build the school and to equip it with the required tools and machines. In the same country, German loans have promoted small industry, and along with

1. Kreditanstalt für Wiederaufbau, XVII. Jahresbericht (1965) p. 62. Cf. "Entwicklungshilfe in Asien," Entwicklungspolitik, Ausgabe I/8, May 25, 1965, pp. 12–14.

French credit, have financed the Nong-Song chemical project. West Germany has also dispatched considerable medical aid, including a hospital ship, to South Viet-Nam; of course, the obvious connection of this assistance with the war and German governmental references to the fact that the medical facilities are looked upon partly as a substitute for German military hardware or troops mark this as something other than development aid in the normal sense.[2]

In 1963, the Federal Republic granted credits to South Korea to expand the country's telephone and telegraph service; slightly less than $5 million was added to the original sum in 1965. Negotiations have taken place for additional investments in water-supply installations and coal mining. Since 1962 German instructors have taught at a technical training school in Inchon.

In Indonesia, West Germany has helped to finance a large dam, a power station, an irrigation project and, to improve internal communication; she has undertaken road and harbor construction, as she has also done in the Philippines. A substantial portion of German aid to Indonesia has been in the form of export guarantees.

To Burma went a loan of nearly nine milion dollars in 1965 for several industrial projects: the most significant were cotton mills (including the generators necessary to power these), a pump-and-motor factory, a brick kiln, and factories to produce containers for foodstuffs.

In Malaysia, the Federal Republic has agreed to furnish a model hospital, which is to function as part of the new medical department of the Kuala Lumpur University. With an investment of some $3.8 million, the West Germans hope to equip the hospital with 756 beds for patients, facilities for treating up to 1,000 outpatients a day, and instructional facilities to enable 110 medical students to complete their studies every year. This should double existing opportunities for medical education in Malaysia.[3] Capital aid has also been promised for an expansion of the harbor at Penang-Butterworth.

In Pnom-Penh, the capital of Cambodia, a slaughterhouse is to be financed; a West German delegation also concluded an agreement in 1964 to begin work on a trade school in Battambang, the country's second largest city. This project was in the planning stage in 1967.

An agreement was reached with Thailand to build a similar trade school under joint auspices in Khon-Kaen, 300 miles northeast of Bangkok. In the

2. "Wirtschaftshilfe für Süd-Vietnam, Kambodscha und Thailand: Arbeitsgespräche einer Regierungsdelegation in den betroffenen Ländern," *Bulletin*, No. 152 (Oct. 13, 1964), p. 1,403; "Humanitarian aid for Viet-Nam," *Münchner Merkur*, Aug. 3, 1966, reprinted in the *German Tribune*, No. 229 (Aug. 20, 1966), p. 2. During 1966 the West German government several times denied East German allegations that members of the Federal Republic's Air Force were carrying out military assignments in South Viet-Nam and emphasized the strictly non-military nature of its projects for refugee relief in that country.

3. *XVII. Jahresbericht*, pp. 69–71.

same region of Thailand several years earlier, the Federal Republic had loaned over $11 million for the Nam Pong project (thirty miles from Khon-Kaen); the chief undertaking was a giant dam to supply the entire province with electricity, while providing irrigation for agriculture. In 1965, the Nam Pong project was given another credit boost by the Federal Republic, and about $5.75 million went toward the expansion of the telephone and telegraph network.[4] The Technical Institute in Bangkok continues to be Germany's largest technical assistance project; the Werahera training center in Ceylon is reportedly the most successful one. In the latter country, West German capital aid has financed a cement factory and the modernization of the port of Colombo.

Afghanistan and Pakistan

In 1965, West Germany put some $40 million at the disposal of the royal government of Afghanistan in the form of capital-aid credits. The largest part went into an ambitious scheme to advance agriculture through the construction of two huge silo installations and thirty-nine warehouses for grain storage; these facilities should increase the incentive for grain production by giving Afghan farmers an opportunity to dispose of any conceivable amount of grain they might grow and so provide the population with a steady year-round supply. Another portion of these credits was earmarked for financing new oil depots and a network of gas stations; this project is of particular importance in Afghanistan, which has neither waterways nor railways to speak of, and is hence much more dependent on its motor traffic than other developing countries.

In spite of Afghanistan's fame and history as a producer of wool—seventy years ago this country exported over twelve million yards of wool annually to India alone—and its considerable production of cotton, the industry was too poorly developed through the early 1960's to turn out enough finished textiles for its own people. Textiles imported from industrial countries were placing a severe strain on the short supply of foreign exchange credits. In the last few years, supported by German credits, the Afghan Textile Company in Gulbahar has taken a long first step on the way toward the modernization of textile production and has provided over 4,500 workers with employment.[5]

Apart from other capital-aid projects (e.g., electrical and telecommunication installations), the Germans have created a number of training centers and trade schools in Afghanistan. The Universities of Bonn and Cologne have sponsored the natural-science and economics faculties in Kabul, and

4. "Wirtschaftshilfe für Süd-Vietnam, Kambodscha und Thailand," p. 1,403; XVII. Jahresbericht, p. 71.

5. Kreditanstalt für Wiederaufbau, Deutsche Kredite für Entwicklungsländer: Afrika und Asien (Frankfurt am Main, 1964), p. 27.

for several years German experts have been engaged in guiding the development of Afghan natural and human resources.

Over ten million dollars in German capital credits went to Pakistan, chiefly to finance a large-scale water project which centers around well-boring in the Indus Basin, an area suffering from new deposits of salt and the formation of swamps. Hopeful estimates foresee an eightfold increase in agricultural productivity as a result of washing out deposited salt, creating sufficient ground drainage, and supplying water from drilled wells. Another part of the same loan was devoted to expanding and improving the Pakastani telephone and telegraph system, which has suffered from a reputation for backwardness even among the developing countries of Asia.

An earlier West German loan of $3.53 million facilitated the construction of a cement plant in Manghopir, which was producing five hundred tons of cement a day by 1964 and is to turn out a thousand tons after completion of an extension. As was the case with Afghan textile imports, Pakistani cement imports had increasingly sapped the country's foreign reserves as building construction, a key part of any national economic development, had increased rapidly in the decade 1953–1963.[6] The Federal Republic has contributed heavily to both Pakistani five-year economic plans and the establishment of numerous technical schools.

India's Needs

From several standpoints India presents the most dramatic case in the program of German development aid: its needs are everywhere acknowledged as the greatest among all the countries of the developing world, and, correspondingly, it has received the largest quantities of aid.[7] India's leaders also have attracted more international attention to the development of their country than have those of any other developing state, not only because of the seriousness of their nation's plight but also because of comprehensive and long-range national economic planning they have attempted.

India has been trying to cure its economic ills in the areas of agriculture and industrialization through a series of five-year plans. While she has made progress in agricultural production, growing population demands are still exceeding food supplies. Her per capita income of $88 a year explains the plight of the 490 million people living in an area where the average density is 390 people per square mile. Since 1951, the country has instituted four five-year plans. Typically enough for the ambitions of developing countries, the objectives of these plans have been to: produce more food,

6. *Ibid.,* p. 21; *XVII, Jahresbericht,* p. 71.

7. The amount of foreign aid received in 1962 and 1963 may have been as large as 4–5 per cent of India's national income, and may have equalled two-thirds of her internal savings. Fritz Baade, *Strategie des Weltkampfes gegen den Hunger,* (Kiel/Bonn: Forschungsinstitut für Wirtschaftsfragen der Entwicklungsländer, 1966), p. 82.

build a broad industrial base, create new employment opportunities, educate its people, improve health conditions, and develop sound social institutions for promoting the general welfare.[8]

The First Five-Year Plan began on April 1, 1951. It was aimed at agricultural improvement, irrigation, land reclamation, and community development. The Second Five-Year Plan, ending in 1961, emphasized direct industrialization. The Third Five-Year Plan gave priority to agriculture because of the population pressures. This plan proved too ambitious, and by 1962 many projects had to be dropped and goals reduced. The overall aim of the plan was to increase national income by 5 per cent per year.[9] Table XXII shows foreign aid to India from selected countries up to December 31, 1961.

Table XXII.   Foreign Aid to India (in millions of U.S. dollars).

Donor	Aid Authorized				Aid Utilized	
	1st Plan	2nd Plan	March—Dec., 1961	Total	Up to March 1961	Per cent Utilized
U.S.A.[a]	518	3,240	142	3,900	2,050	63.3
U.S.S.R.	135	673		808	160	19.8
U.K.	0.8	259	127.2	387	257	99.1
Germany	0	299	125	424	269	89.9

Source: V. K. R. V. Rao and Dharm Narain, Foreign Aid and India's Economic Development (New York: Asia Publishing House, 1963; published in Delhi by the Institute of Economic Growth), pp. 3–4. Dollar values shown in the table are converted for the original at the rate of 4.76 rupees to $1.00.

[a]Includes P.L. 480 Titles II and III, gross value of exports authorized under P.L. 665 and P.L. 480 Title I and Third Country Currency Assistance. Considering these inputs, the U.S.A. figure is deceptive.

It is noteworthy that Germany has played an important role among the countries contributing to India's development. Although she was a late starter in this aid effort, the fact that she rated third in total aid and second in per cent of utilization attests to the presence of an effective program. Germany's efforts are continuing, but there is some doubt that they will increase in the future.[10]

8. U.S. Aid Mission to India, The United States Contribution to Indian Development. (New Delhi: Program Office, 1962); Shankerier Subramanian, Die Wirtschaftsentwicklung Indiens 1951–1961, Kieler Studien, No. 69 (1965).

9. "Progress of India's Third Plan," The Colombo Plan, Vol. 8 (1963) No. 1, pp. 7–8.

10. The West Germans have been accused of foot-dragging in regard to their contribution to India's Fourth Five-Year Plan. Bonn's hesitancy has both budgetary and political reasons as West Germany objects to India's friendly contacts with East Germany. J. Anthony Lukas, "India is Impatient at Slow Bonn Aid," The New York Times, June 18, 1966.

Germany's Aid Role in India

In the middle of the Second Five-Year Plan period, India was confronted by a serious shortage of foreign exchange. The World Bank (IBRD) convened a meeting of countries that had played dominant roles in the Second Plan, and the resulting consortium has met periodically with a view to coordinating assistance to India. These meetings, commencing in 1961, have produced long-range commitments by ten nations to facilitate India's economic planning.

Table XXIII. Consortium Commitments to India, 1961–1966 (in millions of U.S. dollars).

Austria	18
Belgium	24
Canada	173.5
France	120
Germany	644.5
Italy	170
Japan	290
Netherlands	44
United Kingdom	518
United States	2,285
World Bank and IDA	1,185
Total	5,472

Source: International Bank for Reconstruction and Development, "Consortium Communiqué on Aid to India," press release, April 21, 1965.

While the figures in Table XXIII represent only promised funds, for which necessary legislation was not passed in all cases, they did provide a valuable basis for economic planning. As the 1962–1963 commitments were refined, it was decided between Germany and India to disburse $106 million in 1962–1963 and commit $45 million for disbursement in subsequent years. Sixty-one million dollars for 1963–1966 was set aside for proposed extension of the Rourkela Steel Works (discussed below).[11] As this demonstrates, aid from the German government has been primarily in the form of credits, the popularity of which has been increasing. A significant feature of the German credits extended for the Third Five-Year Plan was that—in contrast to German capital assistance elsewhere in the developing world—they were predominantly "untied" both as regards projects and the source of procurement. This has been particularly true in respect to loans for import maintenance funds. Understandably, India considers this a desirable trend and welcomes West Germany's intention of permitting the emerging nations to make interest payments and loan redemptions in local currencies.[12]

Until mid-1963, about 29.6 per cent of all capital aid and 9 per cent of

11. Ministry of Finance of India, *External Assistance—1961* (India, Dept. of Public Affairs, 1961), p. 41.

12. *International Financial News Survey,* Vol. 16, No. 39 (Oct. 2, 1964), p. 343.

technical assistance granted by the Federal Republic went to India. The official Indian figures in the Tables XXII and XXIII do not reflect all of the aid; such efforts as technical training in West Germany and private investments by German firms constitute a greater effort than appears on the surface. At present 75 per cent of German aid to India is derived from public funds and 25 per cent from private sources. India would like to see the ratio shift to an equal amount from each source.[13]

Industrial Development

A predominant amount of German aid is directed toward the industrial sector of India's economy. These efforts create a situation in which Germany can compete more successfully for the sale of capital goods and replacement items to India—as well as realizing sales through tied aid—and can increase imports from India. The end result is bound to stimulate German–Indian trade.

The German-built Rourkela steel complex is an outstanding example of the industrial effort in which about forty German manufacturing firms have participated. The plant was designed in 1954 to produce one million ingot tons of steel annually to be rolled into 720,000 tons of flat products. The entire foreign exchange costs of the project are being met with credits received from the Federal Republic. As of March 1963, the Rourkela steel works had an annual capacity of 91,400 ingot tons of crude steel compared with 91,000 tons at the British-built steelworks at Durgapur and 88,000 tons at the Bhilai steel works built by Russia. Rourkela II, and expansion of the existing works, was being finished in 1966 to bring the total Rourkela capacity to 1.8 million tons.[14] Eventually, Rourkela's annual steel capacity is expected to rise to 2.5 million tons.

The Utkal Machinery Limited, one of India's most modern engineering works, is conveniently located in the Rourkela region. German private investors own 62 per cent of the company's capital shares. As is true of all similar undertakings, the official contribution to aid in this project can be found in the application of the Federal Republic's tax credit system (see Chap. IV) and in treaty guarantees to allow the free transfer of profits realized in the developing countries.

13. The West German contribution to the aid for 1965–1966, promised by the above-mentioned consortium, was $86.8 million and consisted of $23.6 million for the Rourkela Steel Works, $37.9 million for capital aid, and $25.2 million for export guarantees. *Ibid.*, Vol. 17, No. 19 (May 14, 1965), p. 173.

14. Jürgen Burandt, "Rourkela, The Second Stage Commences," *Germany*, Vol. 8 (1963) No. 35, pp. 47–50. Cf. Kreditanstalt für Wiederaufbau, *XIX. Jahresbericht (1967)*, p. 84. Rourkela is one of the biggest German capital-aid projects in the world and thus far has cost more than $250 million. Its construction taught the Germans many a hard lesson as numerous difficulties had to be overcome. Problems arose not only from India's limited financial ability, employment of indigenous labor, and primitive methods of transportation, but also from a Communist propaganda campaign directed against Rourkela and intended to benefit the Soviet plant at Bhilai. The Germans complicated their task by insisting on the use of the most advanced methods of steel production.

The Federal Republic is also active in the fields of coal, oil, gas and electric-power development. As of the end of 1963, German interests were involved in, or had completed 7 power plant projects, 33 turbine projects, 19 generator projects, 40 transformer-station projects, 469 coke-oven projects, three coal-processing plant projects, one large conveyor-belt project, and one oil- and gas-prospecting project.[15] These vary in magnitude from feasibility studies to completed plants, but the number of projects furnish an idea of the extent of German activity. The following are examples of the wide range of projects involved.

In the field of coal development, West Germany has established a program to train nominees of the Indian National Coal Development Corporation in Germany. This effort to develop technical skills was supplemented in 1961 when German experts made a study of the National Coal Development Corporation and prepared plans to improve its efficiency.

In 1960–1961, a German team consisting of eleven specialists carried out seismic surveys. The government bore all expenses for salaries of German personnel, equipment, and compilation and interpretation of field data. The Indian Oil and Gas Commission bore local costs for the surveys.[16]

A typical example of a large completed project, and of the international cooperation such projects entail, is India's Koyna Dam. Located about 175 miles southeast of Bombay, the $80 million dam—largely financed by the World Bank—comprises a power plant and a 2.6 billion cubic-yard reservoir. Two billion cubic yards of the water are used to run the generators which will supply Bombay and vicinity with electric power. The rest of the water goes into a vital irrigation project in the Krishna River region. The project was built with the assistance of the German consulting firm of Salzgitter Industriebau, which has a 50 per cent interest in the Indian firm constructing the dam. A German staff of six persons at the site was responsible for organization only; Indians supervised the work. With this organizational structure, it is probable that much of the material and equipment used to construct the dam and the power facilities came from the Federal Republic. Money from the World Bank flowed to India and then to the engineering and construction firms. Some of the money returned to Germany in the form of purchases and investments, again emphasizing the business nature of the Federal Republic's development assistance, even when the aid extended is not tied outright to purchases in Germany.

Transportation

German aid has permeated the Indian transportation industry. Her involvements include two harbor projects, engineering advice on roads and

15. *Twelve Years of German Development Assistance*, pp. 62–63.
16. *External Assistance, 1961*, p. 44.

railroads, the supply of vehicles, and capital participation in German transportation firms working in the country. The harbor project at Kendla in northwest India is impressive and was handled by Sindhu-Hochtief Limited; the German firm of Hochtief owns 50 per cent of the Indian company. In seven years a quiet creek on the eastern shore of the Gulf of Kutch, north of Bombay, was transformed into a bustling trade center handling hundreds of thousands of tons of goods. The harbor is now one of India's six major ports. As the trade outlet for the northern region, it serves a vast hinterland of three million square miles with a population of fifty million people.[17] The financial implications of this project for Germany parallel those of the Koyna Dam.

As part of the transportation effort, Germany has supplied India with 23 aircraft, 37 seagoing vessels, 5 tugboats, 2 river barges, 1,021 locomotives, 450 coaches and baggage cars, 30 railroad cars and 2,430 freight cars.[18] A similar trend is to be noted in the fact that Germany has delivered 1,380 automobiles, 1,960 trucks, 4,180 tractors and 70 special vehicles.[19] This impact on Indian transportation goes beyond the initial cost of the German vehicles since the relatively high density of German-made equipment generates requirements for replacement parts and maintenance. The business opportunities thus created are apparent:

1. Baja Tempo Limited, Bombay, has produced 3,500 three-wheel delivery trucks. The popularity of these vehicles has created a real demand for more. The German firm of Vidal und Sohn Tempo-Werk, Hamburg, has a 25 per cent interest in the Indian firm.

2. Tata Engineering and Locomotive Company, Limited, produces 12,000 trucks per year. Six thousand of the trucks are exported annually. Daimler-Benz AG, Stuttgart, has a 12 per cent interest in this company.

3. Motor Industries Company, Limited, is producing Bosch electrical parts and products. Robert Bosch of Stuttgart has a share in this company.

4. Stumpp, Schule und Sonapa and International Instruments Private, Limited, are in the automotive accessory field in the Bangalor area.

Similar capital participation projects are carried out in other industries. The business pattern presented here is the key point. Germany furnishes industrial goods, creates a demand for replacement or associated items, and becomes involved in capital-sharing ventures with a resultant involvement in profitable trade and business enterprises.[20]

17. *Twelve Years*, pp. 62–63.
18. *Ibid.*, pp. 86–87.
19. *Ibid.*, pp. 78–79.
20. For the growing stake of German industrial enterprises in India's economic progress see *Hands Across the Sea, passim.*

Other Development Efforts and German–Indian Trade

While Germany has made a start in agricultural development efforts in India, these are not nearly so spectacular as German industrial efforts. This can be explained partly by the fact that German aid to India began during the Second Five-Year Plan, which had industrial development as its goal. Behind this choice lay India's firm conviction that its poverty and most of its unenviable foreign-trade balance are traceable to its role as too much of an agricultural land. The record of Indian trade with the Federal Republic through 1962, when the Third Five-Year Plan first took effect, supports this assumption.

Table XXIV. Trade Between India and West Germany, 1960–1966 (in millions of U.S. dollars).

Year	German Imports	German Exports	Balance
1960	44.0	198.8	154.8
1961	55.5	194.3	138.8
1962	64.0	182.9	118.9
1963	63.7	181.5	117.8
1964	68.0	194.3	126.3
1965	61.0	262.4	201.4
1966	59.8	237.8	178.0

Source: Statistisches Bundesamt, *Foreign Trade,* Series 5, Volumes 1960–1966 (Wiesdaben: W. Kohlhammer Verlag).

As an Indian government publication summarizes trade with Germany: "India now mostly buys from the Federal Republic expensive machinery, equipment and technical know-how but still sells mostly primary and secondary goods which do not contain a high proportion of added value. It is very much one way traffic and India's large negative balance with this country may continue for several years."[21] A glance at the page-long enumeration of Indian exports to West Germany with its entries of "Bristles, Bones, Bauxite, Coiryarn, Cashew nuts, Coarse animal hair..." provides assurance that such a pessimistic appraisal is indeed an honest one.[22]

Still, as much as India would like to stop being a more agricultural than industrial country for the best of reasons, both Germans and Indians realize that India's most immediate worry is feeding more of her people better.[23]

21. Republic of India, Directorate of Commercial Publicity, *Federal Republic of Germany: A Report on Economic and Commercial Conditions* (New Delhi, 1963), p. 15.
22. *Ibid.,* p. 15.
23. The Germans do not conceal their disapproval of India's preference for industrial investment, especially when the latter causes the country to become the largest international debtor without solving in any way its fundamental problem—food. See Hans Roeper, "Entwicklungshilfe für Indien kritisch betrachtet," *Frankfurter Allgemeine Zeitung,* July 9, 1960; and Walter Rau, *Plädoyer für die Landwirtschaft* (Bonn: Bundes-

Perhaps there will be a shift toward agricultural aid as the Fourth Plan develops. German agricultural undertakings so far include three sewage plants, one sprinkler irrigation system, capital participation in two farm-machinery companies, three milling plants, seventeen sugar factories, seven fertilizer plants, two dairy plants, one insecticide and pesticide plant, and large numbers of tractors, cultivating machines and harvesters. Eicher Werke, of Bavaria, has invested large amounts of capital in India. After an initial 1,800 tractors had proved successful, the German producer and Indian enterprises established the Eicher Tractor Corporation (Private) Limited, producing 2,000 tractors a year for local and export markets.[24]

In addition, Germany has started a test program whereby she will supply India with 20 per cent of the fertilizer which the United Nations Food and Agriculture Organization regards as necessary.[25] (Similar programs are being placed in effect in other developing countries.)

The Federal Republic is also involved in two technical training centers in India. On August 8, 1958, Bonn agreed to supply equipment and books worth $3.8 million to the India Institute of Technology in Madras; twenty experts and four foremen were assigned to the effort. The institute is now the largest in India. At about the same time, it was agreed to establish a prototype Production-Training Center at Ohhla near New Delhi for which Germany supplied the necessary training aids, machinery and equipment, tools and spare parts. The director and the necessary German staff of instructors were provided for a period of five years; in the meantime, Indian technical instructors were trained in the Federal Republic.[26] The Germans now have a total of two training centers and four pilot institutions in the country. This, coupled with the training of Indians in Germany, again illustrates the importance Germany places on technical assistance and education.

Aid to India and its Effect on Foreign Policy

Since the late Jawaharlal Nehru first introduced the word "neutralism" into common parlance and, as spokesman for the "unaligned nations," held the respect of commentators on international affairs to an extent rare for a head of state in the developing world, India's favor has been sedulously courted by nations with pressing international problems. This chapter has pointed out that in providing aid to India, Germany ranks an absolute second in aid actually utilized by India and third in aid appropriated—but in the latter case still second among Free World nations. A trend may be de-

ministerium für wirtschaftliche Zusammenarbeit, 1965), pp. 5–9.

24. *Twelve Years*, p. 26.
25. *Ibid.*, pp. 36–39.
26. *External Assistance—1961*, pp. 43–44.

veloping to derive more aid from German private investments and possibly to increase agricultural assistance.

The examples cited demonstrate the extent and intricacies of German aid in this region where the Germans have few historical ties. With Germany's aid projects geared toward creating a demand for German goods and consequently stimulating trade, the Federal Republic intends to work toward the general worldwide socio-political goals of development aid (which Minister Scheel has been fond of referring to) and simultaneously to pursue its own national economic goals. India certainly welcomes German aid; Indian government publications used as source material indicate official interest in and an appreciation of recent West German efforts to make the terms of capital assistance more attractive,[27] as well as to stimulate private investment in India.[28] As West German business investment and trade with India continue to grow in a receptive environment, it is natural to expect that Germany will realize foreign-policy gains in dealing with the Indian government.

But limitations on West German influence in India are clearly set by India's continuing role as the leading advocate of neutralism and, more recently, by her ardent desire—springing from heightened disputes with Pakistan and Red China—not to offend the Soviet Union. And, the Soviet Union, which has its own notion of questions and answers relating to "the German problem," has also been making considerable investments in India. Can the Indian government give West Germany real international support, particularly in regard to West Germany's insistence on sole recognition? On the occasion of a visit to Moscow in the summer of 1966, Mrs. Gandhi specifically confirmed the thesis that there are indeed two German states. Bonn remains hopeful that even though the statement was made as part of the official final communiqué of the visit, it was made only under the pressure of the occasion and that India will in reality continue to accord official diplomatic recognition only to the Federal Republic. But there can be no doubt that India will have a very difficult time in giving West Germany as much support as "some sectors of public opinion" (in spite of the Ministry for Economic Cooperation's repeated cautions not to expect this in short order) feel to be West Germany's just political return on its Indian expenditures.[29]

---

27. What is known about West German development aid in government circles in New Delhi is not shared to any impressive extent by the Indian public at large, which, according to the Indian Institute of Public Opinion, does not give the Federal Republic the credit for its effort which it deserves and expects. Dietrich Witzel, "Deutsche Hilfe in Indien wenig bekannt," *Frankfurter Allgemeine Zeitung*, June 20, 1966.

28. Between January 1952 and June 1964, West German private investment in India totaled DM 82 million. Comparable figures for all of Asia and Latin America were, respectively, DM 223 million and DM 1.5 billion. *International Financial News Survey*, Vol. 16, No. 41 (Oct. 16, 1964), p. 366.

29. "Bonn's relations with Delhi upset: Mrs. Gandhi's two-state theory," *Süddeutsche Zeitung*, July 27, 1966; reprinted in *The German Tribune*, No. 227 (Aug. 6, 1966), p. 3.

CONCLUSION: CRITICS AND THE
PROGRAM'S RATIONALE

Blanket Indictment from the East

The only total condemnation of West Germany's foreign-aid program has come from Communist critics, particularly East Germans, who assert that the whole program is intended to bring developing countries into the orbit of the capitalist West and that Bonn's claim of giving aid without ideological strings is mere pretense. There is considerable truth in this Communist charge, for much of the Ministry for Economic Cooperation's rhetoric focuses on strengthening the free world by making the developing countries friendly to it. The fact is that the West German foreign-aid program has never purported to be non-ideological, if the more careful policy statements of its spokesmen are taken as the criterion. At the same time, however, when the program's advocates yield to the temptation of presenting its justification in broad humanitarian terms, the limits of their altruism are not as clearly defined as they might be. There is a certain amount of Orwellian ("all animals are equal but some animals are more equal than others") logic in many official West German utterances; they insist that Germany has no interest in exporting a Western ideology or way of life to the underdeveloped world, at the same time pointing out that countries which cooperate with the West are to be given more aid than others, and even that the whole aid program may somehow eventually win over the uncommitted nations to a Western point of view. Compare, for example, the following quotations from the same publication of the CDU/CSU Bundestag group concerned with development-aid policy:

> Economic aid for developing countries is in every case an example of intervention into the technical and economic structure within cultures of an often quite different composition. Everything should be avoided that might disturb the country's own cultural development even more. And it must be clearly understood that we attach no importance to exporting our cultural forms and way of life, but rather only to performing a service through our aid toward

124

making the existence of peoples more secure who today are suffering from sickness, malnutrition, and underemployment.[1]

And yet:

> The more quickly and effectively the industrial states of the world succeed in a common effort to secure an adequate minimum existence everywhere, the sooner these underdeveloped peoples will be ready to decide in favor of those values of human freedom and democracy familiar to us. They will then seek a partnership with the West.[2]

As part of their unqualified denunciation of West German foreign aid, Eastern sources also regularly charge that military aid is really part of the West German program, in spite of Bonn's assurances to the contrary. Once again, there is some truth in this allegation; but here, too, it is necessary to look closely at the West German position on this subject. It is easy enough to find West German policy statements to the effect that development aid should be kept separate from military aid; but the context of such statements makes it clear that what is meant is an avoidance of the American system of making economic aid dependent on the acceptance of military aid in something resembling an alliance. As long as it remains reasonably clear that military aid, let alone an alliance, is no prerequisite for capital or technical assistance, the Ministry for Economic Cooperation has no objection to a discussion of economic and military aid to the same country. Who would doubt that imparting funds and technical know-how to a country will enable it to make better arms sooner? Or that arms manufacture is part of the manufacturing-in-general which developing countries are supposed to be learning? Hence there is no reason for surprise at Eastern exposés of such times as a West German company's backing of an arms factory in Nigeria. There is undoubtedly some truth too in the assertion that training by the Federal Republic in the use of weapons *may* produce some tendency on the part of the recipient country to maintain good relations with Germany—other factors being equal, which, as Germany's experience with the Arab states indicates, is not to be counted on. But it can hardly be seriously maintained that giving arms or training will bring the recipient country to the point where it is willing to fight in a cause named by the donor. Certainly by now West Germans and their Communist critics must be equally aware of this.

What other purpose than preparation for fighting in a cause connected with German national interests could West German arms and training assistance to developing countries possibly serve? For one thing, the West German sale of arms to underdeveloped countries, even at such discounts

---

1. Christlich Demokratische Union (Diskussionskreis Entwicklungshilfe der CDU/CSU Fraktion des Deutschen Bundestages), *Die Entwicklungsländer und unsere Hilfe* (Bonn: Presse- und Informationsdienste der Christlich Demokratischen Union Deutschlands Verlagsgesellschaft, 2nd ed., 1961), p. 19.

2. *Ibid.*, p. 15. Cf. Matthias Schmitt, "Die historische Grundlage der Entwicklungspolitik," *Kieler Vorträge.* (Kiel: Institut für Weltwirtschaft, 1963), No. 27.

that the sales can be described as aid, helps dispose of outdated equipment without its being a total loss. Arms replaced by a modern army are surplus and anything salvaged in exporting them is pure gain. Communist critics would have a point if they could show that income yielded for the Federal Republic's budget was disguised from the developing countries or that the prices exacted were exorbitant. But they have not done so.[3]

Another justification for sending aid in the form of arms and training is the constant threat which tribal warfare and the ambitions of guerilla bands present to many none-too-stable governments. In such areas, national armies are advantageously used as oversized police forces; in fact, internal pacification is often their chief function. Since governmental stability in the underdeveloped countries is seen as a precondition for effective Western economic aid, it follows that the Western countries should provide military-training programs and arms to the extent that recipient countries need and can use them effectively. Inevitably, when the government of a developing state uses its forces, strengthened by Western equipment and training, against "popular-front" forces with or without foreign Communist backing, it leaves itself open to charges of acting as a puppet of reactionary, imperialist forces.

The West Germans do, of course, have to be careful about military support given to fellow NATO members Spain and Portugal which still hold their colonies. In the case of the latter, whose territory of Angola remains the scene of constant guerilla skirmishes, West Germany has taken pains to deny that German arms which rebel forces claim to have captured from colonial troops were intended for use in the colony. Here the Germans find themselves with the uncomfortable alternative, quite familiar to Americans, of having to choose between NATO allies and native groups fighting against them for their independence. It is plain that pacification attempts by colonial powers are anathema to leaders of newly-independent underdeveloped countries. For this reason, the Federal Republic not only refuses to send arms to such trouble spots as Angola and the other overseas possessions of Portugal, but also licenses the export of *all* military equipment with a view to turning down applications for export to "tension areas." But the enforcement of such regulations is a different matter. No sensible West German exporter would apply for permission to ship arms directly to a "tension area"; but shipment by way of a third country is very difficult to control.

3. In the most recent comprehensive Communist attack on the West German foreign-aid program, the East German Afro-Asian Solidarity Committee's *The Neo-colonialism of the West German Federal Republic*, a four-page chapter subsection is devoted to "Military 'Aid' as a Lucrative Business" (pp. 111–114). The thorough documentation from the West German press proves the crashingly obvious point that the Federal Republic desires to dispose of its replaced armaments through sale to countries with less technically advanced armed forces. It also indicates that the sales have received wide public discussion and fails to provide any eyebrow-raising information about excessive costs to underdeveloped countries. Originally published as: *Der Neokolonialismus in der westdeutschen Bundesrepublik* (Dresden: Verlag Zeit im Bild, 1965).

DAC Partners: The Charge of Inadequacy

Criticism of Bonn's development-aid program from sources friendly to German national interests usually proceeds from one of two starting points: (1) the general idea of the program is good, but present activities are inadequate because of the government's parsimony, bureaucratic procedures, or lack of planning; (2) the idea of the program is unrealistic and/or undesirable, so that money appropriated for it would really be better spent at home.

The charge that West Germany could do more for the underdeveloped countries than it is doing is, naturally enough, most frequently heard in the capitals of DAC partner-states. The percentage of the West German gross national product contributed to foreign aid is small when compared with that of some other Western states, notably France;[4] also, the gold and foreign-reserve accumulations of the Federal Republic seem to indicate an ability to devote more money to development aid.

Even many prominent West Germans, former Minister Scheel and present Minister Wischnewski among them, feel that West Germany could contribute somewhat more than it does—hence the exhortations to greater financial sacrifice and sharing which emanate from the Ministry for Economic Cooperation. Still, most West German officials believe that the image of a stinting Germany within the OECD or NATO framework is a gross misrepresentation; they argue that high expenditures required for certain uniquely German governmental burdens represent economic aid of a type which at least very roughly parallels development assistance. They contend that before condemning the Federal Republic for stinginess, Germany's OECD and NATO partners should consider some of the following obligations which the Federal Republic must discharge as a result of World War II: costs of equalizing the burden of individual war losses, including large sums spent for the integration of expellees and refugees into the West German economy; restitution payments to victims of Nazi persecution, of which by far the largest part is sent abroad; subsidy payments to keep the economy of West Berlin viable; and, finally, defense costs. A few expenditure subdivisions under these general headings, such as restitution payments to Jews now residing in Israel, could be seen as reasonable substitutes for development aid. On the other hand, sums such as those spent to aid East German refugees in establishing themselves in the Federal Republic go to the same cause as development aid only in the very general way that all measures to provide security and prosperity for citizens of Western coun-

4. See above Table III; Holbik, "West German Development Aid," pp. 7 and 16; Deutscher Rat der Europäischen Bewegung, "Aspekte der deutschen Entwicklungshilfe," *Bulletin*, No. 24 (Feb. 9, 1965), p. 191; United Nations, *International Flow of Long-term Capital and Official Donations 1961–1965* (New York, 1965), p. 17.

tries strengthen the position of the Free World. To equate this sort of expense with development aid is overstretching a point. Ostensibly the German figures show that if all the special expenses of the Bonn government for war-loss equalization, Berlin support, restitution, and defense were added to those for development aid, the German total would make up a larger percentage (8.4 per cent) of the gross national product than the development aid and defense expenditures proportions of England and France (each 7.7 per cent).[5] The intention, however, is probably less to convince others that the supplementary German expenditures really resemble development aid than to show that the Federal Republic has fewer funds free to commit to development assistance than its critics suppose.

Challenges from the Loyal Opposition

Before October 1966, the debate within West Germany on the efficiency of administrative departments dealing with development aid most frequently began when the Social Democratic Party, in its stance of loyal opposition, posed critical questions in the Bundestag; the governing Christian Democrats and Free Democrats felt obliged to answer in detail. Members of the SPD, a party wholly committed to the principle of development aid, concentrated their queries most often on the length of time needed to process applications for development aid, and on the conflicting authorities whose coordination and approval was required. The response of the coalition was downright diffident by German standards: Minister Scheel constantly assured his opposition that the Ministry for Economic Cooperation had as streamlined a set of channels for processing applications for assistance as a limited budget and the novelty of the situation would permit; further, he had constantly stiffened the chain of command to reduce duplications or inconsistencies in the treatment of requests.[6] In 1964, the federal cabinet reviewed his ministry's jurisdiction and confirmed its ultimate responsibilty for the program as a whole but with some important reservations: the Foreign Office should have final authority in deciding all political questions connected with development aid; both the Ministry for Economic Affairs and the Foreign Office should be consulted or asked to participate in working out principles of the program and the coordination of its projects; and the planning and execution of individual capital-aid projects should be the ultimate responsibility of the Ministry for Economic Affairs, aided and advised by other agencies as needed. These principles of juris-

5. *Ibid.* Because the United States spends more than ten times as much for defense as for development aid, its percentage relative to its gross national product for both items together is about 10.5 per cent.

6. Bundesministerium für wirtschaftliche Zusammenarbeit, "Entwicklungshilfe ist keine Giesskannen-Politik: Der Weg zum Kapitalhilfe-Kredit ist genau festgelegt," *Bulletin*, No. 50 (March 20, 1965), pp. 403–404.

diction have also been accepted by the "Grand" (CDU/CSU-SPD) coalition, and so the Ministry for Economic Cooperation retains the last word in overall policymaking while having sole responsibility from start to finish only in the field of technical assistance.[7]

Again before October 1966, another usually partisan charge alleged lack of success by the Federal Republic in gaining the allegiance of countries to which development aid has been offered. This is, of course, a familiar theme to American ears, and both German and American critics of their countries' aid programs have come to refer to Egypt as the classic case in point: How can you give a man like Nasser so much and have him denounce the very country whose aid he is receiving or ignore its vital interests? In seeking an answer to such barbed queries the CDU/CSU-FDP administrations enjoyed an advantage that recent U.S. administrations have not. In the United States, this criticism has come from hard-liners in the Cold War, rigid backers of free enterprise who look askance at any assistance to neutralist or socialist governments; they can point to the negligible good-will effects of aid to Egypt, Ghana, or even India, as proving a point—that aid to these countries "does no good." But in Germany the most vocal critics of "unsuccessful" foreign aid were necessarily the Socialists, partisan opponents of the old coalition.

Of course, the German Socialists were anything but consistent hard-liners; their opposition role led them in the early days of the Cold War to criticize positions toward the East taken by Adenauer, Erhard, and their foreign ministers. This fact took much of the force out of SPD charges that Minister Scheel was unable to ward off opposition or indifference to German national interests in parts of the underdeveloped world. In the earliest stages of Germany's foreign-aid program, the Socialists voiced no objections to it on principle; instead they warned the parties in power against using it to export militant capitalism. Their expressed fear was that the CDU/CSU-FDP coalition, strongly committed to a policy favoring free enterprise at home, might use the program for strengthening its own ideology of liberal capitalism abroad by seeking to impose it on aid recipients. Thus the SPD spoke loudest against a firm tie-in of foreign aid with commitment to an economic set of ideas. But in the international arena, when an underdeveloped country sides with the Communist bloc on a given issue, it is impossible to distinguish the degree to which it is motivated by economic feelings of anti-capitalism as opposed to political ones (resentment over past colonialism, distrust or dislike of the competing party

7. "Zuständigkeiten auf dem Gebiet der Entwicklungshilfe," unsigned article, *Bulletin*, No. 154 (Oct. 16, 1964), p. 1424; "Straffung der Zuständigkeiten für Hilfen an die Entwicklungsländer," unsigned article, *ibid.*, No. 155 (Oct. 20, 1964), p. 1435. Probably the review of responsibilities resulted from disclosures by the Federal Auditing Agency in the spring of 1964 that 231 sections in 15 of the ministries were dealing in some way with development aid. Minister Scheel rejected implied charges of conflicts of authority with reference to the fact that most of the sections in question were simply consulted on matters within their special fields. Interview: "Entwicklungshilfe—Gebot unserer Sicherheit," *Rheinischer Merkur*, No. 19 (May 8, 1965), special reprint.

system associated with the West, reaction to diplomatic slights, etc.). Thus when a foreign-aid recipient showed ingratitude–as Nasser did in publicizing an exchange of visits with Walter Ulbricht and in his espousal of a two-Germany policy in defiance of Bonn's fervent wishes—the SPD's past insistence that no grants and loans be dependent on ideology rendered its accusations that the administration has failed to keep recipients as allies rather unimpressive.

In the Grand Coalition, partisan criticism of the German foreign-aid program has virtually disappeared. When Socialist Bundestag delegate Hans-Jürgen Wischnewski succeeded Walter Scheel as minister for economic cooperation, he emphasized continuity of policy, although, of course, it had been his task in the past, (as the leading SPD expert on development aid) to introduce his party's criticism of the German foreign-aid program to the Bundestag.[8] He identified himself from the outset of his ministerial duties with the work of his predecessor: "Let me say, first of all, that since I already cooperated indirectly on the parliamentary level in making the blueprints for German development-aid policy, no basically new direction will be taken in German development-aid policy, although now in the Administration we are in the process of conducting an inventory, in order to consider what can possibly be improved."[9]

The FDP, with many fewer seats in its opposition role in the Bundestag than the SPD had formerly, will probably not make the Grand Coalition's aid program a matter of partisan dispute, particularly as one of their party members organized and headed the Ministry for Economic Cooperation for five years.

A Questioning of Motives

Finally there is the lament that the German people's hardearned money is wasted in efforts to sate the luxurious appetites of backward potentates: "Money for sheiks, Negro chiefs, and their likes; Nothing is there, 'though, for farmers and dikes."[10] The two pejorative implications in such an objection to development aid are really quite separate, however naturally they may seem to go together: (1) the Federal Republic has financial problems enough of its own, so that development aid demands uncalled-for sacrifices; (2) money spent in the program never reaches the "people" abroad.

Government spokesmen have tended to counter the first objection on an

8. See above, Chap. III.

9. Interview printed as "Positive und konstruktive deutsche Entwicklungspolitik," *Bulletin*, No. 162 (Dec. 29, 1966), pp. 1319–1320.

10. "Geld für Negerfürsten und Scheiche—nur nicht für den Bauern und seine Deiche," cited by Scheel in a radio address, Sept. 12, 1962, Bayerischer Rundfunk, in series: "Politik aus erster Hand." Press release of Bundesministerium für wirtschaftliche Zusammenarbeit, p. 2.

emotional level. Former Minister Scheel in a radio address once compared the markets of a northern German city—blocked by the tractors of farmers protesting the effects of German tariff reduction on agricultural products —with warehouses that he had seen on his Latin American trip, "filled up to the roof with children's coffins, unlovingly nailed together from rough boards, for children who must die, yes, who even today must die because the most primitive prerequisites of life are lacking for them."[11] The theme of "Shouldn't we be ashamed at being so fat, complacent and reluctant to share our prosperity?" is certainly an important one in the rationale for aid of any Western country; and probably because West German agriculture has felt itself so threatened by Common Market measures popularly associated with foreign aid, West German defenders of development assistance have felt compelled to drive this point home harder than their counterparts elsewhere. In contrast, United States foreign aid in the form of surplus agricultural exports has helped to keep domestic agricultural prices up, presumably to the satisfaction of American farmers.

In both the Federal Republic and the United States, admonitions for citizens to be reasonably generous toward the underdeveloped countries are bolstered by grim predictions of what will happen to world peace if the needy nations are not aided. But in reality, the prediction that famine and technological backwardness necessarily leads to war does not seem well founded in history. When "threat to world peace" is mentioned as arising in the underdeveloped world, it is seldom clear, who is threatening whom. Are neglected countries in their projected misery really going to start wars? The fact is that starving illiterate masses have more often been the victims of aggression than the perpetrators of it. Will they be attacked by stronger forces? If so, whose? Will the West attempt recolonization? Will the Communist bloc take them over? Or will the underdeveloping countries be tempted to maul each other because of their deprivation?

We can rest assured that the West is not going to attempt recolonization. That Communist exploitation of the poverty in the developing world and mass discontent may bring about Western intervention and an East-West clash of arms is all too possible; but this is the familiar threat of a Cold War confrontation and should be discussed as such. Those who have singled out wretched living conditions in underdeveloped countries as the threat to future world peace have been most reluctant to associate this threat with the Cold War, which—as the Viet-Nam hostilities currently make plain—is neither entirely "cold" nor demonstrably ending. In short, it is very difficult to pin down exactly how the threat to world peace is visualized by those who profess to see it most clearly emerging in neglected parts of the world and what concrete questions should be asked about it. Actually, the idea that underdeveloped nations may themselves turn into aggressors seems to fit in best with the underlying assumptions and reason-

11. *Ibid.*

ing here, historical precedent largely to the contrary: after all, there *is* the unique phenomenon of Red China, which daily threatens war in the face of mass malnutrition at home. That China does not stand to improve its standard of living by resorting to war is beside the point.

The tenuousness of arguments equating poor material and educational conditions with threats of war does not seem to undermine their force anywhere in the West, least of all, apparently, in Germany. Such reasoning is behind the West German government's 1966 decision (astounding and infuriating to the American government facing China not too indirectly in Viet-Nam) to support the construction of a steel mill in Red China, although the business firms whose credits (and, in effect, profits) were thus guaranteed probably needed no such abstract justification. This would seem to be the acid test: Will steel mills and other technological advances really help in reducing the misery of the Chinese masses in a way that will lessen the aggressiveness of Chinese Communist leadership? Quite possibly we shall see.

The phenomenon of underdeveloped Arab states threatening moderately well developed Israel may also be cited as an example of a menace arising from the desperate pressures of Arab economic deprivation. But is there any evidence that providing the means for Egypt, Syria, and Jordan to become developed countries would remove their reason for desiring to destroy Israel? It is just possible that an economically well developed Arab world, possessing a credible military potential, might be *more* of a threat to peace in the Near East than the present underdeveloped one. This is no argument against continuing to aid the Arab world, which DAC countries must do and hope for the best. But the case for economic deprivation as necessarily causing war and the conquest of economic deprivation as necessarily bringing peace appears as thinly supported after the Arab-Israeli war of 1967 as it did before.

The second implication in the alienated attitude toward foreign aid described above—that the funds for development aid really go to satisfy the excessive demands of a few and ignore the neediest strata of the populations of recipient countries—must be handled with great tact by the Ministry for Economic Cooperation; a few real scandals arising from this type of abuse would probably be enough to turn away the public opinion on which the Federal Republic depends for support of its aid program. Popular impressions that wily leaders from the underdeveloped world are exploiting West Germany's generosity with cynicism and animal cunning are evidently widespread enough to cause the ministry concern: "Twenty-five times during 1965, statesmen from developing countries drove up with an escort to the Ministry for Economic Cooperation in a black Mercedes with a flashing blue light. Now it is said that there are people who believe the following: A statesman from a developing country comes to Bonn for a visit—he picks up a check for development aid. He proposes a visit to

Berlin—the sum in the check rises. He offers to visit the Wall and to state publicly his positive attitude toward German reunification—the check reaches the desired height."[12]

In answer, the ministry has been able to do little more than assure German taxpayers that the government is not easily swayed to grant public money on spur-of-the-moment impulses and that it is cultivating a more realistic image of the Federal Republic in the minds of people in the developing world: "I have made an attempt in these countries visited on a trip to Latin America to reduce, not to say destroy, an image that—whatever the reasons for it may be—had become fixed there, namely, the image of a rich uncle who has endless treasures, which he keeps sitting on just out of meanness without pulling them out right away. Going into this in detail during discussions with all my conversation partners, I attempted to change this image and, I believe, with a certain success."[13]

Minister Wischnewski, a bit more inclined to call a spade a spade than his diplomatic predecessor, has dealt rather sharply with what he felt to be unjustified complaints about the ministry's allegedly excessive generosity. For example, answering complaints in an open letter which documented the businesslike nature of German capital assistance, he accused the protesting taxpayers' group of indulgence in irresponsible polemics and wrote: "Even just a superficial study of information and sources accessible to every citizen would have had to lead to different conclusions than those reflected in the study-report of the League of Taxpayers."[14] Objective criticism of specific mistakes remains, of course, necessary to the improvement of the program. But citizens' emotional alienation from the program is something else again; and the fact that it need not spring from identifiable scandals but can germinate as the result of an abundance of fragmentary glimpses and rumors makes it all the more difficult to counteract.

Trade and Aid

More evident progress of West German trade with (and especially exports to) the emerging nations would doubtless fortify Bonn's arguments in favor of development-aid expansion. However, in terms of both German and international statistics, trade with the developing countries has become

12. Minister Walter Scheel, "Ein Gebot der Fairness," *Bulletin*, No. 7 (Jan. 15, 1966), p. 50.

13. Minister Scheel, "Bewährte Partnerschaft im neuen Stil," press release, Bad Godesberg, Sept. 10, 1962, p. 4.

14. "Offener Brief an den Präsidenten des Bundes der Steuerzahler," *Bulletin*, No. 33 (April 4, 1967), p. 275.

a decreasing proportion of both aggregate West German trade and total world trade.[15]

Given the "third world's" urgent need for development assistance, German authorities have concluded that only a trade and aid policy vis-à-vis Africa, Asia, and Latin America is available to them.[16] The official German view recognizes that development aid constitutes basic investment in the country's future customers and markets. Its continuation and eventual expansion has, moreover, become imperative in the face of both growing international competition among the Western industrialized nations and a worldwide trend toward higher incomes. Thus the Federal Republic's development-aid policy has to be geared to the country's export interests, which Bonn believes will be served well through long-term trade agreements.[17]

Considering the developing countries' substantial purchases of German manufactured goods—which belong not only to the Federal Republic's most valuable exportables but are also indispensable in industrialization —a West German policy of trade liberalization and encouragement can hardly fail to succeed. In fact, such a policy is bound to stimulate German internal economic prosperity, whatever the multiplier (unknown as it is) of the expenditures in question. By definition, all export economies thrive on exports. Table XXV illustrates the magnitude of the strategic investment goods purchased by the developing countries in West Germany in 1964.

Table XXV. Selected West German Manufactures Purchased by Developing Countries (in millions of DM).

	Asia	Africa	Latin America
Machinery	1,490	718	723
Vehicles	589	647	354
Electrical products	512	273	264
Chemical semi-manufactures	444	135	371
Chemical products	368	—	318
Tools	—	200	—

Source: *Ihre Zukunft—Unsere Zukunft* (Bonn: Druck- und Verlagshaus Heinz Möller, 1965), p. 23.

15. Cf. Table X, Chap. II above. Between 1950 and 1964, West German exports to developing nations dropped from 30.7 per cent to 27.5 per cent of total exports; imports dropped from 26.5 per cent to 21.9 per cent, although during the fifteen years total exports trebled and total imports doubled.

16. In 1966, West German trade with the four groups of developing countries amounted to the following quantities in billions of DM: Europe: imports 2.1, exports 4.1; Africa, 4.9, 2.2; Asia: 4.5, 5.0; Latin America: 4.7, 3.8. *Monthly Report of the Deutsche Bundesbank*, July 1967, p. 125. Cf. "Die deutsche Entwicklungshilfe," *Neue Zürcher Zeitung*, Sept. 10, 1966.

17. Walter Scheel, *Neue Wege deutscher Entwicklungspolitik*, (Bonn: Bundesdruckerei, 1966), pp. 11–13; Dieter Vogel, "Neue Strategie für die Entwicklungshilfe," *Frankfurter Allgemeine Zeitung*, June 21, 1966.

It is necessary to stress that many of these materials have been not only aid-financed, but that most of them have been acquired by foreign companies capitalized entirely or to a significant degree by West German industrial giants.[18] That many local banks in the underdeveloped world controlled by large German banks (in Frankfurt and Hamburg) are directly involved in financing imports from and exports to the Federal Republic is well known.[19]

Before Bonn institutes an "aid helps trade" policy as an integral part of its present development effort—if it indeed does decide to do so—encouragement of German *imports* from the emerging nations will continue to rest on West German domestic economic prosperity; balance-of-payments surpluses; tariff concessions (especially those to which West Germany is committed by virtue of its membership in the European Economic Community); private investment; and the relatively new government-sponsored exhibitions of imported products—*Import-Ausstellungen* "Partner des Fortschritts."[20]

While not all West German economists endorse the principle that infrastructural aid (transfer of capital) is the prerequisite for the development of economically backward countries, most of them do adhere to this view.[21] The preceding chapters abound with examples of West German determination to help the developing areas overcome their absolute economic (and trade) disadvantages and secure comparative advantages as a basis for sustained economic growth. There is no doubt on the West German side that trade and aid not only interact but also supplement each other. Nor does the Federal Republic question that the fundamental premise of international cooperation is to promote the realization of gains from trade via reallocation of resources, production expansion, increased efficiency, and rising propensities to export as well as import.

Practical Economics or Idealism?

A problem facing both German and American spokesmen for foreign-aid programs is that no ready answer of a few words can be given to the question "Why have the whole program in the first place?" A recent and thorough analysis of the American rationale for offering foreign aid over the last eighteen years has identified the political motive as consistently dominant; the American Congress has responded to different aspects of

18. For an impressive list of these, consult *Märkte von Morgen, Eine Bilanz der deutschen Entwicklungshilfe* (Bonn: Druck- und Verlagshaus Heinz Möller, 1964), *passim*.

19. *Hands Across the Sea*, pp. 86–87.

20. "Westdeutschland als Partner im Welthandel," *Neue Zürcher Zeitung*, March 24, 1965.

21. Cf. Clodwig Kapferer, "Handelshilfe an Entwicklungsländer durch Förderung ihrer absatzwirtschaftlichen Aktivität," *Wirtschaftsdienst*, Vol. 45, No. 7 (July, 1965), pp. 362–366.

the Communist challenge, from the threat of outright aggression or of the overthrow of a non-Communist government in Turkey and Greece to the much more subtle program of gaining the confidence of peoples in the underdeveloped countries, with greater speed than it has responded to anything else that might justify foreign aid. The author notes: "In view of the acknowledged material motives associated with aid, any claim of self-righteous altruism is certain to invite suspicion of hypocrisy. When, inevitably, the point is raised that eliminating poverty prevents Communism, altruism is unmasked as a political proposition.... Cloaking a political program with an aura of moral responsibility and national 'mission' introduces confusion into the rationale for aid."[22]

All this is certainly true and if recorded debates are any evidence, the political motive is uppermost in the minds of Bundestag members as well as U.S. congressmen. But—and this is due not only to West German desires to avoid a strident militancy in foreign-policy pronouncements—no truthful German advocate of foreign aid can attempt to separate the political motive entirely from that of humanitarianism or mission. Most West Germans, like most Americans, *do* honestly believe that assisting the people of underdeveloped areas to the point that they can utilize Western modes of production and may adopt as much from Western politico-economic systems as they would knowingly choose will be *good* for these Asians, Africans, and Latin Americans. However much disdain economists and political scientists may have for such naive phrasing it is a strong motivation for most citizens. To the precise extent that aid officials believe this and act accordingly, they are indeed altruistic in their rationale for supporting development aid programs.

Today no one has any doubts about why the English or French are granting development aid to their former colonies: to make sure that no opportunity is missed for encouraging the peoples there to develop a way of life in which Western notions of political and economic freedom, as associated in the French or English mind with the culture of France or England, will be respected. There is no reason for Germans or Americans to feel the least embarrassment in doing the same thing, as long as they sincerely feel their aid programs to be both in their own political interest and in the political and economic interest of recipient countries.

For the sake of clarity and forthrightness, Germans and Americans explaining the reasons for the aid programs of their governments might well observe two rules. First, the political motive—namely that of helping the developing countries toward an acceptance of economic and political systems which retain a large portion of free choice for the individual—should be acknowledged without apology as foremost. Secondly, humanitarian justifications should be presented together with or after the evident politi-

22. Herbert H. Aull, "Rationale for Aid," *Naval War College Review*, Vol. XVII, No. 9 (May/June 1965), pp. 35–96.

cal rationale. The point is *not* to pronounce grandly against disease, poverty, and ignorance abroad as if these were the sole enemies under attack only to trail off later into voicing the expectation that raising living standards in the underdeveloped world will thwart Communism, i.e., aid Western political interests there, as if this latter goal were secondary; everyone reasonably familiar with the development of Western foreign aid from the Marshall Plan through the OECD's latest efforts knows this is simply not true.

It should also be made plain that the two Western governments concerned seek to exert a minimum of pressure—there is no purpose in claiming to be able to operate with the impossible "no pressure" here—on the leadership of the emerging states of Africa, Asia, and Latin America; they must recognize the right of countries which have received aid to reject, if they choose, any degree of economic and political freedom. Nonetheless, the unconcealed desire of the Federal Republic and the United States should be to facilitate a broad, popular acceptance of both of these. Any hesitation about governmental intentions cannot help but evoke doubts concerning the donor nation's own certainty of purpose and probably suspicions that its leadership's guilty conscience has something to hide. Why should Western nations be so stumblingly reluctant to admit frankly the primarily political nature of their goals in the underdeveloped world, while the Communists, whose plans for these regions are a matter of their own public record, can claim credit for forthrightness?

As for the association of foreign aid with world peace, there is no imminent threat to international peace in the world of the 1960's from the underdeveloped regions, except the threat that Cold War tensions in these lands will turn into shooting wars as in Viet-Nam or Korea. Palace revolutions and tribal or factional power struggles in the developing countries doubtless bring bloodshed and misery to thousands there; however, to the extent that these arise from misery caused by economic backwardness they are not serious threats to international peace unless fired by Cold War antagonisms. To the extent that they are politically motivated, as in the case of the Yemen Civil War (with or without Egyptian intervention), an increase in economic resources available to the contenders can be expected to sharpen the conflict rather than to help end it.

But, if this is so, doesn't a Western presence in the underdeveloped world fan the very flames of Cold War tensions which threaten world peace? Yes, and necessarily so, assuming that the West can be blamed for responding to its fear of Eastern power in these regions. Either the essentials of Western politico-economic systems are worth promoting in the underdeveloped world—in which case a tension-heightening confrontation with some part of the Communist world is inevitable—or they are not—in which case the whole business of developing Asia, Africa, and Latin America would logically be best left to the East, which knows not only what it is doing there but also how much the risks are worth to it. Thinking in these terms does not imply the widely feared "rigidity" or "inflexibility" in East–West encounters in the underdeveloped world; it does not indicate a refusal to compete constructively with Communist countries in dealing with the developing states. There may be nothing wrong sometimes with settling for considerably less than a victory of free enterprise and representative government in countries receiving aid. Indeed, since freedom of choice, national as well as individual, is such an integral part of the ideology that the West is backing, Western countries may well have to rest content with many an anti-Western decision by leaders of developing nations, particularly in the immediate future. But, again, there is no reason to try to hide the fact that the West thinks of itself as competing for reasons of political commitment which would motivate its foreign-aid steps even if no other reason existed.

When forthrightly stated, there is nothing inconsistent or hypocritical about the real U.S. and German rationale for foreign aid. It can be made to sound as practical and as mutually beneficial as its most enthusiastic backers feel it to be. Frequently journalists and political scientists present foreign-policy steps in terms of two alternatives: "realistic" pursuit of the national interest or "idealistic" contributions to international interests, as if one had to be neglected to advance the other. When this pair of alternatives is applied to economic aid for developing countries, any conceivable program is destined to failure as a matter of course. Should aid sacrifice the interests of the donor country more than it advances them, the donor country could scarcely be expected to continue its loans and grants. On the other hand, should aid sacrifice the recipient country's interest, it could then certainly not be considered aid at all. A choice between the two, then, leaves nothing of aid as a foreign-policy measure.

Regardless of the corner they come from, the thoroughly destructive criticisms of the West German aid program presuppose that such a self-defeating choice is necessary. Communist criticisms boil down to an assertion that recipient countries are necessarily impeded by capitalist-inspired aid measures in achieving the social and economic goals that collectivism would give them more quickly and painlessly. In the eyes of the East, then, Western "aid" is not really aid, but only a self-serving device operating in the particular donor nation's interest.[23] From an entirely different direction, the moans of those who condemn the program as a waste of taxpayers'

23. Nothing has changed the basic Communist view that private investment is rank exploitation if it returns a profit—which is, after all, what it is intended to do. Consequently the U.S. and West Germany cannot expect any Eastern recognition that their aid programs, which give high priority to encouraging investment in developing countries, are helpful to recipients. "Exposing" the fact that U.S. investments in developing countries between 1946 and 1959 had returned their intended profits, Nikita Khrushchev asked in rhetorical indignation: "If this is called 'help,' then what is called 'robbery'?" O national'no-osvoboditel'nom dvizhenii (Moskva: Isdatel'stvo literatury na inostrannykh yazykakh, 1963), p. 25.

money (that would have been much better spent for domestic needs) imply that the best-conceived German foreign-aid plan must serve only the recipient nations to the detriment of the donor's interest.

When, on the other hand, domestic critics focus on alleged frivolous appeasement by the Federal Republic of unenlightened despots in jungles and deserts or on allegations that the West German government fails to reach the people of Asia and Africa with its program of assistance, their plaint becomes essentially one against mismanagement and abuses. Even at their emotional and unconstructive worst, such criticisms do not presuppose any built-in conflict between donor and recipient nations. To allege that the Adenauer, Erhard, or Kiesinger administration has failed to make good on the Federal Republic's pledge to use development aid for enabling the peoples abroad to help themselves is no condemnation of the goal of doing so. The same is true of partisan opposition to the program with its emphasis on bureaucratic delays and duplications or its exposures of the Foreign Office's inability (on occasion) to distinguish between potential friends and implacably hostile forces abroad. In such criticism as this the assumption remains that a better-thought-out program could indeed bring the interests of donor and recipient into harmony. Such criticism may be vague (how would the loyal critics have used the Foreign Office, the Ministry for Economic Cooperation, or any possible combination of governmental organs to "do something" about Germany's unhappy position in the middle of the Arab-Israeli dispute?) but its starting point, the need to seek out improvements in the program, is positive.

It is this type of criticism, affirming the program in the broad outline of its goals, which has carried most weight in West Germany's public discussion of its assistance plans and their implementation. The success of the program will partly depend on the Grand Coalition's ability to sustain enough objective self-criticism to offset the lack of a strong parliamentary opposition. In 1967, while expressing general satisfaction with previous capital-aid projects, it undertook an assessment of all technical-aid projects for the purpose of simplifying the projects, shortening the length of time between their approval and their execution, and weeding out "non-optimal" ones.[24] In the long run, the success of West German foreign aid, like that of the United States, depends on the private sector's response to inducements for much larger investments in underdeveloped countries than have been forthcoming in the past ten years.

24. Minister Hans-Jürgen Wischnewski, Address to the Ausschuss für Entwicklungsländer der Friedrich-Ebert-Stiftung, Bonn, May 30, 1967; text in Bulletin, No. 58 (June 2, 1967), p. 495.

BIBLIOGRAPHY

Sources Treating Foreign Aid without Special Focus on the West German Program

Albert, Klaus. "Rohstoffe, aber kein Kapital—Arbeitsplatzbeschaffung Hauptsorge der unterentwickelten Gebiete," *Europa-Union*, 1956, No. 12.

Alexander, Yonah. *International Technical Assistance Experts.* New York: Praeger, 1966.

Asher, Robert E., *Multilateral Versus Bilateral Aid: An Old Controversy Revisited.* Washington, D.C.: The Brookings Institution, 1963.

_____. *How to Succeed in Foreign Aid Without Really Trying.* Washington, D.C.: The Brookings Institution, 1964.

Aull, Captain Herbert H., U.S. Navy. "Rationale for Aid," *Naval War College Review,* Vol. XVII, No. 9 (May/June 1965), pp. 35–96.

Benham, Frederic C. *Economic Aid to Underdeveloped Countries.* New York: Oxford University Press, 1966.

Bergmann, Jürgen. "Die assoziierten afrikanischen Gebiete in der europäischen Wirtschaftsgemeinschaft unter Berücksichtigung ihrer Entwicklungsproblematik." Unpublished dissertation, Köln, 1958.

Besters, Hans and Ernst E. Boesch (eds.). *Entwicklungspolitik: Handbuch und Lexikon.* Stuttgart: Kreuz-Verlag, 1966.

Birmingham, Walter, and A. G. Ford, (eds.). *Planning and Growth in Rich and Poor Countries.* New York: Praeger, 1965.

Black, Eugene R. *The Diplomacy of Economic Development.* New York: Athenaeum, 1963.

_____. "The New Industrial Revolution," *The Virginia Quarterly Review,* Vol. XXXV, No. 3 (Summer 1959).

Bulletin des Presse- und Informationsamtes der Bundesregierung. "Aufgaben und Ziele der OECD; mächtiger und weltoffener wirtschaftlicher Zusammenschluß," No. 139 (September 11, 1964), pp. 1,297–1,298.

_____. "Bildungshilfe muß der Entwicklungshilfe vorangehen: zum Besuch des Generaldirektors der UNESCO [René Maheu] in der Bundesrepublik," No. 138 (September 9, 1964), p. 1,288.

_____. "Forschungsarbeiten zu Problemen der Entwicklungsländer: Wissenschaftliche Schriftenreihe des Bundesministeriums für wirtschaftliche Zusammenarbeit," No. 47 (April 6, 1966), pp. 370–371.

_____. "Neue GATT-Bestimmungen," No. 24 (February 9, 1965), p. 192.

Castle, Eugene W. *The Great Giveaway: the Realities of Foreign Aid.* Chicago: Henry Regnery, 1957.

Cerami, Charles A. *Alliance Born of Danger: America, the Common Market, and the Atlantic Partnership.* New York: Harcourt, Brace & World, Inc., 1963.

Currie, Lauchlin. *Accelerating Development: The Necessity and the Means.* New York: McGraw-Hill, 1966.

Davidson, Basil. "Africa: the Face behind the Mask," *Horizon*, Vol. V, No. 3 (March 1963), pp. 38–59.

Dittmar, Manfred. *Inflation in Entwicklungsländern als strukturbedingtes Problem.* Berlin: Duncker & Humblot, 1966.

Edding, Friedrich. *Die wirtschaftliche Eingliederung der Vertriebenen und Flüchtlinge in Schleswig-Holstein.* Berlin: Duncker & Humblot, 1955.

Freund, Andreas. "Flow of Funds to Poorer Lands is Termed Inadequate to Need," *New York Times* (January 15, 1965), p. C47:7.

Friedman, Irving S. *International Problems of Economic Development.* Address to the Canadian Political Science Association, Ottawa, Canada, June 7, 1967.

Friedmann, Wolfgang G., W. G. Kalmanoff, and R. F. Meagher. *International Financial Aid.* New York: Columbia University Press, 1966.

Goldwin, Robert A. (ed.). *Why Foreign Aid?* Chicago: Rand McNally & Co., 1963.

Hankel, Wilhelm. "How Does German Capital Assistance Work?" *Germany*, Vol. VIII (1963), pp. 18–21.

Hesse, Kurt. *Wirtschaftliche Entwicklungstendenzen in West-, Mittel- und Ostafrika, sowie in Äthiopien.* Bad Homburg: Auslandskunde-Archiv, 1960.

Hirschman, Albert O. *The Principle of the Hiding Hand.* Washington: The Brookings Institution, 1967.

Holbik, Karel. "An Evaluation of Major Foreign Aid Programs," *Rivista Internazionale di Scienze Economiche e Commerciali,* Vol. 13 (1966), No. 6, pp. 539–566.

Hunold, A. (ed.). *Entwicklungsländer: Wahn und Wirklichkeit.* (In series *Sozialwissenschaftliche Studien,* Vol. VIII.) Erlenbach-Zürich: E. Rentsch, 1961.

Jensen, Oliver, "Who's Underdeveloped?" *Horizon*, Vol. V, No. 3 (January 1963), pp. 116–117.

Kaplan, Jacob J. *The Challenge of Foreign Aid.* New York: Frederick A. Praeger, 1967.

Kirdar, Üner. *The Structure of United Nations Economic Aid to Underdeveloped Countries.* The Hague: Martinus Nijhoff, 1966.

Kristensen, Thorkil. *Die wirtschaftlichen Beziehungen zwischen dem Westen und den Entwicklungsländern.* (Kieler Studien, new series, No. 22.) Kiel: Institut für Weltwirtschaft, Univ. Kiel, 1962.

Little, Ian M. D. *Aid to Africa: an Appraisal of U.K. Policy for Aid to Africa South of the Sahara.* Oxford: Pergamon Press, 1964.

_____ and Clifford, J.M. *International Aid—A Discussion of the Flow of Public Resources from Rich to Poor Countries.* London: Allen and Unwin, 1965.

Lovell, A. H. "How Should Overseas Aid be Given?" *Lloyds Bank Review* (April 1966), pp. 19–32.

Lugard, Sir Frederick. *The Dual Mandate in British Tropical Africa.* Edinburgh: William Blackwood, 1922.

Mason, Edward S. *Foreign Aid and Foreign Policy.* New York: Harper & Row, 1964.

Meier, Gerald M. and Robert E. Baldwin. *Economic Development.* New York: John Wiley and Sons, 1957.

Meimberg, R. "Jenseits der Entwicklungshilfe," *Frankfurter Allgemeine Zeitung* (January 23, 1965).

Mikesell, Raymond F., *Public International Lending for Development.* New York: Random House, 1966.

Millikan, Max F. (ed.). *Income Stabilization for a Developing Democracy: a Study of the Politics of High Employment without Inflation.* New Haven: Yale University Press, 1953.

_____ and W. W. Rostow, with P. N. Rosenstein-Rodan. *A Proposal: Key to an Effective Foreign Policy.* New York: Harper, 1957.

Montgomery, John D. *The Politics of Foreign Aid.* New York: Praeger, 1962.

Myrdal, Gunnar. *Economic Theory and Underdeveloped Regions.* London: G. Duckworth, 1957.

Neue Zürcher Zeitung. "Entwicklungshilfe als Daueraufgabe," (July 27, 1967).

_____. "Die Kapitalbewegungen nach den Entwicklungsländern," (June 18, 1966).

Nossiter, Bernard. "While the Rich get Richer," *International Herald Tribune* (July 22–23, 1967).

Papi, G. U. "A Theory of Economic Development," *Weltwirtschaftliches Archiv,* Vol. LXXXV (1960), pp. 90–111.

Parker, William N., W. Paul Strassmann, E. A. Wilkening, and Robert S. Merril. *The Diffusion of Technical Knowledge as an Instrument of Economic Development.* Washington: National Institute of Social and Behavioral Science, 1962.

Paulsen, Andreas. "Real Capital and Human Capital in Economic Development," *The German Economic Review,* Vol. IV (1966), No. 4.

Pincus, John A. *Economic Aid and International Cost Sharing.* Baltimore: Johns Hopkins Press, 1965.

_____. *Trade, Aid, and Development.* New York: McGraw-Hill Book Co., 1967.

Rao, V. K. R. V., and Dharm Narain. *Foreign Aid and Economic Development.* New York: Asia Publishing House, 1963.

Robinson, Joan. *Economic Philosophy.* Chicago: Aldine Publishing Co., 1962.

Robinson, Ronald. *Industrialization in Developing Countries: Impressions and Papers of the Cambridge Conference on the Role of Industrialization in Development.* (6–19 September, 1964 at King's College, Cambridge). Cambridge: Overseas Study Committee, 1965.

Root, Waverly, "French will not Attend Common Market Parley," *Washington Post* (July 2, 1965), p. 1.

_____. "Paris Quits Technical EEC Talks; Steps Up Campaign to Leave Market or Intimidate It," *Washington Post* (July 6, 1965), p. 1.

Rubin, Seymour J. *The Conscience of the Rich Nations.* New York: Harper & Row, 1966.

Runge, Christian. "The European Development Fund," *Germany,* Vol. IX (1964), No. 38, pp. 18–19.

Sachs, Hans Georg (interview). "GATT Milestone for New Countries," *German International,* Vol. IX, No. 4 (April 1965), pp. 22–24.

_____. "The United Nations Conference on Trade and Development," *Germany,* Vol. IX (1964), No. 38, pp. 11–12.

Schmidt, Wilson E. "The Economics of Charity: Loans versus Grants," *Journal of Political Economy,* Vol. LXXII, No. 4, (August 1964).

Schmitt, Matthias. *Entwicklungshilfe als unternehmerische Aufgabe.* Frankfurt am Main: Fritz Knapp Verlag, 1965.

_____. *Partnerschaft mit Entwicklungsländern.* Stuttgart-Degerloch: Seewald, 1960.

Shchetinin, Valentin Dmitrievich. *Ekonomicheskie soyuzy razvivayushchikhsya stran.* Moskva: Izd-vo In-ta mezhdunarodnykh otnosheniy, 1963.

Stanovnik, Janez. *World Economic Blocs: the Nonaligned Countries and Economic Integration.* Beograd: Edition Jugoslavija, 1962.

Studiengesellschaft für wirtschaftliche Entwicklung. *Entwicklungshilfe innerhalb des Ostblocks.* Frankfurt: A. Metzner, 1960.

Subramanian, Shankerier. *Die Wirtschaftsentwicklung Indiens, 1951–1961. Kieler Studien,* (new series), No. 69 (1965). Kiel: Institut für Weltwirtschaft, Univ. Kiel, 1962.

Zimmermann, L. J. *Poor Lands, Rich Lands; The Widening Gap.* New York: Random House, 1965.

Official Sources on Foreign Aid

Afro-Asian Solidarity Committee in the German Democratic Republic. *The Neo-colonialism of the West German Federal Republic.* Dresden: Verlag Zeit im Bild, 1965.

Communist Party of the Soviet Union. *Programme of the Communist Party of the Soviet Union,* adopted October 31, 1961. Moscow: Foreign Languages Publishing House, 1961, esp. pp. 44–45.

Eshkol, Levi, Premier of Israel. Correspondence with German Chancellor Erhard on Israeli reaction to German technicians' work in Egypt and relation of German development aid to Arab-Israeli conflict. In *News from the German Embassy,* Vol. IX, No. 8 (May 18, 1965), pp. 1–3.

European Community Information Service. *The Facts.* Brussels, 1962.

European Economic Community, Statistical Office of the European Communities. *Basic Statistics of the Community,* 1966.

Frei, Eduardo, President of Chile. Speech in Augustusburg Castle, July 19, 1965, printed together with that of German President Lübke as "Herzliche Freundschaft mit Chile," *Bulletin des Presse- und Informationsamtes der Bundesregierung,* No. 124 (July 21, 1965), pp. 1,001–1,003.

_____. Speech in Berlin, July 20, 1965, printed together with that of Mayor Willy Brandt as "Zur Verständigung der Völker," *Bulletin des Presse- und Informationsamtes der Bundesregierung,* No. 125 (July 22, 1965), pp. 1,009–1,010.

_____. Speech before representatives of German industry and finance, July 21, 1965, printed as "Ein Land aufstrebender Zukunft," *Bulletin des Presse- und Informationsamtes der Bundesregierung,* No. 126 (July 23, 1965), pp. 1,018, 1,020–1,021.

German Democratic Republic, Ministry for Foreign Affairs. "Erklärung über den Neokolonialismus in Westdeutschland," *Dokumentation der Zeit,* 1957, No. 141, cols. 27–30.

India, Republic of, Directorate of Commercial Publicity. *Federal Republic of Germany: A Report on Economic and Commercial Conditions.* New Delhi, 1963.

India, Republic of, Ministry of Finance. *External Assistance—1961.* New Delhi: Department of Public Affairs, 1961.

International Bank for Reconstruction and Development. "Consortium Communiqué on Aid to India," press release, April 21, 1965.

International Monetary Fund. *International Financial Statistics,* September, 1967.

Johnson, President Lyndon B. "Address to Congress" (1965 State of the Union Message). Text in *New York Times* (January 15, 1965), p. C12:1.

Kennedy, President John F. "Reciprocal Trade Agreements Program . . .," *Congressional Record—House,* January 25, 1962, p. 953.

_____. Speech at founding of German Development Service in the Villa Hammerschmidt, June 24, 1963; German text, "Ich gratuliere dem deutschen Volk," *Bulletin des Presse- und Informationsdienstes der Bundesregierung,* No. 108 (June 25, 1963), p. 963.

_____. "Fulfilling the Pledges of the Alliance for Progress," White House press release, March 13, 1962, *Department of State Bulletin* (April 2, 1962), pp. 539–544.

Khrushchev, Nikita. *O national'no-osvoboditel'nom dvizhenii.* Moskva: Isdatel'stvo literatury na inostrannykh yazykakh, 1963.

_____. "Report of the Central Committee of the CPSU to the 22nd Congress of the Communist Party of the Soviet Union," *Documents of the 22nd Congress of the CPSU.* New York: Crosscurrents Press, 1961, Vol. I.

Organization for European Economic Cooperation. *Economic Development of Overseas Countries and Territories Associated with OEEC Member Countries.* Paris: OEEC, August 1958.

Organization for European Economic Cooperation, "Report of the Preparatory Committee of the Committee of the Conference on the Reorganization of the O.E.E.C." Reprinted by the U.S. Senate Committee on Foreign Relations as No. 2 in *Background Documents to the Organization for Economic Cooperation and Development.* Washington, 1961.

Organization for Economic Cooperation and Development, *Development Assistance, Efforts and Policies, 1966 Review.* Paris: OECD, 1966.

_____. *The Flow of Financial Resources to Developing Countries in 1961.* Paris: 1962.

_____. "Die Lage der Eisen-und Stahlindustrie 1963: Unterschiedliche Entwicklung in den OECD Ländern," *Bulletin des Presse- und Informationsamtes der Bundesregierung,* No. 35 (February 25, 1965), p. 278.

_____. *OECD Scientific Research and Education for the Future.* Paris: OECD, 1961.

_____. "Tenth Meeting of the Development Assistance Committee of O.E.C.D., Paris, July 25–26, 1962: Communiqué and Resolution," *Department of State Bulletin,* September 10, 1962, pp. 395–397.

_____. "What is Happening to Development Assistance?" press release, Paris, October 11, 1966.

Thorp, Willard L. Chairman of the Development Assistance Committee of the OECD. *Development Assistance Efforts and Policies of the Members of the Development Assistance Committee.* Paris: OECD, 1964.

_____. "Introductory Statement," Meeting of the D.A.C., press release, July 19–20, 1967.

Truman, President Harry S. "Address of the President of the United States—Greece, Turkey and the Middle East," *Congressional Record—House,* March 12, 1947, pp. 1,980–1,981.

United Nations, Economic Commission for Europe. *Implications for Trade and Development of Developing Countries of Economic Groupings of Developed Countries and/or Preferential Trading Agreements.* New York, 1964.

_____. *International Flow of Long-term Capital and Official Donations 1961–1965.* New York, 1966.

United States Aid Mission to India. *The United States Contribution to Indian Development.* New Delhi: Program Office, 1962.

United States Congress, Senate, Committee on Foreign Relations. *Foreign Assistance Act of 1962, Hearings.* Washington: U.S. Government Printing Office, 1962.

_____. *Foreign Assistance Act of 1964, Hearings.* Washington: U.S. Government Printing Office, 1964.

_____. *Nominations of Christian A. Herter, William T. Gossett, and David E. Bell, Hearings.* Washington: U.S. Government Printing Office, 1963.

_____. *Organization for Economic Cooperation and Development,* in three parts: (1) *Background Documents Relating to,* (2) *Hearings,* and (3) *Report.* Washington, 1961.

United States Department of State. *The Communist Economic Threat* (Department of State Publication 6,777). Washington, March 1959.

_____. *Communist Policy in the Less Developed Areas* (Department of State Publication 7,020). Washington, July 1960.

_____. "Resolution on the First Annual Aid Review and the Future Work of the Development Assistance Committee," *Department of State Bulletin,* September 10, 1962, p. 396.

_____. *The Sino-Soviet Economic Offensive in the Less Developed Countries* (Department of State Publication 6,632). Washington, May 1958.

U Thant, "The Decade of Development," *U.N. Review,* Vol. IX (June 1962).

Official Sources on West German Foreign Aid

Auswärtiges Amt, "Kapitalhilfe für Guinea," *Bulletin des Presse- und Informationsamtes der Bundesregierung,* No. 98 (June 9, 1965), p. 792.

Billerbeck, Klaus, Policy Coordinator in the Ministry for Economic Cooperation. *Instrumente der deutschen Entwicklungspolitik und der Beitrag deutscher Ingenieurfirmen,* press release. Bonn, March 21, 1963.

Blank, Theodor, Minister for Labor and Social Affairs. "Eine Bilanz, die sich sehen lassen kann: Die Sozialleistungen sind noch stärker gewachsen als das Sozialprodukt," *Bulletin des Presse- und Informationsamtes der Bundesregierung,* No. 2 (January 6, 1965), pp. 9–10.

Brentano, Heinrich von, Foreign Minister 1955–1961. "The Principles of German Development Aid," *Germany,* Vol. VI (1961), No. 22, pp. 18–19.

Das Bundesministerium für Gesundheitswesen. "Technische Hilfe für Togo," *Bulletin des Presse- und Informationsamtes der Bundesregierung,* No. 56 (March 30, 1965), p. 450.

Der Bundesminister für Wirtschaft. "Deutsch-saudi-arabische Zusammenarbeit," *Bulletin des Presse- und Informationsamtes der Bundesregierung.* No. 124 (August 7, 1964), p. 1,179.

Der Bundesminister für wirtschaftliche Zusammenarbeit. *Report on Development Assistance Efforts in 1963,* press release. Printed as "Enclosure to letter dated 23-3-1964." Explains tax regulations designed to increase German private investment in developing countries.

Das Bundesministerium für wirtschaftliche Zusammenarbeit. "Deutsch-tunesische Zusammenarbeit," *Bulletin des Presse- und Informationsamtes der Bundesregierung,* No. 123 (July 20, 1965), p. 994.

_____. *Deutsche Entwicklungspolitik im Jahre 1965.* Bonn: 1966.

_____. "Entwicklungsförderung der Bundesrepublik in Äthiopien," press release. Bonn, March 1, 1963.

_____. "Entwicklungsförderung der Bundesrepublik in Tanganjika," press release. Bonn, March 1, 1963.

_____. "Entwicklungsförderung der Bundesrepublik in Togo," press release. Bonn, February 16, 1963.

_____. "Entwicklungshilfe ist keine Gießkannen-Politik: Der Weg zum Kapitalhilfe-Kredit ist genau festgelegt," *Bulletin des Presse- und Informationsamtes der Bundesregierung,* No. 50 (March 20, 1965), pp. 403–404.

_____. "Das Entwicklungshilfe-Steuergesetz: Anreiz und Starthilfe für deutsche Privatinvestitionen," *Bulletin des Presse- und Informationsamtes der Bundesregierung,* No. 25 (February 10, 1965), p. 196.

_____. *Hands Across the Sea.* Bonn: Druck- und Verlagshaus Heinz Möller (1965?).

_____. *Ihre Zukunft—Unsere Zukunft.* Bonn: Druck- und Verlagshaus Heinz Möller, 1965.

_____. "Investitionsförderungsverträge mit Entwicklungsländern," *Bulletin des Presse- und Informationsamtes der Bundesregierung,* No. 30 (February 18, 1965), p. 243.

_____. *Jahresbericht des Bundesministeriums für wirtschaftliche Zusammenarbeit— 1963.* Bonn: 1964.

_____. "Kenia auf gutem Wege," *Bulletin des Presse- und Informationsamtes der Bundesregierung,* No. 133 (August 4, 1965), p. 1078.

_____. "Lehrauftrag für Entwicklungspolitik und regionale Entwicklungsplanung," *Bulletin des Presse- und Informationsamtes der Bundesregierung,* No. 79 (May 6, 1965), p. 630.

_____. "Lehrmaterial für Gewerbeschulen in Entwicklungsländern," *Bulletin des Presse- und Informationsamtes der Bundesregierung,* No. 134 (September 1, 1964), pp. 1,258–1,259.

_____. "Lernen und Helfen in Übersee," press release. Bonn, October 1963.

_____. *Märkte von Morgen; eine Bilanz der deutschen Entwicklungshilfe.* Bonn: Druck- und Verlagshaus Heinz Möller, 1964.

_____. "Das Studium der Studenten aus Entwicklungsländern," *Bulletin des Presse- und Informationsamtes der Bundesregierung,* No. 132 (August 26, 1964), p. 1,238.

_____. "Verstärkte Koordinierung bei der Entwicklungshilfe," *Bulletin des Presse- und Informationsamtes der Bundesregierung,* No. 38 (March 4, 1964), p. 307.

_____. "Verstärkter Handel mit der Republik Kongo," *Bulletin des Presse- und Informationsamtes der Bundesregierung,* No. 140 (August 18, 1965), p. 1,130.

Das Bundesministerium für wirtschaftliche Zusammenarbeit, Wissenschaftlicher Beirat. "Bildungshilfe-Gutachten: Grundsätze für eine Bildungshilfe der Bundesrepublik Deutschland an die Entwicklungsländer," in three parts, *Bulletin des Presse- und Informationsamtes der Bundesregierung,* I, No. 127 (July 24, 1965), pp. 1,028– 1,031; II, No. 128 (July 27, 1965), pp. 1,037–1,040; and III, No. 129 (July 28, 1965), pp. 1,046–1,048.

Das Bundeswirtschaftsministerium, Wissenschaftlicher Beirat. *Probleme einer rationellen Wirtschaftshilfe an die Entwicklungsländer unter Berücksichtigung der von der Bundesrepublik zu treffenden Maßnahmen;* report, January 23, 1960.

_____. *Report on German Development Assistance Policies in 1965* (mimeographed).

Busche, Axel Freiherr von dem, Director of the German Development Service, interview with magazine *Deutsche Jugend.* Text reprinted as "Die Position des Deutschen Entwicklungsdienstes," *Bulletin des Presse- und Informationsamtes der Bundesregierung,* No. 131 (August 25, 1964), pp. 1,233–1,234.

Debatin, Helmut, Ministerial Advisor, Ministry of Finance. "Steuerliche Förderung von Investitionen in Entwicklungsländern," *Bulletin des Presse- und Informationsamtes der Bundesregierung: Finanzpolitische Mitteilungen:* I, No. 144 (August 27, 1965), pp. 1,166–1,168; II, No. 145 (August 31, 1965), pp. 1,175–1,176; and III, No. 146 (September 1, 1965), pp. 1,181–1,184.

Deutsche Bundesbank, *Report of the Deutsche Bundesbank for the Year 1966.*

Erhard, Prof. Ludwig, as Minister for Economic Affairs. "The Significance of Foreign Aid," speech at discussion of the International Bank's 1959 report, *News from the German Embassy,* Vol. III, No. 14 (October 12, 1959), pp. 1–2.

_____, as Federal Chancellor. Correspondence with Israeli Premier Levi Eshkol on Israeli reaction to German technicians' work in Egypt and relation of German development aid to Arab-Israeli conflict, *News from the German Embassy,* Vol. IX, No. 8 (May 18, 1965), pp. 1–3.

Gerstenmaier, Dr. Eugen, *Bundestag* President. Radio interview treating German dip-
lomatic conflict with Egypt, printed as "Sitzung des Bundestags in Berlin: Zur
Entwicklung in Nahost—Eine unfruchtbare Alternative," *Bulletin des Presse- und
Informationsamtes der Bundesregierung,* No. 48 (March 18, 1965), pp. 381–382.

Hase, Karl-Günther von, Director of the Press and Information Office. "Diplomatische
Beziehungen zu Israel: Die Bundesregierung zur Entschließung der Arabischen
Liga," *Bulletin des Presse- und Informationsamtes der Bundesregierung,* No. 47 (March
17, 1965), pp. 373–374.

_____. "Novelle zum Wiedergutmachungsgesetz," *Bulletin des Presse- und Infor-
mationsamtes der Bundesregierung,* No. 99 (June 10, 1965), p. 795.

_____. "Unentschuldbare Ausschreitungen gegen deutsche Botschaft in Irak," *Bul-
letin des Presse- und Informationsamtes der Bundesregierung,* No. 47 (March 17,
1965), p. 373.

Kreditanstalt für Wiederaufbau. *Deutsche Kredite für Entwicklungsländer: Afrika und
Asien.* Frankfurt am Main, 1964 (?).

_____. *XVII. Jahresbericht: Geschäftsjahr 1965,* Frankfurt am Main [1966].

Lübke, Heinrich, Federal President. "Address before Mexican Congress" (text),
Bulletin des Presse- und Informationsamtes der Bundesregierung, No. 152 (November
30, 1966), pp. 1,222–1,224.

_____. "Besonderer Anteil der Deutschen an Afrika," *Bulletin des Presse- und Infor-
mationsamtes der Bundesregierung,* No. 46 (March 16, 1965), p. 365.

_____. "Freundschaftliche Verbundenheit mit Afrika," speech at opening of the Third
German Africa-Week, *Bulletin des Presse- und Informationsamtes der Bundesregierung,*
No. 62 (May 11, 1966), pp. 487–488.

_____. "Mehr Investitionen im Ausland notwendig," *Bulletin des Presse- und Infor-
mationsamtes der Bundesregierung,* No. 51 (March 23, 1965), pp. 405–406.

_____. "Soldaten des Friedens," speech at the Villa Hammerschmidt at reception
for first graduates of German Development Service training program, *Bulletin des
Presse- und Informationsamtes der Bundesregierung,* No. 117 (July 24, 1964), pp.
1,113–1,114.

Sachs, Hans-Georg, Chairman of the Foreign Office Department for Trade and Overseas Development (interview with). "GATT Milestone for New Countries," *German
International,* Vol. IX, No. 4 (April 1965), pp. 22–24.

_____. "Neue GATT-Bestimmungen," *Bulletin des Presse- und Informationsamtes der
Bundesregierung,* No. 24 (February 9, 1965), p. 192.

_____. "The United Nations Conference on Trade and Development," *Germany,* Vol.
IX (1964), No. 38, pp. 11–12.

Scheel, Walter, Minister for Economic Cooperation 1961–1966. "Bewährte Partnerschaft im neuen Stil," press release. Bad Godesberg, September 10, 1962.

_____. "Entwicklungshilfe für Afrika," press release of speech for African Research
Day of the Geographical Society. Berlin, April 4, 1963.

_____. "Entwicklungshilfe für Afrika," press release of speech at opening of Second
German African Week. Bad Godesberg, October 18, 1962.

_____. "Entwicklungshilfe—Gebot unserer Sicherheit," *Rheinischer Merkur,* No. 19
(May 8, 1965); interview, special reprint.

_____. "Entwicklungspolitik im Wandel," press release of speech. Bremen, February
14, 1964.

_____. "Ein Gebot der Fairneß," *Bulletin des Presse- und Informationsamtes der Bun-
desregierung,* No. 7 (January 15, 1966), p. 50.

_____. "Im Geiste menschlicher Solidarität," speech on role of private agencies in foreign aid, June 26, 1964, *Bulletin des Presse- und Informationsamtes der Bundesregierung* (July 10, 1964), pp. 1,033–1,034.

_____. *Konturen einer neuen Welt.* Düsseldorf: Econ-Verlag, 1965.

_____. *Neue Wege deutscher Entwicklungspolitik.* Bonn: Bundesdruckerei, 1966.

_____. "Ein neues Studium des Entwicklungsdienstes," speech at the Villa Hammerschmidt, July 15, 1965, at reception for first graduates of German Development Service training program, *Bulletin des Presse- und Informationsdienstes der Bundesregierung,* No. 117 (July 24, 1964), p. 1,114.

_____ (interview). "New Style in Foreign Aid: 'Promoting Project Groups Instead of Single Projects,' " *German International,* Vol. VII, No. 2 (February 1963), pp. 22, 25–29.

_____. "Politik aus erster Hand," press release of speech in series for the *Bayerischer Rundfunk,* September 12, 1962.

_____. "Rechtsschutz für deutsche Auslandsinvestitionen," *Handelsblatt,* March 13, 1964.

_____. "Wirtschaftliche Zusammenarbeit mit Afrika," press release. Bonn, April 19, 1963.

Schmücker, Kurt, Federal Treasurer, Minister for Economic Affairs in the Erhard Cabinet. "Entscheidende Rolle der Weltbank: Entwicklungshilfe eine politische und wirtschaftliche Notwendigkeit," speech in Tokyo before representatives of the World Bank and the International Monetary Fund, *Bulletin des Presse- und Informationsamtes der Bundesregierung,* No. 139 (September 11, 1964), pp. 1,293–1,294.

_____. "Die Stabilität hat den Vorrang," radio address, January 4, 1965. Text in *Bulletin des Presse- und Informationsamtes der Bundesregierung,* No. 3 (January 7, 1965), p. 22.

_____. "Südamerika als Wirtschaftspartner Deutschlands," *Bulletin des Presse- und Informationsamtes der Bundesregierung,* No. 74 (June 3, 1966), pp. 581–582.

Schütz, Klaus, Deputy Foreign Minister. Interview presenting West German response to East German and Soviet charges of West German backing of Israel prior to Arab-Israeli War of 1967, *Bulletin des Presse- und Informationsamtes der Bundesregierung,* No. 66 (June 23, 1967), pp. 566–567.

Statistisches Bundesamt, "Ausländische Arbeitskräfte einst und jetzt," *Bulletin des Presse- und Informationsamtes der Bundesregierung,* No. 38 (March 4, 1965), p. 307.

_____. "Der Außenhandel im Dezember und im Jahr 1964," *Bulletin des Presse- und Informationsamtes der Bundesregierung,* No. 12 (January 22, 1965), p. 95.

_____. "Der Außenhandel im Januar 1965," *Bulletin des Presse- und Informationsamtes der Bundesregierung,* No. 35 (February 25, 1965), p. 280.

_____. "Das Sozialprodukt 1964," *Bulletin des Presse- und Informationsamtes der Bundesregierung,* No. 19 (February 2, 1965), p. 146.

Vialon, Prof. Friedrich Karl, Executive Under-Secretary in the Ministry for Economic Cooperation. "Der Deutsche Entwicklungsdienst im Rahmen der Entwicklungspolitik: Schaffung einer gemeinnützigen Gesellschaft mit dem Bund als Hauptgesellschafter," *Bulletin des Presse- und Informationsamtes der Bundesregierung,* No. 120 (July 11, 1963), pp. 1,078–1,079.

Wischnewski, Hans-Jürgen, Minister for Economic Cooperation, 1966–. "Aktuelle Probleme der deutschen Entwicklungspolitik," address before the Ausschuß für Entwicklungsländer der Friedrich-Ebert-Stiftung; text in *Bulletin des Presse- und Informationsamtes der Bundesregierung,* No. 58 (June 2, 1967), p. 495.

_____. "Offener Brief an den Präsidenten des Bundes der Steuerzahler," *Bulletin des Presse- und Informationsamtes der Bundesregierung*, No. 33 (April 4, 1967), p. 275.

_____. "Positive und konstruktive deutsche Entwicklungshilfe," interview for German Overseas Radio; text in *Bulletin des Presse- und Informationsamtes der Bundesregierung*, No. 162 (December 29, 1966), p. 1,319.

Descriptions and Evaluations of West German Foreign Aid

Arbeitsgemeinschaft für die Zusammenarbeit mit Entwicklungsländern. *Formen und Methoden der deutschen Zusammenarbeit mit Entwicklungsländern*. Köln: Bundesverband der deutschen Industrie, 1958.

Arntz, Helmut. *Deutschland stellt sich vor*. Bonn: Presse- und Informationsamt der Bundesregierung (6th edition), 1963.

_____. *Tatsachen über Deutschland*. Bonn: Presse- und Informationsamt der Bundesregierung (6th edition), 1963.

_____. *Germany in Brief*. Bonn: Press and Information Office of the Federal Republic of Germany (3rd [English] edition), 1964.

_____. *Germany Reports*. Bonn: Press and Information Office of the Federal Republic of Germany (3rd [English] edition), 1961.

Baade, Fritz, *Strategie des Weltkampfes gegen den Hunger*. Kiel and Bonn: Forschungsinstitut für Wirtschaftsfragen der Entwicklungsländer, 1966.

_____. ...*denn sie sollen satt werden*. Oldenburg: Gerhard Scalling Verlag, 1964.

Behrendt, Richard F. (ed.). *Die wirtschaftlich und gesellschaftlich unterentwickelten Lander und wir: Stellungnahmen aus Wissenschaft und Praxis*. Bern: P. Haupt, 1961.

Bel'chuk, Alexandr Ivanovich, *Vyvoz kapitala iz Zapadnoy Germanii*. Moskva: Izd-vo IMO, 1957.

Bohle, H. "Einig in die Kennedy Runde ... Deutschlands Industrie ist der Gewinner des erfolgreichen EWG Marathons," *Die Welt* (November 27, 1964), p. 14.

Braker, Hans. "Probleme der deutschen Entwicklungshilfe," *Aus Politik und Zeitgeschichte* (Das Parlament), August 29, 1962.

Bulletin des Press- und Informationsdienstes der Bundesregierung, unsigned articles: "Außenhandel der Bundesrepublik mit den Ländern der arabischen Welt," No. 47 (March 17, 1965), p. 374.

_____. "Beachtliche Hilfe zur Selbsthilfe: Finanzielle Leistungen an Entwicklungsländer in den Jahren 1956 bis 1963," No. 40 (March 6, 1965), pp. 317–318.

_____. "Berater für Mexiko," No. 162 (November 4, 1964), p. 1,498.

_____. "Bildungshilfe für Argentinien," No. 160 (October 30, 1964), p. 1,438.

_____. "Die Bundesrepublik und Lateinamerika," No. 147 (September 30, 1964), p. 1,361.

_____. "Darlehensverträge mit Brasilien," No. 125 (July 22, 1965), p. 1,016.

_____. "Die deutsche Hilfe für die VAR," No. 32 (February 20, 1965), p. 253.

_____. "Deutsche Kapitalhilfe für Peru," No. 112 (July 16, 1964), p. 1,072.

_____. "Deutsch-Kolumbianische Zusammenarbeit," No. 143 (September 22, 1964), p. 1,330.

_____. "Der Dienst deutscher Entwicklungshelfer: Die ersten Freiwilligen reisen aus—Zweck und Aufgaben des DED," No. 128 (August 18, 1964), pp. 1,207–1,208.

———. "Entwicklungspolitik ist langfristig angelegt: Die Debatten um das Gesundheitswesen und die Entwicklungshilfe während der Haushaltsberatungen im Bundestag," No. 38 (March 4, 1964), p. 305.

———. "Hilfe für landwirtschaftliche Siedlung in Brasilien," No. 127 (August 14, 1964), p. 1,198.

———. "Privatorganisationen—Partner in der Entwicklungshilfe," No. 10 (July 10, 1964), p. 1,033.

———. "Straffung der Zuständigkeiten für Hilfen an die Entwicklungsländer," No. 155 (October 20, 1964), p. 1,435.

———. "Technische Zusammenarbeit mit Entwicklungsländern: Ein Überblick über Maßnahmen im Mittelmeerraum und in Nahost," No. 226 (December 21, 1963), pp. 2,019–2,021.

———. "Über 7, 8 Mrd. DM Direktinvestitionen im Ausland," No. 5 (January 12, 1966), p. 36.

———. "4283 arabische Studenten in der Bundesrepublik," No. 49 (March 19, 1965), p. 389.

———. "Wirtschaftshilfe für Süd-Vietnam, Kambodscha und Thailand: Arbeitsgespräche einer Regierungsdelegation in den betroffenen Ländern," No. 152 (October 13, 1964), p. 1,403.

———. "Zur Ausweitung der Holzerzeugung," No. 6 (January 13, 1966), p. 45.

———. "Zuständigkeiten auf dem Gebiet der Entwicklungshilfe," No. 154 (October 16, 1964), p. 1,424.

The Bulletin (English-langauge weekly of the Federal Republic's Press and Information Service), "Bonn Outlines Near East Policy: Fairness to All," Vol. XIII, No. 11 (March 23, 1965), pp. 1–2.

Bunkina, Margarita Konstantinova. Vneshnyaya ekonomicheskaya ekspansiya zapadnogermanskikh monopoliy. Moskva: Sotsekgiz, 1958.

Burandt, Jürgen. "Rourkela: The Second Stage Commences," Germany, Vol. VIII (1963), No. 35, pp. 47–50.

Christlich-Demokratische Union, Diskussionskreis Entwicklungshilfe der CDU/CSU Fraktion des Deutschen Bundestages. Die Entwicklungsländer und unsere Hilfe. Bonn: Presse- und Informationsdienste der Christlich-Demokratischen Union Deutschlands Verlagsgesellschaft mbH., 2nd ed., 1961.

Deutscher Akademischer Austauschdienst. "Austausch von 132 Professoren mit 13 Ländern: Kontinuierlich ausgeweitertes Austauschprogramm . . .," Bulletin des Presse- und Informationsamtes der Bundesregierung, No. 80 (May 7, 1965), p. 639.

Deutscher Rat der Europäischen Bewegung. "Aspekte der deutschen Entwicklungshilfe," Bulletin des Presse- und Informationsamtes der Bundesregierung, No. 24 (February 8, 1965), pp. 189–191.

Deutsches Wirtschaftsinstitut. "Die westdeutsche neokolonialistische Wirtschaftsoffensive," Bericht 23, Vol. XII (1961), pp. 441–464.

Diepholz, Otto. "Kein Entwicklungsland wie andere" (on German development aid to Israel and diplomatic relations between the countires), Frankfurter Allgemeine Zeitung (April 1, 1966), p. 2.

Domdey, Karl-Heinz. Entwicklungshilfe oder echte sozialistische Hilfe. Leipzig: Urania-Verlag, 1961.

Donner, Otto. "Germany's Part in the World Bank Aid," Germany, Vol. VI (1961), No. 21, pp. 29–31.

Ehlert, F. O. "Lateinamerika will mehr Entwicklungskredite," Frankfurter Allgemeine Zeitung (April 16, 1966).

Erhard, Ludwig. *The Economics of Success.* Princeton, N.J.: Van Nostrand, 1963.

Fack, Fritz Ullrich. "Mehr Kompetenzen für Minister Scheel," *Frankfurter Allegmeine Zeitung* (October 10, 1964).

Frankfurter Allgemeine Zeitung. "Das größte deutsche Entwicklungsvorhaben; Das Bewässerungsprojekt von Tinajones in Peru . . .," (April 21, 1967).

Funkenberg, Alexander. "German Participation in Multilateral Development Projects," *Germany,* Vol. IX (1964), No. 38, pp. 17–18.

Gache, Paul. *L'Allemagne et l'Afrique: Analyse d'une pénétration économique contemporaine.* Paris: Editions des relations internationales, 1960.

German International. "East and West—20 Years After," Vol. IX, No. 4 (April 1965), pp. 9–14.

_____. Brochure compiled from articles, 1963–1964: *Twelve Years of German Development Assistance.* Bonn: Heinz Möller, 1964.

_____. "How to Make Five Marks out of One," Vol. IX, No. 4 (April 1965), pp. 25–26. Deals with two-year history of the German Development Company.

Germany. "The Principles of German Development Aid," Vol. VI (1961), No. 22, p. 18.

_____. "Partnership Criteria in Development Policy," Vol. IX (1964), No. 37, p. 11.

_____. "Technical Assistance," Vol. VIII (1963), No. 35, pp. 20–22.

Götz, Hans Herbert. *Weil alle besser leben wollen . . .* Düsseldorf: Econ-Verlag, 1963.

Handelsblatt, article translated as "Arabian West Wind: Contacts with Arab World Still Lively," *The German Tribune,* No. 185 (October 16, 1965), p. 2.

Hankel, Wilhelm. "How Does German Capital Assistance Work?" *Germany,* Vol. VIII (1963), No. 35, pp. 18–21.

Hartmann, Helmutt. "Entwicklungspolitik ohne Illusionen," *Wirtschaftsdienst,* Vol. 45 (1965), No. 2, pp. 59–60.

Helborn, Rudolf. *Der westdeutsche Imperialismus erobert Westeuropas Markt.* [East] Berlin: Akademie-Verlag, 1963.

Hesse, Helmut. "Strukturwandlungen im Außenhandel," in *Wandlungen der Wirtschaftsstruktur in der Bundesrepublik Deutschland.* Berlin: Duncker & Humblot, 1962, pp. 249–286.

Hesse, Kurt. *Entwicklungsländer und Entwicklungshilfen an der Wende des Kolonialzeitalters.* Berlin: Duncker & Humblot, 1962.

_____. *Plannungen in Entwicklungsländern.* Berlin: Duncker & Humblot, 1965.

Hickmann, Ernst. *Die Wirtschaft des Auslandes: die Entwicklungsvorhaben der Gegenwart.* Darmstadt: Hoppenstedt, 1959.

_____. *Aufbaupläne und wirtschaftlicher Fortschritt in unterentwickelten Gebieten.* Bremen: F. Trüjen, 1954.

Holbik, Karel. "West German Development Aid—The Means and Ends," *Quarterly Review of Economics and Business,* Vol. V, No. 4 (Winter 1965), pp. 5–19.

Holzer, Jochen. "Easing the Way for Private Investment in Developing Countries," *Germany,* Vol. IX (1964), No. 37, pp. 5–6.

_____. "Principles, Form and Scope of Technical Assistance," *Germany,* Vol. IX (1964), No. 38, pp. 20–23.

Hunck, J.M. "How Good is German Foreign Aid?" *German-American Trade News,* June 1965.

International Financial News Survey. Statistics for German aid to India, Vol. XVI, No. 39 (October 2, 1964), p. 243; Vol. XVI, No. 41 (October 16, 1964), p. 366.

Jacobs, Alfred, and Ernst Hickmann. *Pläne von Entwicklungsländern: eine ökonomische Analyse.* Darmstadt: Hoppenstedt, 1961.

Kapferer, Clodwig. "Handelshilfe an Entwicklungsländer durch Förderung ihrer absatzwirtschaftlichen Aktivität," *Wirtschaftsdienst,* Vol. XLV, No. 7 (July 1965), pp. 362–366.

Kermann, Karl G. G. *Landwirtschaftlicher Aufbau in unterentwickelten Gebieten.* Bremen: Bremer Ausschuß für Wirtschaftsforschung, 1954.

Kopp, Ferdinand. *Unsere Welt im Umbruch.* Bonn: Eichholz-Verlag, 1965.

Lamby, Werner. "German Development Aid in 1963," *Germany,* Vol. IX (1964), No. 38, pp. 15–18.

Lojewski, Günther von. "Die Konkurrenz der Hilfsbereitschaft: Über 250 Organisationen teilen sich in der Bundesrepublik in die Aufgaben der Entwicklungshilfe," *Frankfurter Allgemeine Zeitung* (December 2, 1964).

Lukas, J. Anthony. "India is Impatient at Slow Bonn Aid," *The New York Times* (June 18, 1966).

Majonica, Ernst. "Deutschland und die dritte Welt," *Für Sie gelesen,* No. 22, May 1965, pp. 17–19.

Münchner Merkur. Article translated as "Humanitarian aid for Viet Nam," August 3, 1966, *The German Tribune,* No. 229 (August 20, 1966), p. 2.

Natorp, Klaus. "Würde und Geld," *Frankfurter Allgemeine Zeitung,* (March 21, 1966), p. 1.

Friedrich Naumann Stiftung zur Politik und Zeitgeschichte (Schriftenreihe). *Bildungshilfe für Entwicklungsländer.* Stuttgart: Deutsche Verlags-Anstalt, 1963.

Neue Zürcher Zeitung, "Die Deutsche Entwicklungshilfe" (August 17, 1965).

_____. "Stabilität und Wachstum als wirtschaftspolitische Aufgabe" (February 9, 1967).

_____. "Westdeutschland als Partner im Welthandel," March 24, 1965.

Niggemeyer, Hermann. "Wer hilft, muß richtig helfen," *Frankfurter Allgemeine Zeitung* (September 7, 1961), p. 16.

Olsen, Arthur J. "Erhard Sums up Germany: Position One of Stablest and Healthiest in World," *New York Times* (January 15, 1965), p. C53:1.

Pol'shikov, Pyotr Ivanovich. *Ekonomicheskaya expansiya Zapadnoy Germanii v Afrike.* Moskva: Isdatel'stvo Instituta Mezhdunarodnykh Otnosheniy, 1962.

Rau, Walter. *Pladoyer für die Landwirtschaft.* Bonn: Bundesministerium für wirtschaftliche Zusammenarbeit, 1965.

_____. "Warum Entwicklungshilfe?" *Für Sie gelesen,* No. 35 (June 1966), pp. 1–13.

Roeper, Hans. "Entwicklungshilfe für Indien kritisch betrachtet," *Frankfurter Allgemeine Zeitung* (July 9, 1960).

Scala international: Sonderheft Entwicklungshilfe, December 1963.

Schmidt, Johann Lorenz. *Probleme des Neokolonialismus; die Besonderheiten des westdeutschen Neokolonialismus.* [East] Berlin: Akademie-Verlag, 1963.

Schmitt, Matthias. *Die befreite Welt; vom Kolonialsystem zur Partnerschaft.* Baden-Baden: A. Lutzeyer, 1962.

_____. "Die historische Grundlage der Entwicklungspolitik," *Kieler Vorträge,* No. 27, new series. Kiel: Institut für Weltwirtschaft, 1963.

_____. "Ein Schritt ins Ungewiße," *Frankfurter Allgemeine Zeitung* (October 23, 1965).

Schuster, Hans. *Wirtschaftliche Zusammenarbeit mit unterentwickelten Ländern: Probleme, Erfahrungen und Möglichkeiten im Rahmen des Punkt-Vier-Programms.* Bremen: F. Trüjen, 1951.

Seelmann-Eggebert, Rolf. "Pindorama in Brasilien," *Frankfurter Allgemeine Zeitung* (July 30, 1966).

Der Spiegel. "Auslandshilfe," No. 40 (September 27, 1961), pp. 78–81.

———. "Entwicklungshilfe: Die Steppe ruft," Vol. XV, No. 35 (August 23, 1961), p. 30.

Sonnenhol, G. A. "Größe und Elend der Entwicklungshilfe," *Für Sie gelesen,* No. 20 (March, 1965).

Sterner, Siegfried. "Sünden der Entwicklungspolitik," *Frankfurter Allgemeine Zeitung* (March 3, 1965), p. 21.

Süddeutsche Zeitung. Article translated as "Bonn's relations with Delhi upset: Mrs. Gandhi's two-state theory," July 27, 1966, *The German Tribune,* No. 227 (August 6, 1966), p. 3.

Tillmann, Heinz and Werner Kowalski. *Westdeutscher Neokolonialismus; Untersuchungen über die wirtschaftliche und politische Expansion des westdeutschen Imperialismus in Afrika und Asien.* [East] Berlin: Rütten & Loening, 1963.

Vogel, Dieter. "Neue Strategie für die Entwicklungshilfe," *Frankfurter Allgemeine Zeitung* (June 21, 1966).

Der Volkswirt. "Technical Assistance, Focal Point of German Development Policy," 1963, Special Supplement No. 38.

White, John. *German Aid.* London: Overseas Development Institute, 1967.

Winckler, H. J. *Die Entwicklungsländer.* Berlin: Otto-Suhr-Institut an der Freien Universität Berlin, revised ed., 1961.

Witzel, Dietrich. "Deutsche Hilfe in Indien wenig bekannt," *Frankfurter Allgemeine Zeitung* (June 20, 1966).

Zimmer, Norbert (ed.). *Deutsche in Entwicklungsländern.* Hofheim/Taunus: Verlag des Auslands-Kurier, 1966.

Capital Aid Loans Extended by Kreditanstalt für Wiederaufbau to Developing Countries in Latin America, through 1965.

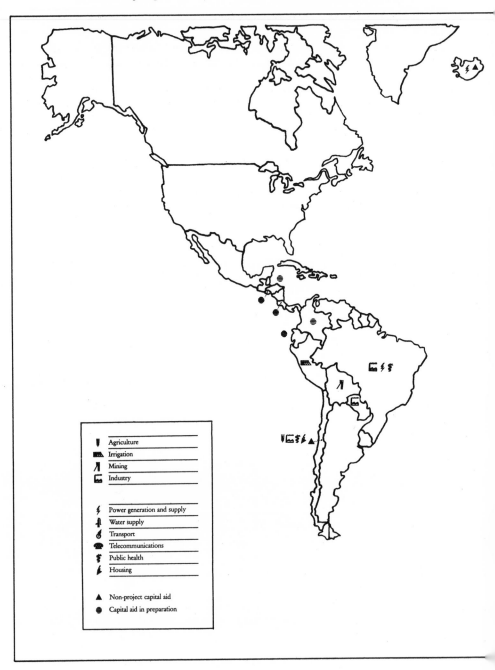

	Agriculture
	Irrigation
	Mining
	Industry
	Power generation and supply
	Water supply
	Transport
	Telecommunications
	Public health
	Housing
▲	Non-project capital aid
●	Capital aid in preparation

Capital Aid Loans Extended by Kreditanstalt für Wiederaufbau to Developing Countries in Africa and Asia, through 1965.

Agriculture

Irrigation

Mining

Industry

Power generation and supply

Water supply

Transport

Telecommunications

Public health

Housing

Non-project capital aid

Capital aid in preparation

INDEX

Fleming, OECD Chairman Donald, 7
Foreign Office, 45, 61, 68, 128, 139
France, aid to colonies and former
colonies, 6, 11, 18, 42, 100–101,
127, 136
Free German Party, 37 n., 128–130
Frei, Chilean President Eduardo,
104–106, 111 n.
Frobenius, Leo, 91–92

Gabon, 93
Gandhi, Indian Prime Minister Indira,
123
General Agreement on Trade and
Tariffs, 45
German Academic Exchange Service, 62
German Company for the Furtherance of
Developing Countries, 62
German Development Service, 62, 69,
78–81, 96, 108
German Foundation for Developing
Countries, 62, 69
German Institute for Development
Policy, 62, 69, 74, 77, 80
German-Iranian Chamber of Commerce,
61
German Red Cross, 61
German Southwest Africa; see
South-West Africa
Great Britain, aid to former colonies,
6, 18, 24, 42, 118, 136
Greece, aid to, 3, 7, 8 n., 26, 60, 70
136
Guinea, 38, 93
Guther, Max, 97

Hallstein Doctrine, 38, 47
Hase, Director of Press and Information
Office Karl Gunther von, 87–88

Iceland, 8 n.
India, 42, 52, 60, 69, 115–123
Indonesia, 69, 113
Interministerial Review Committee for
Capital Assistance, 61, 66
International Development Agency, 59
International Development Association,
83
International Finance Corporation, 59
Investment-encouragement treaties, 57
Iran, 69
Iraq, 86–87
Ireland, 8 n.

Israel: German restitution aid to,
82–83, 127; conflict with Arab
countries as complicating factor in
German aid program, 86–89, 132
Izvestia, 88

Japan, 9, 24
Johnson, U.S. President Lyndon B., 4,
12
Jordan, 132

Kennedy, U.S. President John F., 5 n.,
6, 78, 81
Kenya, 70, 94
Khrushchev, Nikita: on peaceful
coexistence, 2–3; on Western foreign
aid, 138 n.
Kiesinger, Chancellor Kurt, 37, 139
Korean War, 19, 137
Kristensen, OECD Secretary-General
Thorkil, 7, 8 n.

Labor unions, role in foreign aid, 61
Länder, in educational assistance, 32,
61, 68
Laos, 2
Latin America: aid linked to political-
economic reforms in, 102–105;
relative success in inducing private
investment in, 107–108; fear of
competition from Common Market
countries in, 110–111
Liberia, 70
Libya, 70, 80, 83, 86, 88
Lubke, President Heinrich, 37, 55, 78,
80, 105, 111
Lugard, Sir Frederick, 1

Malaysia, 113
Marshall Plan: as analogy for West
German foreign aid, 44, 46;
counterpart funds, 49; political
motivation of, 137
Mexico, 108
Ministry for Economic Affairs, 60, 62,
128
Ministry for Economic Cooperation, 32,
42, 43, 52, 60–62, 70–71, 74, 79,
94, 108–109, 110, 123, 125, 127,
128–130, 132, 139
Morocco, 84–86